BOOK
Craft

Cut the Fluff. Keep the Magic.

How to write books readers love,
from first draft to final polish.

DEREK MURPHY

Contents

My best words come at night.

When soft music is humming and birds or bats are chirping and dusk or dawn is peeking above the horizon. When the story is written and the deadline is looming; when I'm going through it one last time experiencing each scene in its totality; when I can feel the wonder and lean in, exploring its darkest depths. When I alter the hue and sharpen the edges. When I saturate the images or bring out stark relief.

My best words come when I'm sleep-deprived and stressed, or first thing in the morning when my mind is murky, and coffee bites my tongue. Before I've faced the world or after I've tuned them out. When I can disappear into my story and the walls holding me in disappear.

When my spelling is awful and my fingers don't keep pace with the landscape of my inner eyes, when I stumble and stutter and ramble and spit, clicking and clacking away at plastic keys with luminous letters, churning out stars and oceans.

My best words come when they want to, not when they're called. They linger at the edge of my settled mind, nervous to be employed, skittish about the idea of being tamed. But when I sit still and tell a story, they come closer to listen, and sometimes can't help but reveal themselves.

– Derek Murphy

Preface

This is not a book. *It's an initiation.*

You're here because you love the alchemical process where your creativity and inspiration bleed onto the page. You've witnessed the power of using letters to communicate ideas and cast spells, bewitching readers and captivating them with the powers of your mind.

You've got a taste for it, but you want more. So you've sought me out, and here we are. This information took me decades to uncover, and I don't reveal it lightly. Not every author is ready to hear the valuable lessons I'm about to share with you, but this book isn't for them. *It's for you.*

Who am I? We'll get to that later. Right now, let's talk about you and what's holding you back. You're determined to improve your writing, because you respect your audience enough to give them your best work. You're excited about the story you're composing, but not sure if you have the right skills to do it justice. You want to sell more books, without selling your soul or giving up the reason you started writing in the first place: that magical feeling of discovery, when the pages come alive in unpredictable ways. But you're afraid.

Am I good enough?
Does anybody want this?
Am I wasting my time?

YOU'VE BEEN CALLED

You have a gift, but it's not enough. Deep magic isn't a spontaneous explosion of creative energy. That burns too hot. It's unstable and unpredictable. Real power comes from deliberation, skill and craft. You need a guide to unlock a writing practice that ignites your true potential. ***This is it.***

This is not an easy book to read, it's a tome. While the knowledge contained within may be of interest to many people, it will only be as useful as the effort and energy you put into it. If you have the requisite amount of need and are pure of heart (in a state of optimistic expectation; an open, willingness to participate), it will reveal its secrets. If writing a book is a passing flight of fancy, some of the material in this book might seem daunting. The good stuff is near the end, but you've got to earn it.

"If there is a magic in story writing, and I am convinced there is, no one has ever been able to reduce it to a recipe that can be passed from one person to another."
– *John Steinbeck*

Induction

LEARNING TO SPELL

One time I brought a magic trick to elementary school. It was a coloring book, where the pages would show as blank, then illustrated, then full color, depending on how it was displayed. I performed a few times, astounding my friends.

But then at recess, a classmate snuck into my desk, stole the trick and showed everyone exactly how it worked. I was mortified.

"It's a trick," she showed everyone. "It's not real magic."

* * *

Some people say great writing can't be taught, that there is no secret formula, that nobody really understands the creative process enough to teach it. That's why most writing guides narrate the completely unreplicable creative process of a handful of famous authors, with zero guidelines to actually make the work easier, more enjoyable and objectively better. They opine about how real art is hard and there are no shortcuts; that you need to suffer painfully for years wrestling with each word, even as the whole world spurns you.

According to Anne Lamott, very few writers know what they're doing until they've done it. Booker Prize winner John Banville says writing a book is like "wading through wet sand, at night, in a storm, with no lantern to guide one's steps and no lighthouse to warn of the submerged reefs and wrecks that lie ahead."

All of this is inspiring, but none of it is helpful. Few writing guides share the secrets of the *craft*, the wordplay, the form and function, the plotting or organization. The emphasis is on the muse and mystery and magic, none of which can be codified or taught.

Since there are no rules, the only practical advice writers can give each other is persistence and passion. Because the only way to be a writer is to write. They say if you gave a million monkeys a typewriter, eventually they'd write Shakespeare – and that's exactly what we have; a million monkeys banging out manuscripts and the *one* out of millions for whom that strategy produces a masterpiece. Maybe it's the only way to produce masterpieces, but it's brutal, difficult, and unnecessary. It breeds false ideologies, like the harder you work, the better it will be or the more readers will enjoy it.

The majority of books on writing are secretly selling authors the dream that anybody can do it, because nobody knows how it's done: conveniently ignoring the hard truth that most authors never sell more than a hundred copies.

When I started writing, I thought I was a genius. I thought my natural talent would be universally recognized. I shamelessly followed the whim of my intuition. And I realized that writing a book was *hard*.

Or at least, it can be. Sure, sometimes the words flow like magic, pouring out of your soul onto the page until you've suddenly got half a manuscript. But then during the revision, the editing, the rewrites, the insecurity and fear about whether it's actually any good takes over and has you questioning everything. The creative process flickers between unbridled optimism and terrifying inferiority. One good day of writing might be followed by a week on the couch eating ice cream.

This struggle to capture or enhance raw talent into the reliable productivity necessary for sustained greatness isn't new. In 1695, the poet John Dryden asked, *what is genius*, and notes the subtle tensions in the creative process:

> "It depends on the influence of the stars say the astrologists; the organs of the body say the naturalists; a particular gift of heaven say the divines. How to improve it, many books can teach us; how to obtain it: none. That nothing can be done without it all agree."

In other words, genius is a gift or a birthright. It can only be expressed, or accessed. It can't be acquired through effort or will alone, even though it is vital.

For this reason, writing has always been seen as a kind of magic; a state of willing acceptance as the words flow through you. The founding texts of the Western literary canon begin with the incantation, *Sing, Muse*. Egyptian scribes were said to have offered a single drop of their ink each day in Thoth's name.

In the Middle Ages, when most people were illiterate, writing was the work of priests and magicians. The word *spell* was used to refer to deliberate and intentional speech; to call into being through an utterance. But it could also mean "work in the place of another," as in a sign or symbol that replaced the tangible with something silent and mysterious.

To spell was to create invisible meaning through the learned rearrangement of inscrutable symbols; mystifying signs with hidden meaning that conjured and transferred wisdom and knowledge, without speaking them out loud.

A simple leather bag containing 26 magical runes could be arranged into infinite possibilities. Once learned, it gave a practitioner the power to create worlds, and to transcribe meaning across time. As Pulitzer Prize-winning novelist Jhumpa Lahiri writes,

> "Surely it is a magical thing for a handful of words, artfully arranged, to stop time. To conjure a place, a person, a situation, in all its specificity and dimensions. To affect us and alter us, as profoundly as real people and things do."

Creativity is already a kind of sorcery; bringing something into existence out of nothing. But magic implies the intervention or assistance of a supernatural force—an inexplicable raw power, not yet understood.

And there *is* something magical about writing. The unplanned, spontaneous flash of insight, the sudden discovery which feels to come from beyond, just outside of our limited capabilities.

The problem is, most authors think this is the only valuable part, and that everything else, not invested with the muse, isn't real, is worthless; that touching this magic is the *only point* and the *only way* to write.

Attempts to explore or demystify the inner workings of this esoteric process are often resisted or denigrated, because if writing is a sacred process, contingent on the impetuous arrival of supernatural inspiration, it cannot be sought out, it can only be gifted. You cannot choose to write, you can only be *chosen*. If writing is the purview of the muse, handing out boons, then all attempts to understand this power, control it, and wield it must be sacrilegious or profane. It's not real magic. It's just a trick.

But what if it didn't have to be this way? What if inspiration is like lightning? An awesome, mysterious flash in the sky that scorches the earth; yet it can also be studied, harnessed and diverted into productive energy. What if inspiration is like a rare bird that sometimes passes your window; that can be tamed with scattered seeds and a wooden house?

The truth is, there's another path that doesn't depend on supernatural intervention, or the raw talent apportioned at birth that sets limits on your creative abilities. And while it's considered inferior by the literary purists, it also allows for unlimited potential to those who would command it.

THERE ARE TWO KINDS OF MAGIC

The first is ritualistic, formulaic, dependable, safe. It takes years of training to learn the exact steps and procedures. Mostly it's about the transference of belief, repetition and letting go. Trust in the process. Expecting the results.

Then there's the explosive magic. Unrestrained, wild and innate. It's *probably* true that explosive magic is more powerful. The problem is, it's unreliable and dangerous. Also, it's probably not very useful. You may have energy and power – but without purpose, form and intention, it can give someone goosebumps or light a fire in their soul. It's better suited for poetry, not the successful completion of a powerful book.

Which is why, even powerfully great magicians still need to learn ritual and structure; to properly channel the creative energy. Good writing usually does flow. The best writing. The art, the passion. But you need the skill, the craft, to contain it, from one awful long sentence of wordplay into an enjoyable novel.

> "There are two men inside The Artist, the poet and the craftsman. One is born a poet. One becomes a craftsman."
> – *Emile Zola, French novelist*

The Greeks already had a rich discussion about precisely this issue, and decided that *ingenium* needed to be coupled with *industria* (hard work) and *ars* (acquired mastery).

Plato explicitly denied that poetry was an art (whose rules could be learned and intricacies perfected by practice and the accumulation of skill) because in his view, all good poets compose and utter their work not from *ars*, but caught up in grips manic possession, or the *furor poetius*. A poet would become temporarily insane, in *ek-stasis*, standing outside oneself. According to Plato, this irrational inspiration was potentially dangerous. In the *Republic* he argues that such poets need to be censored or even banished.

More recently, a special edition of *Time Magazine* on the science of creativity, distinguished between the "analytical" and "intuitive" modes of creative thinking:

> One is to think it through deliberately, analytically, to come up with a possible answer; the other, the seemingly magical way, is simply to stare at the words, let them roll around in your head until – bang! – the answer presents itself. It's no contest that the intuitive feels better, more exciting, more creative. The brain arrives at the answer and gives itself – and you – a reward in the form of a sense of surprise and satisfaction.

Most writers accept that even if writing is an Art, certainly it's also a Skill; and there's probably no harm in getting better at the thing you hope people will pay you for (if even this innocuous statement causes you to balk, take a deep breath and a long look in the mirror and repeat to yourself, "Readers love to pay for good books.")

It shouldn't be controversial to claim that authorship, like magic, requires a deliberate practice: and if you're already on board and eager to learn more about the craft of writing, feel free to skip the rest of this introduction. In my experience, however, the majority of would-be authors deeply believe that anything other than the pure, untainted expression of personal inspiration is a sure sign of moral weakness. So if it seems I'm unnecessarily belabouring this point, it's only because I've spent years helping authors transcend limiting beliefs, only to be routinely dismissed or criticized for my efforts.

What I discovered, after years of struggling to make it as a starving artist, is that real magic is the useful application of creative energies, not just the zealous expression of personal experience. And while these definitions have been fluid, current conversations often divorce the craft from the art.

Art is a messy affair, that can only be experienced naked, deep in the woods, when you throw yourself at the mercy of the writing gods, pleading for inspiration. *Craft* is the artisanal-impulse to create higher value.

One you can get better at with work, knowledge and practice. The other is a sensitive void of a thousand eyes that must not be probed because it eats hearts. One leads to consistent, measurable excellence. The other is a one-in-a-million crapshoot: a million monkeys and a lot of time.

Art is about self-expression.
Craft is about technical mastery.

Art controls you.
Craft is a tool you wield.

Art is a gift.
Craft is a power.

Art is the *why*.
Craft is the *how*.

Can you get better at both?
Allegedly, no.

Shouldn't you get better at the one you can?

I think the answer is yes.

This doesn't mean you have to choose between them, or have the one without the other. That's not what I'm saying at all. But, according to most other books on the subject – the skill is worthless even if it's well paid; and the art is priceless even if nobody will pay for it.

Writing *can* be an art, if you define art as self-exploration, or a passion fueled torrent of words (Wordworth's "spontaneous overflow of powerful feelings.") It can be that. That's a choice most authors make, without recognizing that it's a relatively recent ideology, that revolutionized thousands of years of standard creative process, and is not at all suited towards book writing.

It's *empowering*, because it allows writers to do the work without worrying about the reception. But it's *impractical*, because they assume passionate writing will automatically be of higher quality and higher value; that the path to great writing is by refusing to conform to any rules or expectations; that real creativity requires no skill or preparation, only insight and inspiration.

But writing can also be a practice: the calculated mastery of technique and ability. The intentional cultivation of sustainable, reliable bouts of creative genius, in order to get more of your best words on the page, with less of the fears, doubts or indecision most writers face. This book aims to resurrect the ancient truth that the muse comes to those who are prepared and willing; that magic needs focus, ability and attention; and that all true magic requires work and sacrifice.

Book Craft is an invitation to become worthy of respecting the craft that is and always has been the ritualistic basis for literary excellence. But it is also a call to arms against those literary elitists that claim skill, education and execution, when offered in the service of quality and value, even or especially when the authors choose to use those hard-won abilities to create books readers love, are somehow diminishing the purity of their artistic vision.

Unlike most other writing guides, this book is not about finding courage or chasing fairy dust. It's about building a reliable, craft-based writing practice, based on rules and shortcuts and templates and story outlines, so you can finish more of your best work faster and unlock masterful prose that will bring you enduring rewards.

The tips and writing advice in this book are not meant to replace or minimize the magic. But they will help coax the magic in, and teach you to unleash it effectively. I'll give you the tools and strategies you need to cast powerful spells over your readers. In the end, I hope to show you that *real magic* and *just a trick* aren't so different: but there's no trick here. I want you to become a master conjurer. A sorcerer of words.

With the right magic, and the right ritual, you can get a specific result: so instead of charming your car into a pumpkin or turning your family into a pack of exploding rats, you can create the effects you actually want: publishing success, professional fulfillment, and a small army of fans who are eager to support your writing career.

Steinbeck might be right; maybe there's no way to teach the magic of story. Maybe I can't teach you how to write *great* books. But you *can* teach the craft. And I can definitely help you improve your writing, by avoiding predictably common, amateur mistakes. That final bit of magic and moondust it takes to go from good to great, that's up to you. But if you practice the craft, and strive to get better, the magic will show up. That's just how it works.

MAGIC STIRS WITHIN YOU

Most writers, when reading this book, will feel some resistance. They do want to become better, they do want to write better quality books, so they can sell more copies and make a living, but they may resist the idea that there is any kind of structured process for that to happen that doesn't completely ruin the experience. They may say things like "well some authors can do that, but I never could. I write for the love of it, the passion. I'm creative. My mind just doesn't work like that." It's not enough to promise them accolades, positive reviews, or sold out new releases, because for them it's not about the money. They may be willing to pick up a few new tricks, but only if it doesn't threaten their deep-seated belief that real art cannot be constrained, and good writing is nothing if not real art.

In the following pages, I will attempt to show that you can be even more creative and inspired when your writing is supported by a structured practice. I'll be doing my best to cast a spell over you, while also showing you exactly how I'm doing it. The challenge is, revealing how the tricks works without spoiling the magic. Going from amateur (one who does for love) to expert (one who does from experience) without losing the joy of writing.

"There is nothing more disenchanting to man, than to be shown the springs and mechanism of an art." – *Robert Louis Tevenson*

A magic trick is simply a bunch of steps that produce a predictable result for those who don't see the secret mechanism behind it. For the magician, it can be performed without inspiration. For the viewer, it creates a powerful illusion, something *impossible*, something *astounding*.

Magic is just something we don't yet understand: the surprise and delight our ancestors felt when the accidental collision of stones caused sparks. In other words, magic is a wondrous state of unknowing. Don't be disappointed or discouraged once you see how the tricks work. It won't make them any less powerful, because the truth is, magic isn't what's performed or how. It's what happens when the viewer's imagination engages with the material being presented. Seeing behind the curtain won't negate the effects, though it may take away some of the charm.

Induction is the process for welcoming new recruits and supporting them as they adjust to their new roles and working environments. It may also refer to the creative process of bringing something about. An induction stove heats up food faster, while remaining cool to the touch – no fire, no heat, yet safe and effective. I don't need to understand the science behind it, or *believe* in it, in order to make my life easier.

By revealing secrets of the craft, and witnessing the hidden mechanisms, you may even feel threatened or incredulous, and that's fine: sit with those feelings. In fact, I'm going to start with a three-part guide to creative confidence that will help you process some of that discomfort, and widen your capacity for growth.

I will assume you're a frog in hot water: nervous about learning something new, and not even sure you really want to be here. I'll distract with interesting quotes and historical minutiae. I'll introduce you to some previously unpublished works of 18th century literary canon. I have to be non-threatening enough to get you to keep reading, which means I need to coax and cajole. With any luck, I'll be slowly chipping away at your defenses, so that you'll be open enough to the *idea* of improving your writing to take action and try out something new.

Because, here's the important thing: *real magic* can only happen within ourselves; it's the friction that causes growth, awareness and personal transformation. Magical initiation relies on repetition and ritual, that inspire enough courage to go beyond current limitations and believe that anything is possible. As Lisa Marie Basile writes in *The Magical Writing Grimoire*,

> "The magic is actually the change that happens within you when you direct your energy, when you show up for yourself and put in the work (even without immediate result), and when you decide to write and feel and encounter all the layers of self."

It should feel a bit like *Inception*: just when you think we can't go any deeper, that there isn't another fresh writing insight or insane historical piece of trivia, whenever things are getting stale or boring, I'll surprise you. You may feel unmoored. If you feel *at all* I'll consider this project a success, as I can't hope to mentor you unless I reach your hearts.

And remember, I'm not asking you to choose. A teaspoon of sugar makes the medicine go down. We do need the magic. I don't want you to get rid of it. I just want you to harness it, by supporting your muse, with systems, rituals and strategies to develop a reliable writing process. While no two writers will use the same words, good writing shares identifiable patterns that you can learn to implement, without stumbling through the dark by yourself. The only thing I'm hoping to achieve at this point is to prepare you for the arduous task ahead: because while inspiration is universally cherished, few authors have the patience to do the work. As Jonah Lehrer points out in *Imagine*,

> "Artists have a vested interest in our believing in the flash of revelation, the so-called inspiration... shining down from heavens as a ray of grace. In reality, the imagination of the good artist or thinker produces continuously good, mediocre, or bad things, but his judgment, trained and sharpened to a fine point, rejects, selects, connects... All great artists and thinkers are great workers, indefatigable not only in inventing, but also in rejecting, sifting, transforming, ordering."

If you want to be a writer, you need to write. But this isn't a magical, instant transformation, and we aren't just writing an inspired poem in a ten-minute frenzied burst. We're going to need *more* than inspiration. More than an inkling of desire or a passing whim. We're going to need an all-encompassing purpose, burning through obstacles like a meteor, an impenetrable shield of courage, and an armory of resistance destroying weapons. That's why this book cannot simply be a basic how-to guide, because writing is not simple, and your biggest obstacles are already inside you, bristling uncomfortably in the darkness.

METHODS OF MADNESS

When I first launched this book, the negative reviews came swiftly. Authors were frustrated by the theme and personal stories I included to make this book hit on a deeper, emotional level: especially those used to my much simpler online resources. Others complained I took too long to get to the point, or spent too much time in the beginning laying out the importance of learning the craft or writing books readers enjoy.

Everything I've added has been intentional, and some authors love how this fresh approach allows them to reconsider their writing from a new angle. But I absolutely don't want the writing style to be an impediment, so I've decided to add a much clearer outline here, along with a simplified, topic-based table of contents.

If you find yourself getting bored or frustrated, please skip to the parts you need most. I think chapters 4 and 6 are the most useful, though 8 is my favorite. If you're only looking for a quick checklist of writing tips, I consolidated all of the practical summaries into an optional Study Guide, which comes with a bonus video series. You can find them at *writethemagic.com*.

If you're already familiar with my Plot Dot formula or detailed chapter outlines, the first few chapters will feel familiar: but they're important to set up a basis for everything that comes later. The 12-chapters in *Book Craft* work well as a weekly plan to write a book in three months – with most of the writing done in the second month. That's pretty fast for just about everyone, so go at your own pace, but remember to give equal time to each section. A 3-month book writing goal is tight, but possible. If you give yourself a year, you'll waste a lot more time. For best results, read a chapter a week, and take action (implement your insights) before proceeding to the next step. That will allow a deeper and fuller learning experience.

The following outline uses simple language for each practical step in the writing process, rather than the magical words and creative themes I've given to each chapter heading, but they will give you an idea of how this book is organized. Rather than trying to do everything at once, we'll break the journey down into manageable stages.

It's always a challenge to predict how a book will take shape, and this beast was a hydra, with teeth that raised skeletons from the dead. I've structured it to the best of my ability, but I'll be pulling back the veils, one by one. It's meant to be experienced as a ritual process, inspiring spontaneous personal realizations; each section building towards a new surprise or deeper insight. Careful preparation, followed by dazzling revealment. You don't need to know where we're going in order to discover value. You just have to pay attention.

WEEK 0: MINDSET

Before we even get started thinking about writing a book, we need to check your mindset and remove any limiting beliefs that are going to slow you down: so I'll introduce you to a framework for generating creative courage, overcoming anxiety and writing with purpose.

Prepare

1: FICTION BASICS

You'll learn what it takes to create a good story, what a story actually is and includes, how to make sure readers are paying attention, leaning in and listening. We'll also learn about the most popular genres, and what readers expect from each; how to make sure you're writing a book that they will care about; estimating the market potential; and figuring out the heart of your story before you write it.

2: IMPOSSIBLE QUEST

Most (but not all) commercial fiction has one main protagonist or point of view; this is the character of greatest change. We need to figure out where the story begins and ends; why it matters; how much to include. We need our story to hit major turning points so our readers have confidence that we're taking them to an emotional payout; that the plot events in the story matter; and that interesting things are happening.

3: PLOTTING YOUR BOOK

Most plotting resources fail because they're too general. They aren't wrong, they're just unspecific. They don't tell you what to do at each point. And while this gives you more freedom, it can also leave you feeling like your story is missing something crucial and you're not sure how to bridge the gap. I've gone in the opposite direction by creating a hyper-specific 24-chapter plot outline. Use it to get started, then allow your story to unfold the way it needs to.

4: RAISING THE STAKES

Having a tight structure or plot outline is just the beginning. Lots of cool things might be happening, but it won't matter unless the events have real consequences. We need to figure out what the protagonist wants and why they aren't allowed to have it, so that through the story they are forced to change. We'll learn the *most* important thing: how to create suspense and intrigue so readers keep turning pages.

Produce

Once we've mapped out all the big stuff, we can write forward, knowing where we're going. Unexpected things will still pop up, and that's fine. We're allowed to stop and take breaks or detours whenever something interesting happens. As long as we don't lose track of the final destination. The first section was about preparation: now we'll focus on writing the rough draft, and go deeper into each stage of your novel.

5: POINT OF NO RETURN

In this section we'll be writing towards the first major turning point that launches our story. If you don't get people to care about your story or characters in the first quarter of your book, they'll give up long before things get interesting. So we'll also include a big list of weak writing mistakes to watch out for.

6: MIDPOINT

Then we'll write towards the middle of your novel, when the protagonist is forced to question who they are and what they want. We'll be establishing the world and making readers fall in love with your characters, leading up to a crucial turning point for your protagonist.

7: DARK NIGHT OF SOUL

Finally we reach the critical, identity-shattering event. The protagonist has been building a house of cards, or juggling with porcelain plates, and here it all comes crashing down. Now they're forced to change, to grow, to choose – usually giving up on youthful optimism, and deciding to play for keeps.

8: EPIC CONCLUSION

This is the satisfying, emotional pay off when it all comes together. You can hold reader's attention with fun banter and action, or literary distractions and nice sounding words, but by the end of the book it should all mean something and hit them on a deep emotional level. If it doesn't, they'll either feel cheated, or they'll feel apathetic. You want them to be thinking about your book months later.

Perfect

Once you have your book written and your story holds water, then we can finally start to make it good, or even great. We do this by improving and deepening the scene description, conflict and suspense, and using my checklists to make sure each scene is powerful and necessary, before doing a final proofread or polish. This is the stuff a very qualified developmental editor might do for you. Editing your own book can be tricky, but I've established a powerful 3-step revision system, with a fourth round for editing and proofreading.

9: FIXING THE STORY

After I finish a first rough draft, I'll go back and fill in any gaps or fix narrative problems, focusing on the events or incidents. Getting things in the right order so they make sense, so readers can read through the book without feeling confused or disoriented. Plot events need to happen in the right order, or else more polishing is useless. I also want to add as much conflict and tension as possible.

10: CHARACTER MOTIVATION

Once I'm pretty sure everything is in the right place, I'll pay attention to the motivations: why does this happen, why are characters doing these things? I'll need to create backstory, plant clues, establish facts. If they need a pair of scissors in the last chapter, I'll make sure to add one into the right scene earlier so it doesn't just appear. I'll make sure everything makes sense and is believable.

11: SCENE DESCRIPTION

In the third stage of revisions, I'll consider how things actually look, and describe the setting, character movements, clothes and scenery. I want to make sure readers can picture it clearly. I want to avoid reference points ("small items") and change them to real descriptions ("a pot of tea, spools of thread and an orange crayon). I'll make sure I'm using expressions and postures, without overdoing or repeating any too often.

12: FINAL POLISH (EDIT & PROOF)

Through that process, I'm also fixing any typos or mistakes I find, but I'm not actively seeking them out and I won't worry too much about word choice or sentence structure. But in this final section, I'll give you some advanced editing and proofreading tricks to avoid weak writing and make your story shine.

Nonfiction Authors

I have an extensive guide to writing nonfiction, with specific strategies and suggestions, but I struggled to figure out a way to include it holistically in this edition of *Book Craft*. I intend to publish it separately. This will allow a better, deeper exploration of the inherent issues and challenges of writing nonfiction. That said, there's a *lot* of relevant material in this book that can be applied to nonfiction, so I hope you find it useful.

ARE YOU READY?

This book, like all books, is equal parts skill and magic, art and craft. The best writing probably came in a euphoric flood and flash of brilliance. The less inspired passages were probably sweat into being as I wrestled my muse into submission; dragged out of my psyche with a pickax. During edits, it's easy to say, take out everything that isn't *great*. But in truth, a book is rarely all great. It's *greatness* supported by a good deal of *good enough*. And that's okay, because the only thing that really matters is the one thing I can't control: the insights, epiphanies, and realizations that this book sparks out of you, which help you move forward with more confidence and ability.

If you're a long-term, career writer who has already published a lot of successful books, first of all congrats! You probably already have a lot of magic inside you. I give you a nod of writerly respect and gratitude. You probably also have a great deal of experience writing good books intuitively. But I'll bet there are a few places where you struggle with the process, or spend days on a stubborn plot hole.

If you're reading this right now, it's because you've encountered *limits*, and are frustrated by the unique challenges that writing a book can pose. You'd like to get better, and are ready to find some new tactics and strategies that make your writing practice easier, more enjoyable, and your stories more captivating.

Many of the tactics in this book were hard-learned, when things *didn't* go easily, when the writing wasn't effortless. While they may feel vaguely familiar, and perhaps you've already experienced them on your own, you've probably never encountered them boiled down to simple formulas you can understand easily.

No matter where you are in your writing journey, whether you're writing for fun, pleasure or profit, fiction or nonfiction, creative or commercial, whether you're writing your first book or twentieth, you will find effective strategies in this book that you can implement immediately, which will have a profound impact on your writing.

Even so, some of you will resist. Some of you may quit halfway through. You'll go back to doing it your way, the way that's comfortable and unscripted; that makes you feel good. I don't blame you. This a big book. Mastery isn't easy. It requires diligence, and change can be scary. The real magic, the deep magic of writing is how it changes *you*. But only you get to decide who you want to become.

> "The degree to which a person can grow is directly proportional to the amount of truth he can accept about himself without running away." – *Leland Val Vandewall*

PS. If you're sick of all the theatrics and magic talk, I get it. I think if you finish reading this book, you'll understand why it was important. But we're only at about 5%. The vast majority of this book is tactical, with specific guidelines that are mostly unique to this book, because I invented and pioneered them. Even if you are an experienced writer who has studied craft for *years*, there will be a secret somewhere in this book, just for you, which is the key to unlock the next level of your spellcraft. So if you're ready...

Take my hand.
Take a deep breath in.
Turn the page.

You walk under the moonlight, your feet bare, the grass tickling your skin. You can hear the ocean over the hill, and step into the crumbling ruins of a forgotten tower. You're here for a reason, something important, but you can't quite remember, like you're waking from a dream.

A sparkle catches your eye, and you discover a bronze dish with a white candle tucked away on a dusty shelf. You fumble in the darkness, hearing a soft rattle as your fingers disturb a box of matches. You light the candle, protecting the whispering flame as it crackles to life, revealing an imposing door. A gust of wind tickles your neck as you push it open. Despite your uncertainty, you step forward into the unknown.

You have earned…
★ The Talisman of Ambition ★
Art is the passion of creation.

You've earned your first totem! These tokens are rewards, meant to energize and chronicle your progress. Desire and inspiration will carry you through the initial stages towards increased mastery of your craft, so this token is a reminder to focus on your joy, that you *want* this for yourself.

Courage is taking action despite the unknown; being aware of gaps in your knowledge or experience, which will make the journey both more difficult, and more necessary. When things get hard, remember to keep the torch of your inspiration lit. This is your *what*: what do you intend, what do you choose? Be specific with your goals, and hold firm to the inner vision of your mind's eye. You can do this.

Sanctify your space: the magic of writing happens inside you, but it's easier to channel that energy with rituals or consecrated tools, set aside for one noble purpose. Our environment shapes our moods in unseen ways, so throughout this book I'll be recommending small, physical tokens you can use to remind yourself what it feels like to be in a state of creative power; leaving yourself touchpoints so you can back into that expansive mindset as quickly as possible. Ideally, this will be something that *stays* in your writing space, even if it's something small. This first one is easy: get yourself a nice scented candle, that you can light while writing and douse when you're ready to move on to other tasks. Consider it as a visual representation of your personal muse.

0

CREATIVE COURAGE
Start Before You Begin

That's right, we're starting with *chapter zero*, because there are some things that must be said before we proceed. Before I can tell you exactly how to write books that matter, we need to agree on some basic tenets, regarding the *purpose* of writing. Otherwise, you may resist some of the strategies I'm about to share, due to things you've been told, and things you believe. You'll feel them when they come up, like tapeworms writhing in discomfort, twisting in your intestines when you read things that feel untrue for you. Like cat parasites or zombie cicadas. They are altering your behavior.

By 1770 BC, the Egyptians had a symbol for zero in accounting texts. The symbol *nfr*, meaning beautiful, was also used to indicate the base level in drawings of tombs and pyramids, and distances were measured relative to this point, as being above or below. So that's what this chapter is: a baseline.

I can't possibly hope to change your beliefs about art and literature, but I want to make you aware of them, while

1

giving you a new framework with which to overcome some of the inherent challenges you may encounter during the creative process.

So we need to talk about not just what to write but *how*, and I'm not talking syntax or structure, I'm talking mood, intent and awareness. What you believe will impact how you feel, and how you feel will impact whether you write well, or whether you write at all.

If you're new to book writing and haven't yet experienced the soul-crushing effects of writer's block; if you just want quick and dirty writing tips without a historical overview of the creative process and the *necessary* anxieties that come with it; if you're determined to write your book your way and immune to harsh critics and negative reviews—then you might want to skip this step and come back to it once you've Suffered For Your Art long enough to be ready for a change.

One of my favorite books is *Divine Fury*, which is basically an academic study of the history of genius. The most fascinating thing was that, once upon a time, the state of genius was perceived to have physiological symptoms that resided in the body. Today we might associate these with a manic episode: wide pupils, sweating, bold declarations, god-like confidence that the universe was conspiring in your favor, that you had a divine mission that must be fulfilled, and it had to be done *now*: no time for bathing or sleeping or eating or anything else, there was only the work.

I'm sure you've felt some version of this yourself, what is more commonly known today as being in the flow or in the zone; when time flies and you're productive and immersed in the creative process.

2

"We all start out knowing magic. We are born with whirlwinds, forest fires, and comets inside us. We are born able to sing to birds and read the clouds and see our destiny in grains of sand." – *Robert R. McCammon*

This reckless enthusiasm and inspiration is important, because it's what actually prompts the *work*. Without the faith that you can do this, that it matters, that you're not wasting your time, the work may go unfinished.

This is why a priest prescribes rituals, why magicians or musicians have a practice. Some days, the magic or muse appears and fills the work with supernatural fervor. Some days, it doesn't. But the more days you can sit there and do the work, the less you need to rely on supernatural entities: or more precisely, the more you come to realize that *you are* the supernatural entity, it resides inside you, and you can tempt it out with rituals that shift your mood and mindset.

But what happens when doubts and fears steal this enthusiasm from you? How do you keep going when you're feeling stuck, lost, inferior, worthless?

CREATIVE FEAR

In my opinion, all creative fear is based on two basic insecurities:

1. Are you good enough? (quality)
2. Your true worth (value)

The interesting thing is, these two critical fears are universally experienced, while also being universally discounted or ignored: the common advice to authors is to *just keep writing*. If all you have is the magic, the sensitive, feeble flicker of your capricious inspiration, then the solution is avoidance. You put your head in the sand, duck into your writing cave and ignore whether your writing is any good, whether it has any value, because that's not why you write anyway, right?

You might consume memes about courage and persistence and perseverance, but that's a trap: courage is a limited resource that needs to be constantly refilled. Courage belongs to those who know they are lying to themselves; the painful anxiety of forcing yourself to do the thing while also recognizing that somehow, eventually, the other shoe is going to drop. An infernal deferment of practical considerations in favor of artistic ones, a bold negation and refusal of the final reception, deliberate as a sword, ferocious self-protection, bent on survival.

3 ORDERS OF WRETCHEDNESS

When I was finishing my PhD in Literature, I came across a list of books Herman Melville had on his bookshelf at the time of writing *Moby Dick*. One of them was called the *Genius of Solitude* by William Alger. I couldn't find any modern reproductions, so I spent months typing out and editing an old badly-scanned copy, and discovered a unique theory of the creative anxieties most authors face.

Alger begins by referring to the competition that forces internal doubts: motivated by external rewards, but threatened by revealing reflections.

> "The endless multiplicity of competition in modern society, at every point a prize, at every point a glass — tends to

force us inordinately on our own notice. If we could but gaze at the prize alone, and break or blink the glass!"

Then he identifies the roots of creative unhappiness; what he calls the "three orders of wretchedness."

1. I have nothing to live for! (purpose)

The first challenge is finding a worthwhile purpose or goal. The meaning of life, if there is one, is to make life meaningful. As Goethe writes: "Wouldst lead a happy life on earth? Thou must, then clothe the world with worth."

According to Alger, the true zest of life is an absorbing object. He writes, "Happiness is the successful pursuit of an aim." But this leads to the second challenge: how do we choose?

2. If I could wish, I could do! (plan)

How do you know which project has merit? How do you find time for creative pursuits, when you're already overwhelmed with responsibilities? Maybe you feel driven to some greater purpose, but you have no idea what it is or how to get started. According to Alger,

> "The greater the number of the interests a man carries, and the greater the number of external relations he sustains, the more delicate and arduous becomes the problem of harmonizing them, fulfilling his duties, and satisfying his desires."

Unfortunately, there is no universal cure for indecision, and nobody can tell you what to do with your life.

However, *any* decision is better than indecision. Doing something is better than doing nothing. Given the importance of #1, the best advice is to choose something that fascinates or excites you, and commit to it.

3. *Why should I wish? I could not do! (skill)*

This third one is the most frequently met by creatives: the disparity between our personal ability and our creative vision. Skills are developed over time, and budding creatives are commonly frustrated by their inability to express, communicate or capture their ideas.

Mastery takes time and determination. Many writers give up too early, unwilling or unable to bear the harsh truth that they aren't as good as they think they are; that they aren't able to do this, or aren't really cut out for this. In order to become proficient at something, first you must produce badly. This can jar uncomfortably with the ideal of ourselves that we have, when our best efforts are so far below our ideal ambitions.

> "Unhappiness results when the imagination outruns the heart. When great faculties have no correspondent desires to animate and use them; also when great energies have no adequate motives and guides."

I also love this quote, which might resonate with you if you've ever had trouble expressing your ideas to your own satisfaction: "Her soul was a noble engine filled with insufficient fuel and fire and the incongruity produced agonizing want. Her spirit was effusively expansive: her nerves scantily furnished. The aching voids of defective vitality continually recalled her attention, and every meditation ended with vacancy and death."

JOY, VALUE, CRAFT

In a response to the *3 Orders of Wretchedness*, I've developed a simple framework that I hope will serve as a remedial potion, meant to instill a temporary path through the wild uncertainties of the creative process.

Purpose: Joy (motivation)
What energizes you

Plan: Value (market)
Respect your readers

Skill: Craft (mastery)
Practice your craft

Other books will tell you, you're either a hack or an artist. That if you write for money, you're selling out your creative soul, your worth, your value. I won't name them, because I don't want to encourage such filthy literature.

According to this unfortunately common stereotype, the artist is the literary purist who writes from their soul's private voice; while the hack is the skilled manipulator who writes books readers love to buy. That it's *better* to be a starving artist than it is to be a celebrated hack; and somehow egregious to write good books on purpose and get paid for your writing mastery.

This limiting mindset assumes you cannot create quality on purpose, only on accident; that the value of the work is in the *process*, not in the end result. It's bad advice, nearly guaranteed to failure—both in terms of financial renumeration, but also in terms of objective quality, which will be verified by a pile of rejection letters or a stack of brutal, negative reviews.

The false dichotomy between a *hack* and an *artist* have no place in this book, so I'll replace them with a more suitable pair borrowed from the Tarot tradition: the fool and the magician.

A fool has a dream, but no map, no plan, just hope and boundless enthusiasm. He sets off in any direction. It doesn't matter, because he doesn't know what he wants. He's counting on help, and filled with courage.

A magician has a specific goal and experience; she's aware of the difficulties, but she's prepared and ready to adapt. She's counting on herself, and filled with confidence.

Everybody begins a fool, and it's not meant as a negative term: there's incredible power in chasing your joy. But at some point, you may decide you want more. This will lead to a determination to harness your creativity and use it effectively, with purpose and intention, by providing value. This quest may be difficult, but with practice and experience, you will improve your craft to the point of mastery.

A good book awakens the reader's mind, is stimulating, is thought provoking, is magical. But *you* do not get to dictate how this magic happens, or if it happens at all. The strategies in this book will help you narrow the gap, but *only* if satisfying readers by providing value is your goal.

My hope is that this three-step, confidence generating framework might help us agree on a very general, shared intention: choose joy, aim for value, practice your craft. You don't have to accept it right now, but I may refer back to these concepts later on.

Prepare

INCANTATIONS

The premise of this book is "books readers love, from first draft to final polish," and I've divided the sections up to help you fulfill those targets accordingly. Thus, in the first section, we'll be tackling *books readers love*.

I've already laid out a little groundwork on *why* you should aim to enchant readers; that magic is a gift you share. But one of the main themes of this book is that magic requires personal autonomy. You can't force readers to love your books by telling them how great it is; the work must stand for itself. You can seduce them, but only if they're paying attention and open to your literary advances. You can be enchanting, but it doesn't follow that others will be enchanted by you. This is the magic that can only be invoked. We'll get to that later.

For now, we'll focus squarely on the craft: the *incantation*. Put simply, these will be rituals or formulas you can study, practice and repeat to evoke and channel your own magic and give it form. The goal is to contain it, not constrain it. These aren't necessarily rules to follow, so much as writing prompts and triggers that will spark your own imagination through friction. So if you resist them at first, that's fine: just don't *ignore* them. They serve a purpose. While some of this is foundational material, only a little of it is basic or vague.

You may find better strategies or formulas of your own; but starting with these will serve you well until you're ready for something more advanced. They may not be perfect, they are definitely not universal, but they *work*. If you put them into practice, you will see results.

That said, like learning any new skill or ability, they may not work immediately. At first, they may seem troublesome, pedantic or even frustrating. They may take repetition, practice and discipline before your words start to glow with power and meaning.

Before we unlock the cabinet of truly powerful magic, we need to start with an introduction to the more basic tools and resources, the safety precautions and utilitarian seminars presented in a secure, classroom setting. It may feel stifling to sit and study instead of doing the *creative* magic that only you can do.

I'm not trying to trivialize your unique experience, abilities or desires. But I do hope to establish some groundwork and set some boundaries; it's very easy to follow the bliss of your inspiration and end up lost in the infinite, labyrinthine hallways of your unfettered imagination. Think of these strategies as Ariadne's thread: they'll help you get through the maze before confronting the minotaur.

BASIC TERMS

- Spellcraft: weaving words together to create meaning
- Writecraft: telling powerful stories on paper
- Bookcraft: creating a long-form masterpiece

Take notes, highlight passages, implement and see where you end up when the dust settles. Notice anything that seems unfamiliar, fresh, new or uncomfortable, that stirs feelings of repulsion or recognition. Sit with your discomfort. Acknowledge it. Thank it. It's served you well so far. Now take a breath, count to three, and let it go.

> "If you would be a real seeker after truth it is necessary that at least once in your life you doubt, as far as possible, all things." – *Rene Descartes*

At the end of each chapter, I've added a short summary of the main points for quick review, as "grimoire" notes. These may include links to additional resources that don't fit within the main content.

> "
>
> The pen is a magic wand.
> Just as the slight flick
> of a conductor's baton
> commands symphonies,
> so too, with a curl
> of your finger,
> vanquish armies.
>
> BOOK CRAFT

1

FICTION BASICS
Filling Your Cauldron

What makes a good story? Imagine a four-year-old is trying to tell you something. They are excited about sharing their experiences with you and having your undivided attention, but as the story keeps going, you're losing interest. Desperation enters their eyes, and they speak loudly and wave their hands around, trying to command your attention, but you've stopped listening. Why? Because the story didn't have a point, or a purpose, or an *end*.

It wasn't building towards a meaningful resolution. It wasn't a story, it was a loose collection of life incidents with no unifying theme or purpose; an endless entanglement of episodic scenes, a torrent of unrelated information. Our brains are *built* to look for meaning and connection, so this deluge of information is almost a kind of mental torture.

We can write whatever we want, but unless we do it in a way that *allows* readers to lose themselves in our story, unless we make it easy and enjoyable, they will get annoyed, bored or exhausted trying to figure it all out.

For an effective spell to work, it has to be crafted with purpose and intention. There are infinite episodes or intriguing scenes that may be interesting enough to share with readers, but it's your job as the author to figure out what fits and what doesn't. And to make those editorial decisions, you have to decide what you're hoping to achieve.

This gathering of elements should be seen as a sacred practice, not a tedious task. A sorcerer's apprentice, for example, might first be trusted with the gathering of materials, because being able to identify useful ingredients is a crucial skill on the path to mastery.

An amateur florist will pick and place pretty flowers together because of how they look. A botanist will understand their deeper meaning, their uses and effect, their risks and dangers. They will have the information, without the practical intention. An apothecary, however, will respect the knowledge of their craft, and see the deeper connections and effects of potions or herbal remedies. They will go beyond the aesthetics, to the effects. They will recognize which ingredients are necessary, and which are poisonous.

You can't start brewing a spell without a full cabinet of potential ingredients; and you can't cook with an empty pot. *The Stone Soup* is a European folk story in which passing travelers convince the people of a town to share a small amount of their food in order to make a meal that everyone can enjoy. It's meant as a parable on the value of sharing, but it has a deeper meaning. By themselves, the travelers would still only have stone-flavored water. They create a delicious stew by slowly adding in common elements, that by themselves have little value, but together create a bountiful meal.

So in this section, we will be *on the lookout*. We will become literary hunter-gatherers. Our goal will be to build an apothecary's cabinet, which some authors refer to as plot fodder or story seeds.

> "When I'm reading, I'm looking for something to steal. Readers ask me all the time the traditional question, 'where do you get your ideas from?' I reply 'We are all having ideas all the time. But I'm on the lookout for them. You're not.'" – *Philip Pullman*

Before you begin writing a novel that matters, you have to ask yourself, what are you trying to do, and what do you need to make that happen? Which elements you choose depend on the results you're trying to achieve: and this is not something you get to decide. Every element has its own attributes, function, qualities, rich history and unique flavor. Licorice might enhance an herbal tea but ruin a pot roast.

To write with intention, you have to understand the qualities and effects of your ingredients. You need to understand what readers are trying to feel when they read their favorite genre. These essentials elements can be uniquely combined, to brew novel tensions and flavors. But choose wisely, because they can bring your story to life or take it from you.

GATHER YOUR INGREDIENTS

You can imagine this part like *filling your cauldron*. Throwing random stuff in your pot is a good way to burn off your eyebrows.

But there are common, basic ingredients for story-telling that will help give your novel shape. So over the next few chapters, we're going to simplify, starting with this:

> Your story is not about your character.
> It's about your character's *problem*.

What problem? The problem so big it can't be fixed.
The problem that forces the character to *become*.

According to E.M. Forster, the ingredients of fiction are "human beings, time, and space." And while that's technically true, it misses the point. Why should readers care about what happens to those characters? Why should they keep reading? What makes a novel boring, versus gripping?

Aristotle reduces drama into just two elements: pity and fear. We have to *care* about the characters enough to *worry* what happens to them next. This means your character must face a challenge or problem.

In my opinion, if a story is worth telling, this problem will be greater than the character. If the character is greater than the problem, it's an incident, an anecdote, an episode, something cool that happened once. This is fine, but it's not *great*. It's interesting, not devastating. For a memoir or biography or historical fiction, sure there will be lots of historical nostalgia about life and culture back when... but it should *also* involve one critical core conflict that shatters the character's sense of identity, awareness, understanding, and forces a real change. You can't just show a determined character who succeeds; you need to show a determined character who is destroyed.

We'll talk more about drama and tension later, but for now let's start with a basic introduction of story elements. Here are the things I think a good book should include.

1. **Story:** a unifying narrative (things that happen and are tied together).
2. **Purpose:** a goal worth pursuing and necessary (by someone we care about).
3. **Drama:** conflict, suspense and intrigue (the outcome is unclear).
4. **Structure:** a comfortable reading experience with clear signposts (what's happening & why it matters).
5. **Resolution:** a concluding event with positive emotion (goal achieved).
6. **Credibility:** mastery, smooth reading experience, trust.

That last one may seem better suited towards nonfiction, and it is – but I'm leaving it here because it'll be important later: basically, even if you have all the right elements, it can still be poorly written and turn off readers. Readers need to trust that you know what you're doing; that the story is going somewhere and will deliver an emotional payout worth the time invested. This is why the writing and craft is so important, but *alone* the writing is meaningless, without a strong story.

A good story has a beginning and an end. Sometimes, like in short stories, the ending is abrupt, leaving you with compelling images and questions; it's something to muse over, something that sticks with you. But a novel needs to do more than give you something to think about, because you're committing more than just five minutes of your time. The longer the story drags on, the more readers will feel a nagging skepticism about where the author is taking them.

There are a lot of elements to putting a story together, but I want you to keep this one thing in mind: a good novel is generally about one episode that has a major emotional impact in a character's life, presented them with an impossible moral choice, and forced them to become greater than they knew they could be.

Why that episode matters, how it all came about, why it was so important – everything else is just there to give context to that one big event.

LIKEABLE PROTAGONIST

Most books will have one main protagonist, hero or heroine. This is generally the character through which the story is told; either as a witness, narrator, or POV (point of view).

Readers have to *like* this character enough to care what happens to them. Luckily there are some quick and easy tips you can use to make your characters likable. If you watch any movie or TV show, the one-minute introduction, before the story even gets started, is probably focused on "good person" signals.

They stop to feed the homeless; they pick up trash that wasn't theirs; they wait patiently in traffic even as someone else cuts them off. They may not be *heroic* yet, but they are *good*. This is often shown through contrast. Not only are they good, but they are also different from their peers (this goodness is who they are, not how they were raised).

You also want to make them sympathetic (someone vulnerable that invites feelings of empathy). Despite being a good person, their life is hard. They are doing the best they can.

And then, you want to make them unique and interesting. Don't overdo it here, with clownish, radical antics, but do make sure you don't have a cardboard cut-out or "Mary Sue" character who is mostly a blank slate or mirror to events. Often, the protagonist is actually kind of boring at first, shy and timid— and it's another character that is more flamboyant and outgoing.

Here's a quick checklist of main character attributes:

- quirky habits
- self-consciousness
- getting bullied
- being brave or clever
- standing up for someone weaker
- saving pets, children or elderly
- burdened with problems & responsibilities
- unique hobby, style or totem
- fatal flaw, fear or lack (shard of glass)
- oppressed or repressed

A "totem" is a writing device I like to use, where a character will have a keepsake or souvenir that has profound personal meaning; it may be related to their backstory (the big event that made them who they are today, probably a loss of some kind) or a favorite memory. They may also have a unique style, but how they dress should be related to their lifestyle and habits (they shop second-hand so they can donate to the soup kitchen).

I also like to think in terms of oppression or repression: in some way or another, they are *not free*. Either because of physical limitations in their environment, or interior anxieties about their worth or ability. They *want* things, like everyone else, and would *try* to get what they want, probably, but not right now, because they have too much responsibility, duty or other excuses.

A lot of writing guides focus too much on character development – if you have tons of backstory on your characters, you'll be trying to squeeze it in even if it's not relevant. However, it is necessary to give your characters proper motivation. They should have deep reasons for doing things and feeling things, but these don't have to be revealed right away.

A great character will also have what's sometimes called a fatal flaw or shard of glass. They start at a disadvantage: with a lack they're trying to fill, often tied to an earlier failure. A tragic science fair event, which led to an irrational terror of lizards. The final *change* that happens may be tied to this fear or lack; a way to right the wrong, wipe the slate, heal the wound by removing the shard of glass that's been keeping it open. If the character is terrified of lizards, maybe they are forced to swim through an alligator pond at the climax in order to save someone they love (or prove that their love is greater than their fear).

Through the course of the book, their flaw holds them back. They succeed when they're able to overcome that limitation, or realize it was never a real barrier at all (they've changed and grown to the point where the limitation no longer applies to them, or they're forced to confront their deepest fear or relinquish the thing they want most). This is the figurative "death of self" after their greatest setback or fear is realized; then they come back stronger, reborn, ready to triumph.

This isn't absolutely necessary, but it's an effective writing device. To make the story matter, to show how *this challenge* is so important and critical for *this character*, you can make the experience that much harder and more threatening by starting your protagonist off with a unique deficit that perfectly matches the zenith of the ordeal: this story matters *to them* because the events threaten their personal identity at a deep, critical level.

BIG DREAMS THAT FAIL

Many stories begin when one path closes. Characters will need or want something enough to take action; but should fail, at least in the beginning. They must be incapable of fulfilling their desires; or have an inability to get what they want. For our story to matter, we have to show how profoundly challenging the narrative is, at least to our protagonist.

In the first chapter, which we'll talk about later, you want to introduce the character through action and plot events, not backstory or humdrum reality. There should already be inherent conflict in their current, normal situation or environment; conflict they perhaps ignore or avoid because they're waiting for *this one big thing* that will change everything for them.

Beginning your story when that one big thing fails to materialize is a great starting point: if they've been hoping for years to get into college, show them opening the rejection letter. If they've been waiting for a big promotion at work, show them getting fired. If they've been dreaming of a big wedding to the perfect guy, show them getting left at the altar. Stories often *begin* with characters out of their depths, cast aside, floundering for purpose, disillusioned and emotionally wrecked.

Characters must be faced with a threat, barrier or challenge *so big* that they cannot currently overcome it. The story is the process through which they grow strong enough to actually overcome the obstacle. But smart characters won't take big risks unless they are desperate. So first, take away the safe, easy path, and force them to pivot onto a more reckless path they wouldn't choose under normal circumstances. They may still be chasing the same dream or goal, but the stakes are higher, and the risks greater, and the outcome uncertain.

Hint: if they are capable of defeating all the challenges without changing... your story probably isn't big enough.

Active antagonist: your story may need an antagonist, who is trying to get, achieve or do something that puts him at odds with your hero.

INTERESTING CHARACTERS

Your cast or ensemble will be critical for adding emotion into your story: relationships, betrayal, lies, promises, romance, friendships or enemies drive the drama. Your protagonist should be torn between loyalties and need to make difficult moral decisions. You may find characters come into being later, when you need them most, but it would be a good idea to brainstorm some potential characters before we begin plotting, even though the story we are telling is probably the journey of the character who is forced to change the most.

Think of them like puzzle pieces. You're cutting up different bits of cardboard of different shapes and sizes. Later you'll try to sort them together into a larger panel; then you'll paint details over the panel. Create the pieces you might need now and see how they fit, trim or discard them later. Here's a list of potential roles and important characters.

Ensemble Cast

- the main character (MC)
- best friend (supporter, optimist)
- best platonic friend (these three form a non-romantic trio, though sometimes the platonic friend actually wants more or vice versa)
- skeptic (a non-supportive friend who doubts and questions: pessimist/rationalist)
- comedian or jokester (provides comic relief)
- teacher (in a literal sense)
- mentor (wise role model who introduces them to the new world)
- boss
- parents
- siblings
- nosy neighbor
- nemesis
- cute sidekick
- main antagonist
- antagonist's henchmen
- cannon fodder (a faceless horde to slaughter)
- traitor (someone on their team who plots against them)
- natural catastrophes or monsters (can be character-like); a sudden storm, lion mauling, etc.

PS. Don't rely on "bad luck" often, but it's okay if accidents happen a few times when necessary.

PERSONALITY ATTRIBUTES:

To bring your characters to life, you'll have to give them unique identities. I'm not a fan of creating huge "character bibles" for each role, but it can be really helpful to make a quick list of main attributes to keep track of everything.

- where they live
- what they wear
- hair/eye color
- an object they treasure
- something they love
- something they hate
- something they'd never do
- a unique skill or ability
- a weird habit
- what they want (immediately, and permanently)

Characters often develop as the story begins to manifest itself, so they may tell you who they are when they appear. Interesting, strong characters that readers care about, will probably have individual identities that clash together, creating drama and tension you didn't fully predict. It might be useful to begin deliberately, by casting your major characters into personality archetypes.

When I read the *Brothers Karamazov* for the first time, I was struck by how unique the characters are, and how well they match up to astrological traits. Whether or not you believe in astrology or other more popular systems of personality like the Myers Briggs or Jung Archetypes (which are based in part on the Tarot's higher arcana) they can be useful in fleshing out characters and giving them consistent temperament and behavior.

Just for fun, I tried to merge these together into one collective list, even though they don't actually match up perfectly. Start with this, if you like, or dig deeper into each particular system (there are handy graphs online). Myers Briggs has 16 personality types, while the other systems have 12.

Concerned With Personal Issues:

1. **Aries:** Pioneer, she starts.
   Ruler, control.
2. **Taurus:** Creatrix, she makes.
   Everyman, belonging.
3. **Gemini:** Lovers, she connects.
   Joker, enjoyment.
4. **Cancer:** Protectress, she takes care.
   Caregiver, service.

Concerned With Larger Community

5. **Leo:** Leader, she inspires.
   Hero, mastery.
6. **Virgo:** Professional, she discerns.
   Sage, understanding.
7. **Libra:** Diplomat, she mediates.
   Lover, intimacy.
8. **Scorpio:** Investigatrix, she delves deep.
   Rebel, liberation.

Concerned With Universal Issues

9. **Sagittarius:** Adventuress, a free spirit.
   Explorer, freedom.
10. **Capricorn:** Keeper of tradition, she organizes.
    Magician, power.
11. **Aquarius:** Revolutionary, she makes way for the new.
    Innocent, safety.
12. **Pisces:** empath, she feels.
    Creator, innovation.

These can be divided more broadly into core ambitions like *achievement, belonging, freedom,* or *control*. To add more friction, choose opposite characteristics or fundamental motivations for your main characters. Friends can share interests and values, while also having deeply divided principles that will create conflict and drama when you apply pressure.

If you want readers to care about what's happening, then you'll need to create characters that care. You need to flesh out your characters to the extent that you plan to cause them pain.

Think of it like a voodoo doll. If you just draw a face on it and stick it with pins, it won't hurt, we won't be able to picture it harming our enemies. The more detail and backstory and motivation you give your characters, the more readers like them, the more they will feel the pain.

If you are going to hurt a character, they must have a reason great enough to make the pain and suffering worth it; they have to be motivated to fight for what they care about, and endure the suffering willingly. Otherwise you're just bringing strangers into the plot for a bit of torture porn. (If you're not familiar with this term, don't worry I'll explain it later – but basically, it's sadistic brutality without a deeper purpose).

OBSTACLES & CHALLENGES

Whenever your main characters try to do something, they should run into as many obstacles as possible. Rewards must outweigh the risks (they must want the goal enough to overcome dangers, and be completely committed to action). Pressure forces action and keeps the momentum.

We'll discuss plotting *ad nauseam* later, but a very simple framework might look something like this:

1. Beginning: *knocked off course.*
2. Middle: *forced to fight.*
3. End: *sacrifice to win.*

In other words, unexpected things happen that encroach into the main character's experience, until they are forced to respond to an uncomfortable situation. Along the way, they become embroiled into the conflict until they can no longer extricate from it without destroying a piece of themselves (and through the ordeal, gain deeper wisdom, insight or power).

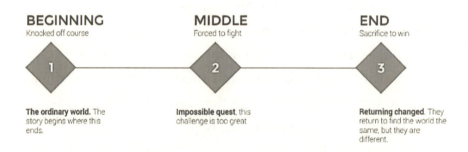

BEGINNING
Knocked off course

1

The ordinary world. The story begins where this ends.

MIDDLE
Forced to fight

2

Impossible quest, this challenge is too great

END
Sacrifice to win

3

Returning changed. They return to find the world the same, but they are different.

Many types of commercial fiction do not absolutely depend on the internal change of the protagonist, and that's okay. A great book should still feature a very *difficult* or *meaningful* encounter that leaves a lasting impression on a sympathetic character; that brings out the very best of what they are capable of; that affects them on a deep, emotional level.

The circumstances of the unfolding drama should include a level of intrinsic autonomy, as we'll discuss more later. *This* story is profound for *this* character because they are attached to the narrative in a way that feels inevitable. It isn't just a series of events happening to them; they are also in some sense responsible for the outcome.

> "The order of events should spring from decisions the characters make. Create situations of conflict in which characters can only ever get out of if they decide on something, even if they make the wrong choices."

While I absolutely agree with this quote from screenwriter Ben Scharf, I don't think it's enough. Yes, your character's choices should direct the chain of events; but that only happens if you're also creating situations of conflict.

In many genres, the plot is really the prime story driver, and the character's reactions are secondary. It may not even be smart to dwell on the deep psychological soliloquy of self-doubt or self-loathing. Readers might get bored or frustrated with a modern Hamlet character. Whether you're more comfortable with plot-based or character-based fiction, keep in mind that *conflict* is the primary driver for narrative momentum, and most books will feature an escalating series of crises leading to one crucial moment.

Momentum and urgency are easier to handle when *each scene* or chapter is crucial for activating the next bit of action. Something happens or changes; the characters are forced to respond or react; then something else happens. Think of them like links in a chain. One weak link and the whole endeavor will fail when the pressure becomes too great. A tight plot on its own might be engaging enough. But if it's *all* action or survival, it won't have the emotional punch or depth of greatness.

UNIQUE SETTINGS

Your setting or scenes needs to be vivid and different enough to keep readers interested: they will also provide obstacles and challenges, or give us a deeper understanding of your characters. Always try to show the setting as characters interact with it, and only during low-stakes scenes. Only show what's relevant, or what the characters notice. We'll talk a lot more about description later, but it's a good idea to brainstorm key scenes that you might feature in your story.

You need to present readers with things they've never seen before. Try to think visually: what are the coolest, most epic things that could happen? What kind of scenes would make an excellent movie? Basically, we're building a sandbox our characters can play in. We need to establish the rules of the world, what kind of creatures or magic or technology exists there. If it's contemporary fiction, we can add amazing settings and locations, where neat things can happen. We're not thinking about plot yet, this is just *wouldn't it be cool if...*?

For my first novel, I wanted the heroine to use a whale as a weapon and have it destroy a castle. I had to spend the whole book building up her powers and magic so that it didn't come off as ridiculous. In the book I'm working on, I want my protagonist to face a massive sea creature (like Andromeda, except she saves herself), so I need to figure out:

1. where the monster came from and why it appears now
2. how she's going to defeat it when nobody else can

They don't have to be magical, but pick a setting that makes you feel all the emotions. Even your basic settings (job, home, school, park, hospital, police station, grocery store) can be interesting settings. What's the most emotionally stunning thing that could possibly happen there?

*   running into an ex
*   a robbery
*   slipping on spilled milk and knocking out a tooth
*   being embarrassed in front of someone attractive
*   your dad having a heart attack
*   witnessing a kidnapping
*   an infestation of rats

You don't have to make everything emotional, but things should happen – books readers love are entertaining; they can't just be life-as-is. They need to reflect the deepest, most honest, most vulnerable parts of human existence (the less magic and action, the more emotional depth you'll need).

If it's a political thriller or space odyssey or urban fantasy, you can dazzle with adventure, charming characters, magical abilities, historical trivia and secret societies, and keep readers interested without all the emotional angst (there should still be some emotion, but it doesn't have to be dripping with it). If it's just a story about life, and small challenges, it's going to be harder to keep the readers caring about what's going on.

Make a list of ten favorite scenes from other books in your genre. Think about the scenes that stick with you, the scenes that you remember – those are the good ones. Then take all your ideas, characters, potential locations, and dream up some epic scenes. Remember it's not just about what happens or how cool it is, it's also about the character's emotional motivations: why it matters. See how you can increase the conflict.

THEME

According to Jerry Jenkins (author of the *Left Behind* series), "What happens is your plot, and why it matters is your theme." But as K. M. Weiland points out in her writing blog,

> "These days, theme is the orphaned child of the storytelling world. Everybody tries to be kind to it, but because nobody knows quite what to do with it, it mostly just ends up sitting in the corner playing with itself."

I've never found discussions of theme particularly useful; for me it represents *what the author intends to convey* or why *they* think their own work is important or meaningful, but understanding or acknowledging the theme rarely increases the enjoyment of the work, nor does it help authors figure out what actually happens in the story.

There's already far too much garrulous discussion about the *meaning* of a particular book or novel, which gives pundits and professors something to dissect and argue about, but much of this meaning is generated outside of the text of the book. While it can make for deeper discussions about why a particular book is meaningful or relevant, it won't matter if nobody is reading it.

Certain genres will have more theme; and nonfiction books or memoirs almost always *do* need a theme, so it's not just a collection of information or anecdotes. But nobody will care about the meaning if the content is boring.

All that matters is whether the words on the pages succeed in creating the desired effect, whatever it may be. That's why I've focused on a step-by-step, systematic and practical approach to writing a book that doesn't leave much room for navel-gazing or lofty ideals about creative production.

GENRE TROPES & CLICHÉS

We've talked about the elements of a good story, and they are important. Any story will have the right batch of ingredients. Whether or not you mix, prepare, bake and decorate those ingredients into a successful novel, we'll focus on later, but definitely a piece of the puzzle is *genre*: in other words, where does this book fit on the shelf? What is your audience looking for, and how will they recognize it when they see it?

A lot of authors will say, well my book is kind of a speculative fiction genre mashup that doesn't follow any rules. Why should I have to conform with genre at all, I don't *want* to use tropes or clichés, I want to write something totally different!

And I get that, but here's the thing, if someone is looking for recommendations for the best books in their favorite genre, while it's true some of those might subvert stereotypes and stretch the rules, *most* of them will have basic, common, universal motifs, tropes and clichés that are the basis of what constitutes that particular kind of reading experience: if you don't use these, you are not writing in that genre.

Think of it this way: nearly every piece of art or literature that we herald as works of great genius did not come out of nowhere: each was and is important to us because it's representative of a movement; of a shift in literary style. Art is rarely a spontaneous, isolated explosion of creativity. It's a reaction and synthesis. It's a great ocean wave, crossing the world and back again, cresting and breaking.

Great artists had peers and rivals that they openly or secretly copied from. While the other supporting pieces in that wave disappeared or faded, their existence created the space and rising interest for one perfect work that could encapsulate everything people craved. Writers and artists are often trying to do the same thing to satiate demand, but only a handful have the skill and inspiration to become immortalized. Books that succeed, almost without fail, are those that have become popular, whether or not they were expected to.

"The ugly fact is books are made out of other books."
– *Cormac McCarthy*

However, that doesn't mean "writing to market" needs to be a compromise of your artistic virtue. Just as your readers have been influenced by current changes in the consumer landscape, influenced by TV Shows and Culture and Media, *so have you*. The things you love, they love. The things you enjoy and find cool, they do too! You exist as a product of the times. Whatever you want to write about, whatever thrills you, there's an audience who will appreciate it out there.

> "If only you'd remember before you ever sit down to write that you've been a reader much longer than you were ever a writer. You simply fix that fact in your mind, then sit very still and ask yourself, as a reader, what piece of writing in all the world would you most want to read." *– J. D. Salinger*

Keep your story, that's fine! But there is a crafty way to tell it, that maximizes the dramatic impact and improves the reading experience, and a weak, amateur, inexperienced way. On the one hand, the words on the page are purely technical. All presentation and packaging. They aren't the *main* thing. On the other hand, they are the *only* thing. The story is that magical thing that is generated by them.

A rainbow doesn't exist outside of human experience. It's a miracle, an accidental moment, when our color receptors perceive a combination of elements in our environment in a specific way. According to Pythagoras, seven is a magical number, made up of the material (4) and the spiritual (3). We see the primary colors red, yellow and blue, and mix them in our brains to create the composite hues of orange, green, indigo and violet.

A rainbow is generated by the precise arrangement of predictable elements. But whenever it happens, for the person viewing it, it's a magical experience. Likewise, in your writing, if you put everything in the right places, the "rainbow" will be the magic happening between you and the reader. Something greater than the words on the page. The integral factors are common and technical. The personal experience is breathtaking.

LET THEM EAT CAKE

Let's say you're making a cake. First, you get the recipe and ingredients right, so that it tastes good. Because that's the main point. Then, you can mold it into a cake-shape and add some frosting. You can do this real rough with a butterknife at home and have a lopsided, homely, but delicious cake; or you can spend all day curling tiny little frosted flowers and decorations until it's gorgeous.

The better the decoration, the more value – because people will usually pay more for your time if you've added more craft or artisanship. But the cake will taste the same. If your cake tastes bad, it doesn't matter how good it looks.

Now imagine, you don't want to conform to a *type* of cake. You create an epic masterpiece, but it's not quite chocolate, or carrot, or red velvet... it's a mashup of everything, with intriguing flavors and unexpected structure and everything is new and different. It's *Art*.

But now that it's done, how do you market it? Cake lovers might be skeptical. They might ask "what kind of cake is it?" and you'd say "it's the quintessence of cakeness without being limited by a rigid definition of taste or flavor."

And they might politely take a bite, and it would be a unique culinary experience, and they might applaud your bravery and artistic courage, but they probably won't buy a slice and sit down to eat it, or more importantly, they wouldn't eat it every single day because of its unusual flavor.

That's what happens when you avoid genre conventions or basic, universal principles of story architecture and narrative. So let's say you start over, and think, "now that I know how to make cake, what *else* could I make?" You do some research and find out chocolate cake is the universal favorite and gets more searches than anything else. There is a bigger audience of chocolate cake lovers than any other type of cake.

Wonderful. Because you want to use your skills to create the most value, you determine to create the world's *best chocolate cake*. First, you study the competition. You sample the ten highest rated chocolate cakes and get a feel for their flavor and texture.

You define the "chocolate cakeness" that they share, and notice the interesting features that make each unique. You also notice any problems that fans aren't loving, by reading the negative reviews (too dry, too sweet, not enough chocolate sprinkles, dried fruit and nuts are disgusting, etc).

Then you set out to combine all the winning features by avoiding all the negatives. You aren't trying to "game the market." You're just trying to provide chocolate cake lovers with the *perfect* chocolate cake eating experience. You want people to moan and gush and react like your cake is the one they've been dreaming of their whole life.

This isn't necessarily about *craft*, though you do want to polish and design and pay attention to the aesthetics. Just like cake, part of the reading experience is flavored by expectations.

If you really wanted to do this well, instead of making ten different flavored cakes for multiple audiences, you'd stick with one. You'd also test and fail quickly, by setting up a "free cake day" for chocolate cake fans. You'd try a new formula every week for a year getting feedback until you'd perfected the recipe (without wasting time on stuff that's not important).

Then when you had the flavor and texture just right, you'd hire the best cake designer (assuming that baking and cake-decorating are separate skills, and while you could master both, you really want to focus on your own sphere of genius, and do what you do best, while partnering with someone who is already a master).

After all of that – you'd be ready to market. But all you'd really have to do is give out free samples to a few cake enthusiasts, and your cake would be so damn good they wouldn't be able to stop talking about it.

You can absolutely do this with books. In fact, this is the way it's done. Don't worry about being derivative: including common genre elements is only the base level of creating a book readers enjoy. You have to know what the audience wants – and once you've found it, *readers* determine what they like and dislike; the similarities between popular books in a given genre aren't because authors are stuffing tropes, but because readers are responding to books with those tropes in common.

In my baking example, everyone is going to use the same ingredients, because chocolate cake eaters are expecting a chocolate cake eating experience. If you try to get carrot cake eaters to enjoy a chocolate cake by putting carrots in the chocolate or chocolate in the carrots, that's unlikely to satisfy anyone.

Sometimes I may slip up and use the term *commercial* to designate popular books, but this shouldn't be a negative term. It just means, can you communicate the benefits of your book enough to convince people to pay for it? If not, nobody will want it, and it will be impossible to find. A book like this won't belong on any shelf, and will probably get stuffed in the back somewhere under the miscellaneous pile. You'd have to ask a bookstore clerk, excuse me, but I don't like any of these genres. I'm looking for something that doesn't fit in a box. Do you have anything *else?*

Some authors proclaim that they don't enjoy popular genres themselves, and are writing the stories they want to read. There's nothing wrong with that, unless it's connected with the belief that popular books are inferior, and the general reading public is simply too uninformed to recognize true literary brilliance. This attitude is common among writers, but thinly veiled disdain for your audience won't get you very far. You don't create a better story by avoiding tropes. You create a non-genred story that appeals to nobody. Don't be like Marie Antoinette, feasting with pleasure in the imagination of your creativity palace, while your kingdom starves.

DON'T AVOID, TRANSCEND

The key to excelling in your genre is to include and *transcend* common elements into a rich and original narrative. But you can't achieve this without first recognizing the crucial elements of your particular genre.

How do you know what to include? *You read.*

> "Read, read, read everything—trash, classics, good and bad, and see how they do it. Just like a carpenter who works as an apprentice and studies the master. Read!" – *William Faulkner*

Terry Pratchet gives the same advice more succinctly: "Read with a mind-set of a carpenter looking at trees." Once we have a basic idea of our genre or subject, we can browse relevant categories for common elements. We need to know:

1. How other bestselling authors describe their books
2. What readers are using to search for books they want
3. The popularity of each keyword and category

When I started writing young adult fantasy, I read everything in my genre and took notes of the similarities. I did keyword research, and came up with a word cloud of the most popular topics.

Out of that list, I wrote a very short summary. It's not a book, but it's the beginning of a potential story, that ticks the right boxes. It has legs. It has foundation. Execution is something else, but it's a good place to start:

> Once upon a time there was a girl with silver eyes that reflected the moon and the stars. Her brothers were Devils, who could turn into panthers. Their kingdom was divided between her people, the fae and an ancient race of dragons. One night as she was walking through the silent woods, near a powerful waterfall, she met a vampire prince with a severed hand. She made him fingers of pure magic and became his bride, but her father forbade the match and her brothers hunted them down. The girl with silver eyes and her vampire lover passed through the veil beyond the grave, where their love could bloom forever. One kiss and he gave her the gift of death, making her an immortal like him in the exclusive city. Children still whisper about the girl with

silver eyes who gave up everything for love and became a secret legend.

Besides keywords, there will also be common tropes and motifs: not *what happens*, just literary elements that increase the conflict. In a lot of YA books, the sexy love interest has captivating magical powers over mortal women. But for some reason, they don't work on the protagonist. She's immune. He can hear everybody's thoughts... but hers. She's a mystery, a puzzle, that drives him crazy, because her existence defies his prowess and hints at some inner weakness.

This is often the basis for his attraction to her. Echoes of this permeate through the romance genre, where he "looks at her like a puzzle he can't figure out" or even "you're not like other girls." The protagonist is unusual, special, intriguing, and unexpected. It's that scrutiny and attention, being seen, being watched, that heightens the erotic tension. This is a trope or cliché, which could be used in a thousand different ways, but its inclusion is shorthand – immediately familiar to readers – and if it's overused, it's because it's so effective.

Another simple one is a *smirk*: love interests are often shown as infuriatingly handsome and cocky. A smirk is a facial expression that communicates this confident, teasing personality. You can easily let readers know who the love interest is by having him toss out a devastating smirk early on.

Likewise, the trope of a guy leaning against the wall and blocking the heroine's path is so common it has become a Japanese meme. Kabe-Don (Kabe, "wall", and Don, "bang") refers to the action of slapping a wall fiercely. It's commonly used to heighten romantic tension.

You can use tropes effectively, without seeming cliché or cheesy, as long as you don't use them too much. There are also shared plotting devices that feel common and familiar. Be careful not to use any singular, unique story event from another author, but you don't need to avoid all of the general tropes and clichés that define the genre. For example, nearly all young adult paranormal romances go something like this:

1. Heroine is uncool, unnoticed.
2. Parents died or are missing.
3. Discovers secret powers/ability/unique history.
4. Has a friend of the opposite sex who wants more from them, but they aren't interested "in that way."
5. Has a romantic interest split between two ideal people, both really want her – one is "safe" and one "bad."
6. They discover they have a unique role to play in a secret war or struggle.
7. They discover something shocking about their parents.
8. The bad guy usually turns out to be the father, mother or uncle.
9. They are scared of their powers and begin to think they might be bad or evil.
10. Build up to the "final battle" or the face-to-face conflict, but the bad guy gets away so the story can continue in the next book.

There are reasons this template fits hundreds of YA books. They aren't just copying or recycling motifs. They are including powerful plotting or story devices that generate the greatest intrigue, and heightens the reading experience for a specific audience.

If you think this is just about commercial, popular fiction, you'd be wrong. Here's a simple one I made for more literary or contemporary YA novels:

1. The protagonist is a shy girl or guy who meets
2. an adventurous/outgoing girl or guy who
3. brings them out of their shell, teaches them to live…
4. and then dies.

Also known as the *Bridges to Terabithia* model. My point is, don't avoid the most effective techniques just because they've been done. Instead, figure out how you can use them to your advantage to enhance your story.

> "Adapt what is useful, reject what is useless, add what is specifically your own." *– Bruce Lee*

FULFILLING THE EXPECTATION

Do you know the difference between urban fantasy and epic fantasy? The difference between paranormal romance and supernatural suspense? Each genre has its own rules and tropes and expectations. If you aren't using them, you aren't writing that kind of book!

A romance ends with an HEA – happily ever after. If not, it's not really a romance. Within the romance genre, there are tropes. Some popular ones include: second chance, fated mates, forbidden love, arranged marriages or enemies to lovers. And then there are common situations or elements that allow the story to heat up faster, like being stuck together in a confined space. For each subsection, there are expectations: a particular itch the reader wants to scratch. This might be the idea that anybody can find love, at any time.

A *young adult* contemporary romance, at least the literary kind, has a different expectation: the love interest dies in the end. The message is that you are already dying, and the future is unknown and unexpected, so why not seize every beautiful moment while you can in rebellious defiance to a cruel and unjust world? As Shawn Coyne writes in *The Story Grid,*

> "The only way to write a Story that works is to know exactly what Genre(s) you are exploring and deliver exactly what is required from those Genres. You must know what your reader is expecting before you can possibly satisfy her. And yes, if you are writing a Story, you must think of your audience. A Story means nothing if it is not experienced."

WRITING TO MARKET

If you're planning to publish, you are already writing to market. Your book will be put in a box, on the shelf, according to the nearest plausible category. If you're having trouble defining it, you're probably writing speculative literary fiction: a small genre with very choosy readers. Do you know what they like, what they're looking for? Do you know how to reach and satisfy them? Don't assume the readers will do the work of finding you. They won't.

"When we say, "here, I made this," we're not seeking credit, we're taking responsibility. To be seen, to learn, to own it, to do it better next time. Hiding is too easy. And hiding is a trap." – *Seth Godin*

Not choosing a genre is hiding. If you don't aim for a target, you can never miss; never be compared; never be read. All I'm saying is, you need to read books in your genre and their reviews, to understand what readers like and why. Consider the opposite, which is how most authors operate:

"I didn't write this to be commercial; I actually hate all the tropes and things that popular books do. I wrote this book because of how it felt to me and what I liked. I understand it doesn't have any of the things that you're used to or that other books in the genre have, but if you're looking for a new, different reading experience, that doesn't fit neatly into a genre category, you should read my book."

Why though? Why should they? What's the benefit? Is it the writing quality? The uncomfortable and unfamiliar reading experience? People rarely read for style, they read for story.

If you're not writing a genre-based story, that's okay – but you'll have to make up for it in dramatic tension and scene description. The further you stray from the quick and easy fruit of tropes, clichés and genre considerations, the more work you'll need to do to carve out precious gems, and even when you've collected them, you may find frustratingly that your reader's palates don't appreciate the extraordinary lengths you've undertaken to bring them something new or unique. *Nobody asked you to.*

It reminds me of the piano player who refused to stop playing on campus until he got his girl back. Some people saw it as a grand romantic gesture; others decided it was creepy, manipulative and controlling. Zealous dedication does not *earn* the right for affection or loyalty, though many authors operate from this assumption: because I didn't follow the instructions, because it's more creative, people should like it more!

And they *might*. But if they don't, it's not their fault for not appreciating your creation; it's yours for not valuing their time or interests.

THE VAN GOGH MISTAKE

One of the most interesting things I learned at the Van Gogh museum in Amsterdam was how blatantly commercial Van Gogh tried to be. We only remember his struggle and his eventual, unique style. But he started by copying everything. He copied impressionists with bright colors and pointellated riverscapes. Then he copied Japanese print art with bold colors and severe lines. Less well known is the time he decided to go all-in on weavers: because *nobody else* was doing them.

He thought to stand out, you had to find something novel and new, an untouched space. He was also convinced that *portraits* were destined to become the single greatest form of artwork, because cameras were causing a stir, but according to him a machine could never capture the soul:

"Always the same conventional eyes... painted portraits have life, deep in the soul of the painter and where the machines can not go."

If I may be so bold, I would guess that deep down in your heart of hearts, when you say you intended to avoid tropes, demands of the market or commercial appeal, you secretly think you're touting the benefits of your book—that your book is *more valuable* for precisely this reason, that readers who also hate all the tropes and garbage out there will flock to your grand disavowment of popular literature. In other words, you very deliberately are writing what you feel is a product with commercial appeal. What the market *needs,* if not what the market *wants.* You wrote it for yourself, but you want and expect it to sell for precisely that reason.

If this is you, don't worry, this is completely normal and expected, given the things you've been told about writing. But in almost all cases, it doesn't work out (yes there are outliers, of course there are! But that doesn't mean I'm wrong).

The good news is, you're already on board with making something people want enough to pay for, but like Van Gogh, you've made an error in judgment. Unlike him, we have an infinite capacity to research. If, on the other hand, you absolutely do not want your books to sell, or care if anybody likes or appreciates your work, keep doing what you're doing: but from this point forward, you also have to stop posting humble brags about how you're in it for the art or poignant, wistful laments about how terribly basic the reading populace has become. You're asking them to read a book that *they don't want*, without any of the features that they like, simply because you enjoyed writing it.

ELEVATOR PITCH

Your elevator pitch, blurb or sales copy should include the most relevant genre designations, the intended audience, and the intriguing elements that make your book unique and memorable.

A premise with inherent conflict, the primary stakes, and the main story question. It should include some of the keywords or categories to make the genre obvious. It should not be about the story details or what actually happens. If someone asks, "what's your book about?" and you can't answer without launching into a full plot summary, that's an indication you lack clarity around your book's potential audience. Readers won't read the book to figure out what kind of book it is. Figuring this out is your responsibility.

I'm not going to discuss how to write a winning blurb here, but I'll add some formulas and resources in the *Grimoire* section. I would suggest creating something before you start writing: it'll serve as a guide during the development of your story. In other words, you can go wherever you want, as long as you pick a direction. Otherwise, you'll probably end up going in circles.

YOU CAN'T NUMBER THIS

Medieval scholars used to argue about how many angels can dance on the head of a pin. In my understanding, it was part facetious and part Zen, meant to quiet the grasping mind with an unsolvable riddle. But some bookworms didn't get the joke and tried to do the math.

Normally, I would recommend picking a genre and calculating the demand, so you have some slim indication of how many books it might be possible to sell. But we're far too early, and genre is not nearly enough. I've seen books launched well that had a great cover, good writing and a commercial blurb – and still bombed. I've seen new authors boldly proclaim that they don't need to follow any rules or best practices because *they* are going to build a loyal audience who loves whatever they write, because *they* follow authors, not genres.

There are always outliers who don't appear to be following the rules, who discovered it all the hard way after decades of struggle; and even most of them got lucky with an accidental hit that was trendy enough to be ravished or applauded. It's emboldening to ignore all the noise and concentrate on that, because *why shouldn't I be as successful? Why couldn't I get lucky?* There's nothing wrong with magical thinking, unless it blinds you from doing the work. You feel excited, you feel confident, you feel special. I get it, I've been there too. It feels like you can create worlds with your hands and mind. You *can*.

But everything else, everything after, is going to depend on whether readers can access those worlds, and the vast majority of authors never get good enough at their craft to keep readers reading. You're in for a brutal wake-up call either way, the difference is, after reading this book you'll understand what you did wrong and what to do next time. But if you skip the important bits, the devastation will sink in deep, shattering your confidence.

If you're still determined to forge your own path and write a book that doesn't seduce readers with common genre considerations, pay *very close attention* to the rest of this book: this is only the beginning, and I've stressed this point because it will make the journey easier. If you've chosen the arduous route, the tools and strategies within this guide will be even more vital to drafting a compelling story. As an anonymous samurai once said, "The more you sweat in training, the less you will bleed in battle."

EMBRACE THE CHAOS

When you're being creative or inspired, you are not pulling out of the void of nothing; your subconscious is drawing from every experience you've ever had. Your brain is stimulated by excess, not emptiness. Many artists write in order to avoid popular conceits and invent something entirely new, but as Mary Shelly discovered, "Invention, it must be humbly admitted, does not consist in creating out of void, but out of chaos."

In order to create a winning book, we need to read widely, in a specific genre, and aim to impress readers who enjoy that type of story by including elements they love. This doesn't mean copying or plagiarism. It's inevitable that we produce variants of the work we consume and are influenced and inspired by what we read.

> "If you stuff yourself full of poems, essays, plays, stories, novels, films, comic strips, magazines, music, you automatically explode every morning like Old Faithful. I have never had a dry spell in my life, mainly because I feed myself well, to the point of bursting." – *Ray Bradbury*

Creative magic is not the absence of essential ingredients, it's the novel combination and skillful implementation; the subversion and synthesis of tropes into intriguingly new stories. It's the bubbling overflow of shared resources, not an empty pot full of water and a stone. Filling your cauldron is a way to make sure you have enough raw material to satisfy your audience with a compelling story. As Nietzsche writes, "One must have chaos to be able to give birth to a dancing star."

MEMORANDUM

- A character worth caring about (avatar)
- Something they want, and an inability to get it
- An event or challenge they cannot overcome
- ...that forces them to change.
- A barrier or active antagonist
- A setting (description)
- Interesting characters (cast)
- Obstacles (challenges)
- Difficult decisions
- A beginning and an end
- Epic scenes
- Fulfills genre expectations
- Consistent tense / POV
- Linear timeline

Grimoire Notes Added

As a deeper example of genre research, I've added some detailed breakdowns of the genres I write in, mostly YA paranormal romance and dystopian. I've found that exceedingly pedantic case studies can be tremendously useful, but also bog down the flow and thematic power of the main content of each chapter, so when necessary, I'll add them as bonus material in a section called the *Grimoire*. Look for them at the end of this book.

2

IMPOSSIBLE QUEST
Plant The Seeds

When I was young, my family liked to take us camping. The problem was, in Oregon it's nearly always damp or raining, so I had to learn to make a 'one-match fire.'

The flame of a match will last a few seconds, so you need to build an environment for the flame to flourish. Stacking up a pile of sticks and twigs won't work, because it's not just about the *fuel*; it's about the space between them, the organization of elements. The hungry flame will flicker upwards, searching for fuel, and then burn out and down until it hits the wet soil.

So first, you'd build a platform; then a small pile of kindling. I liked to surround that with a teepee of smaller twigs inside a log cabin of large sticks, then frame it all with chunks of split timber. The kindling will burn away in minutes, providing just enough fuel for the fire to smolder into the larger logs. If done right, the fire will keep burning for hours, with no maintenance or added wood.

I've also seen it done wrong: by casual outdoor enthusiasts who can't start a fire with lighter fluid, fire starters, cardboard scraps or lighters. When everybody is hungry and wet and cold and waiting to eat and relax, and five people are kneeling by the fire pit blowing their lungs out and shifting the wood around. If they were *really* incompetent, they'll add moss or bark or pine cones and create a blinding cloud of toxic smoke as well.

I won't try to convince you that writing a novel is exactly like building a fire, but the point is this: your reader's *attention* will be like a single match for the first few pages. Fickle, feeble, a little wobbly. The slightest distraction could snuff it out. Kindling might hold their interest for the first few pages or even a couple chapters, but unless they meet the stability of a well-crafted structure and "settle-in" for the long haul, they may never finish reading your story.

It's possible to dump a huge pile of kindling on the dry earth and invite everyone to toss their matches in. Some of them will probably catch. The fuel will be consumed. But it'll burn away quickly, the ash blowing into the wind, the readers scurrying off to find new warmth and comfort elsewhere.

If you've been writing for a while, you're probably already familiar with the basic concept of plotting, and if it makes you uncomfortable, I completely understand! When I started writing, I just wanted to tell my stories. But I found I got stuck in the middle, I didn't know what happened next, or how to make the ending as satisfying as I wanted. I had great *scenes* but not enough structure. This meant that after I had stumbled my way through a basic rough draft, it still needed so much work I'd drown in heavy revisions for months.

I spent months reading everything I could about craft. I studied every plotting structure and organizational tool I could find. But all the books were different, and mapping out the details for every chapter was exhausting – plus I didn't *know* what happened, that's why I needed the guides!

The common advice on plotting or story architecture were repeating the same tired templates; more suited to screenwriting than novel writing. And they were *broken*. They just didn't work. It wasn't until I combined a few plotting systems together with some significant adjustments that I found a formula that fit the majority of popular genres.

Eventually, I reduced it into a simple framework. The little stuff could change or evolve, but as long as I hit these major turning points, I'd have a strong, well-balanced story. It's based heavily on other plotting traditions, but with some crucial modifications.

At a writing conference in Ecuador, I made some videos walking through the system, published them on my blog, and later turned it into a little ebook I made available for free. At first I was afraid people would be upset that it was too basic or derivative. So I was surprised when I started getting supportive comments like these.

> "Fantastic book for any writer who wants to create sound, believable plotlines. Invaluable information. Just made it to the top of my writing reference book list."

> "I've read several books on writing plots and this is by far the best! The author takes you step by step and makes it

much easier to understand and create a bestselling plot. I highly recommend this to all writers."

"A ton of research distilled into a simple storytelling framework that works for any novel. You won't be disappointed no matter how long you've been writing."

I loved that the book was helping people and am so grateful for the reviews, but I was also confused. There were much bigger, more comprehensive books on writing from famous authors. I knew my book was *useful,* but I was surprised people were calling my framework one of the *best* outlining strategies.

But I finally realized, authors didn't need another complex book about writing; they needed a simple to understand, easy to implement structure that supported their creativity without tripping them up or interrupting the creative flow. That's why for many writers, my concise resources have allowed them to ignore the overwhelm and actually start writing again

"I have been on the fence with starting a novel but did not know where to start. I would research and plan to avoid feelings of guilt from procrastination but never really started a project. With this outline I feel like any barriers have been removed. I have started writing again for the first time in years. Thank you for getting me back in the saddle."

Despite its simplicity, I believe my 8-point structure can help you even out a stubborn plot. Think of it like spokes on a bicycle wheel, stretching out the rubber. The wheel turns smoothly because of the rubber, but without the internal structure, the wheel wouldn't turn at all (or it would be a bumpy ride).

If you need another metaphor, think of weaving a straw basket: you start with the base, just four thick reeds crossed at the middle; around these you weave the lighter strands or threads of your story, in and out, around and around, tightly woven narrative threads. When the book is finished, you can't even *see* the original base, which is now invisible, but it still holds the whole thing together. (Now imagine trying to weave those threads or reeds together with no base or structure; you'd end up with a tangled knot).

While my formula may seem similar to other plot structures, it's not identical. If you're reluctant to ease into a plot outline because they've never worked for you before, that's because they're confusing. For example, what's the difference between the first plot point and the inciting incident? If they're the same, then nothing at all happen for the first 25% of the book (which is lame). Simple plotting graphs lump the second pinch point and final battle together under "climax," but they each have a unique function.

This understanding of story was a breakthrough for me, and finally let me map out a successful story after years of struggle, but it may be different from what you'll learn about plotting elsewhere. I've used language taken from screenwriting, especially *Screenplay* by Syd Field, but adapted some of the principles as I understood them.

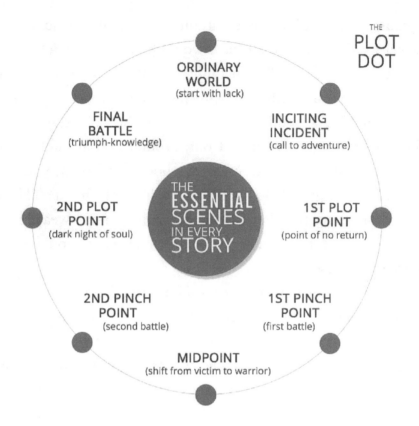

But wait, isn't this just the hero's journey? Well no, actually. You're probably familiar with Joseph Campbell's hero's journey, first set out in the 1949 *Hero With a Thousand Faces*. But he was influenced by Jung's psychoanalytical models for human consciousness, which were based on Freud's psychoanalysis, and Freud was coked up and seeing penises everywhere.

In 1909, Otto Rank wrote *The Myth of the Birth of a Hero*, where he took fifteen hero stories, all from the west and all male, and developed a unifying pattern from common elements. However, as a close friend and peer of Sigmund Freud, he felt that to truly understand the formation of such hero myths, one must go back to their ultimate source: the individual imagination. In other words, the universality of the hero pattern was believed to result from a commonality in the human psyche, which could only be investigated through psychoanalysis.

Hero myth narratives go back at least to 1871, and the anthropologist Edward Burnett. Campbell's "monomyth" has 17 points. Others have followed in his footsteps, with varying results, often dividing the points into a three-act structure. But it's worth pointing out that this tradition was rooted in a colonial agenda towards assimilation and cultural erasure; and that it's linked with nascent views of a collective unconscious, which now seem a bit outdated.

This doesn't make it useless, however: we could easily contend that great myths share a common structure because, over thousands of years of vocal storytelling, all of the *greatest* elements of story were shared, remembered and repeated, until most great myths contained similar themes and structure.

Simplified, Campbell presents his story this way:

"A hero ventures forth from the world of common day into a region of supernatural wonder: fabulous forces are there encountered and a decisive victory is won: the hero comes back from this mysterious adventure with the power to bestow boons on his fellow man."

It's true this model can apply to a great many ancient myths; but ancient myths do not have the same structure as modern novels. And while the hero's journey, as a basic narrative structure, is often the basis for blockbuster Hollywood movies, these are also a different narrative medium than words on the page.

The hero's journey *does not work* for contemporary, commercial fiction; even though those elements might often be present in great works of popular literature, they are too vague and disorganized to be helpful in creating new books.

Not every story will include a hero's journey narrative, and later we'll talk about a few fiction genres that break this model. But *most* commercial fiction, and nearly all popular TV pilots and movies, have common elements and devices. Even if there aren't literal battles or antagonists, there must be a few things for your book to hold a reader's attention:

1. a likable, sympathetic main character
2. things that happen that force action or change
3. difficult decisions (a crisis of conscience)
4. a final resolution

The more exciting action, drama, interesting characters and settings, witty banter, and romance, violence, suspense or humor you can add (depending on the genre), the better. Some of these plot points can be psychological or metaphorical, but make sure things are happening (external and internal conflict).

To simplify, you can think of it this way: every *good* story has a *hero*. According to Campbell's definition, a hero is "someone who has given his or her life to something bigger than oneself."

As I mentioned in the last chapter, a meaningful story is not just about a particular character, but about a specific ordeal, challenge or event that forces the character to become more. The story is the process through which they grow strong enough to actually overcome the obstacle; as well as all the incidents that directly led to that fateful and crucial event, or influenced the character's choices along the way.

A hero is someone who goes through a change that forces them to give up what *they* want in favor of something selfless and external, what others want – whether this means saving the galaxy or learning to put their lover's needs first.

Every great story is an *impossible* quest, which, through the journey, bestows upon the character the skill, strength, will or motivation to persist in a uniquely heroic sense.

A good story will lead to a reckoning and a resolution – if it doesn't, it would be more of a vignette, which are pretty unsatisfying. The main character is changed by the experience; even if it's merely to shift his understanding or viewpoint. The story *matters*; it left an impression or mark. Otherwise, it is literally unremarkable.

However, the deeper and more important this change, the more time and space is needed to communicate the transmutation. We can't just show the final battle. We have to show the whole journey; how far the hero has come and what the victory cost. We need the context, otherwise, the shift won't be believable or won't make sense. The *Plot Dot* solves this problem by focusing on the big turning points that provide supportive scaffolding for this personal transformation.

STRUCTURED CREATIVITY

After posting this image online, I received comments from a few skeptical writers, who refused the idea that every story is a hero's journey. One writer said, "I reject your picture and decide to be creative." Another said, "I need structure? I just want to write."

But the truth is, most great works of fiction have a predictable plot structure, and books that fail to capture readers' imaginations are missing the key turning points that generate momentum and escalating stakes. Experienced pantsers (who write from the seat of their pants) can go scene by scene and work their way to the end, but especially if you're working on your first novel, having a little structure can really help you reach the finish line.

Think of structure as training wheels—they'll help you map out the broad strokes, in roughly the right place for maximum emotional impact, based on cues readers have come to expect after consuming thousands of books and movies. This doesn't stop you from being creative, though it will probably prevent months of feeling stuck and unnecessary frustration. This is a system that has worked for me personally, and it's based on tons of research, but if it doesn't work for you or it feels constrictive, you're free to try something else.

In an article by T. M. Luhrman published by Cambridge, the author writes that "manuals which purport to train novices in the magical arts, break rituals into actions, words and imagination."

> The use of a characteristic ritual form is an engaging technique, to substitute internal commitment for external authority. Ritual is often depicted as if the rite is easily transferred symbolic knowledge and ineffable experience to willing neophytes.
>
> In a simple sense, a ritual will be moving to the performer if he wants to be moved.

In other words, this "ritual" formula of plotting a novel may work even if you don't *believe* in it. You don't need to commit in order to see its unique benefits. It's merely a symbol, through which to focus the power of your creative imagination and unlock your own unique magic.

> "A spell is projected energy through a symbol, in order to bring about a desired change. Props may be useful, but it is the mind that works magic." – **Starhawk,** *The Spiral Dance*

Book Craft is not a *dogma*, it's a *practice*. And while there's no common formula that applies equally for everyone, there are effective tools that can be put to use as you develop your powerful abilities. Magical gestures and sacred words have negligible effect unless the practitioner approves of them, but it's enough to be willing to try them out and see what happens.

We'll start with the eight major plot points—they're the biggest, most powerful scenes in your novel, the bones of the structure. As long as you get these eight points right, your story will have a strong foundation.

PLOT-BASED STORY

Plot: things that happen in a restricted period of time.
Plot Dot: The 8-point guide to major plot events.

Something big happens with a major impact on the protagonist.

1. Ordinary World (start with lack)

Your First Act sets up your main character (MC) in their ordinary, mundane environment. You'll introduce their friends and family members, their home, school or workplace, in the first few chapters. But you need to show what's missing. You don't want to start with a perfect, happy character who has everything (unless you're going to take it all away, which is fine).

You need to give them space to grow. Maybe they have unresolved emotional issues. They're probably shy, awkward, clumsy or embarrassed, or unpopular. Maybe they hate their job or just got dumped. You need to show what they want, their secret desires. What are they working towards? They probably have daydreams about things they don't think will ever happen.

Spend some time developing the protagonist, but show their personality and attributes through action and conflict. We'll talk more later about where exactly your story should begin, but I would focus on a "big day" – a significant or meaningful event or occasion that they've been preparing for; and an unexpected twist or surprise that disrupts their ordinary world experience.

What are they afraid of or worried about? How is their environment a reflection of their inner flaw? What is their favorite object or possession? Where are the sources of conflict?

Start on a "big day"
- preparing for an important event
- already facing fears and challenges
- demonstrate the world and culture
- hook with sympathy & kindness
- oppressed or repressed

2. Inciting Incident (call to adventure)

In most books, the inciting incident should actually happen in chapter one or two. It's an intrusion on the ordinary world.

Something big changes. Maybe a stranger moves to town, or a family member dies, or there's an earthquake. It might be an invitation, or a friend inviting your MC to a party. It can't be a huge crisis, but it will be annoying and noticeable, or exciting— it's the beginning of your plot. You want to get the ball rolling pretty early, otherwise nothing will be happening. Avoid writing a lot of history or backstory. Start your book as near to the inciting incident as you can. But don't think of it as just one scene or chapter. It's an unexpected element that exacerbates or draws out existing conflict or tension in the ordinary world.

The "call to adventure" is usually followed by denial or refusal. The MC doesn't trust it, or doesn't want to make a decision. They'll ignore it and continue focusing on their previous goals. They just want things to go back to normal.

Something weird or unexpected
- doesn't fit into "normalcy"
- unusual and hard to forget
- points towards an unknown world or conflict
- threatens status quo
- an invitation or offer
- possibly puts the character off balance
- might be responsible for bitter failure
- a path opens...

3. 1st Plot Point (point of no return)
Things have been getting weirder and more intriguing for several chapters. Your MC tries to ignore the problems, but they keep interfering with their normal agenda. They get roped in, and something happens that forces them into the action.

Everything changes, and there's no going back to the ordinary world. They might have met a teacher, or they might have seen something that changes their perspective: a revelation of supernatural abilities; a murder or death; an accident or robbery or attack or disaster. Something pretty big, that shatters what they thought they understood of the world, and makes them feel vulnerable and exposed. This will be one of the major scenes in your book, so make it unforgettable.

This is your protagonist stepping off the cliff, or venturing down the rabbit hole. It may not be a physical change of location; it may be a step off the path, a risky move that they wouldn't have considered previously. Also, this is the end of Act I, about 25% of your book—by now all the major characters should have already been introduced, or at least hinted at.

Can't ignore the weirdness
- steps into the unknown (often forced)
- the way back is lost
- doesn't know the rules or what's happening
- normalcy is broken; the new world takes over
- hesitation or refusal

4. 1st Pinch Point (first battle)

After the 1st Plot Point, there will be several chapters where the protagonist is learning about the new world. They might be doing research, or discovering things in conversations. There needs to be conflict and tension, which builds up to the 1st Pinch Point. This doesn't have to be a literal battle, but it is the first major interaction with the antagonist. The antagonist might not be visible yet, but they should be the one wielding the strings.

The antagonist (AC) is after something, and that something is tied to the MC somehow. Maybe the AC wants something the MC has, or needs the protagonist to do something, or has a score to settle.

The MC probably still has no idea what's happening, but they find themselves at the center of some greater conflict. They probably don't win, but they do survive. Now the stakes are clear. You should make them as dire as possible, almost inconceivable. Ask yourself, what's the worst thing that could happen? Then ask, how can I make it even more difficult for my protagonist? The stakes should always seem life and death to the protagonist: they represent a complete change, the "death" of the former self, which is why the MC resists them. If your protagonist doesn't have their self-identity shaken to its roots, you need to make this scene bigger.

This is the first major interaction with the antagonist or the forces of evil. It demonstrates what's at stake. What can you add to make the setting reflect the mood? What's remarkable about the setting?

The stakes are real
- dangerous opposition
- the larger forces at play
- the antagonist makes a move
- they survive, maybe thwart the antagonist, which could make them a target
- deepens the mystery (what were they after?)
- show off courage or weakness
- forced to choose sides

5. Midpoint (victim to warrior)

After the 1st Pinch Point, the protagonist continues to face new challenges, but they are in a defensive role. They might be making some plans, but mostly they're waiting for something to happen and reacting to events or circumstances beyond their control. If they try to solve any issue, they end up making things even worse. They might accidentally hurt someone, or their friends and family begin to fear and distrust them, because they are keeping secrets.

They begin questioning their identity and worldview, which triggers a personality crisis, which leads to a shift in perspective. This is about halfway through the novel, and marks the point where the protagonist decides to start taking action. They stop being a victim and reacting to events, and vow to do whatever it takes to win. They'll probably form a new goal, and even if they aren't sure how to achieve it yet, they'll feel a deep conviction towards the attempt. This might be based in rage or anger towards the antagonist, a newfound perspective, or increased self-confidence.

This could even literally be the protagonist looking at themselves in a mirror, questioning their reflection. So far, they've been refusing their quest. But now they're pissed off. They decide to fight back.

Shift from victim to warrior
- deep self-reflection
- identity crisis / shift in perspective
- shocking reveal
- what have I become?
- antagonist's plans revealed

- committed to the cause (even knowing risks)
- takes an active role, even if not a true believer
- personal vengeance

6. 2nd Pinch Point (second battle)

The fulfillment of new goals and plans bring them towards a second confrontation with the antagonist. It still may not be the main villain; it could just be henchmen that represent the main villain's interests. It could be an attack, or the result of the MC taking action, such as setting a trap for the AC (or vice-versa, the villain can set a trap for the MC, for example by kidnapping a friend or relative).

The protagonist is determined to see this through, and feels personally responsible, even though the chances of success are slim. The conflict erupts into an open battle, with escalating consequences; or it could just be something really bad that happens, as a result of the antagonist's actions. This confrontation makes the protagonist realize that everything is much worse than they thought, and they realize they've underestimated the antagonist's power. They rally with new determination, and might even score a seeming victory—even if it's just escaping with their lives. In this scene, the antagonist defeats the protagonist's forces, or foreshadows what's at stake in the next major encounter.

Heavy Losses
- take (sneaky) action
- everything falls apart
- unexpected conflict with antagonist's forces
- critical failure, personal responsibility

- guilt and remorse
- new information that makes everything much worse

7. 2nd Plot Point (dark night of soul)

The plan failed. The secret weapon backfired. The hero's team was slaughtered, or they lost their one advantage, or the AC's evil plan succeeded. The antagonist has won. Alternatively, the 2nd Pinch Point can be elevated conflict that demands an urgent response.

Maybe the antagonist has stolen something or kidnapped an ally. They rally the troops, and try fix things, but things keep getting more and more dire, leading to a total, devastating loss. Usually, this process happens over several chapters. But at the 2nd Plot Point, everything the MC feared could happen, has happened. They are destroyed. They cannot win. They give up hope.

They lose the battle, with serious consequences. Someone the protagonist cares about got hurt, and they feel guilty. The failure might be tied to their character flaw or a lack of knowledge. This marks a period of depression, prompting a change in mindset. They realize that the thing they've been holding on to (often it's just wanting to get back to the ordinary world, back to normal) is completely gone. There is no chance for victory. The only way forward is through. They are forced to change and go in a new direction. When they figure out what they've been holding onto, what's been holding them back or limiting them, and when they're prepared to sacrifice what they want, for the greater good, they finally become the hero they need to be to defeat the villain (even if the "villain" is simply their own shard of glass or limitation).

This is the second major interaction with the antagonist. The protagonist knew this was coming, and thought they were somewhat prepared, but they were wrong. Make this scene heart-wrenching by taking something permanent from them or one of their allies (destroyed house, lost limb, a death).

All hope is lost
- hero gives up; doesn't see a way forward
- their secret plan or weapon backfired
- loses a piece of their heart or self-identity
- antagonist has taken everything
- the hero is responsible for the villain's success
- serious losses or casualties
- escalating stakes have led to greater losses
- self-pity or self-destructive behavior
- fights or arguments
- an ally gives them a pep-talk

8. Final battle (triumph-knowledge)

Often the MC needs a pep talk from a close friend, to "gird the loins." They need a reason to fight, even if it's hopeless. Even if they don't see how to defeat the enemy, there's no choice but to confront them. But now they are prepared. They might have gained a valuable piece of knowledge or information. They might have been given a new weapon or power, or learned the villain's weakness. Or they might simply go into battle on faith, and whatever they need materializes in the critical moment. The final battle scene often includes a "hero at the mercy of the villain" scene, where the hero is caught, so the villain can gloat (or this can come earlier, just before the 2nd Plot Point).

It's not a clear, easy victory. They fail at first, the hero is captured, the enemy gloats, then the hero perseveres simply by not giving up. With resolve and tenacity, the hero escapes and overpowers the villain. The final battle scene may include a "death of the hero" scene, where the hero, or an ally/romantic interest, sacrifices themselves, and appears to die, only to be brought back to life in joy and celebration. This doesn't have to be a literal "battle." It's just the last, final straw, the most dramatic part of your story. It's what forces the MC to make a realization, change or grow. And it's the place where the MC has a victory.

The antagonist is fully revealed. The protagonist rides off to meet their fate. At first they fail, and are captured—all seems lost, but in a sudden twist, the protagonist reaches into themselves and finds the motivation to persevere, unlocking access to their secret weapon, and defeating the antagonist.

Sacrifice to win
- risks all, despite likely doom
- slim chance at success
- the true antagonist or plan is revealed
- enemy's weakness discovered
- their one hope is taken, the plan fails
- hero at mercy of villain
- the protagonist alone must persevere
- saved by act of sacrifice, unlikely ally, new knowledge or power, or simply refusal to quit

Epilogue (come home changed)

The hero returns, changed. They've won, though it's probably temporary (this villain was defeated, but he or someone new will return). The safety is short-lived and bittersweet. The hero once again faces the small challenges or bullies from the beginning of the story, but they seem trivial now. The hero is no longer lacking; they've grown in confidence and understanding, and now have a group of new friends, and a new hope for the future.

How far we've come...
- the hero returns home changed
- contrast their earlier self
- reflect on what's been lost
- show the challenges ahead
- melancholic reflection
- fill in plot holes or open loops (mysteries)
- it could be a *new* home or status quo
- from alone to supported
- from afraid/weak to powerful
- (sometimes standing up to former bullies)

MAGIC BEANS

If this outline feels vaguely familiar and disappointingly unhelpful, I did warn you that the pragmatics I share may feel like *just a trick* at first. To counter the initial doubt or frustration you might be feeling, because this structure seems too easy, too simple, too basic, imagine it like the *wax on, wax off* scene in The Karate Kid. The basics can be powerful when masterfully applied; but first they must be practiced until the unfamiliar becomes ritual.

I've had people tell me they spent weeks unpacking this simple framework before it all clicked for them. We're going to be moving *much* deeper, and I promise we'll get to some craft strategies you've never heard before, but everything will refer back to this basic structure so take a few moments to become familiar with it. See if you can map out your major turning points using this formula.

Great stories have been told for thousands of years, and readers *respond* to stories that are structured in a certain way. Once you put my formula into practice, I think you'll find it works better than others, because it *is* different. As I mentioned earlier in my fire metaphor, it's all about the spacing and depth between the elements, which will be crucial later on. The structure creates space for your story to flourish. If the *cauldron* was your collection of useful story elements, the Plot Dot is the well-structured stack of kindling that will allow the heat to build, the tension to ignite, the sparks to fly.

> "Why can't we as storytellers 'be creative' and simply violate these conventions? Because each of these (and every other convention in every other genre) is a station in that genre's version of the hero's journey. And the human psyche takes in and evaluates every narrative it sees or hears according to how closely that narrative comports to the beats and structure of the hero's journey. Be groundbreaking, be experimental if you want. But remember, the human psyche is deeply conservative and rigid as a rock." – *Steven Pressfield*

The idea came to me in a dream, that these eight plot points are like the magic seeds from *Jack in the Beanstalk*. Your current, comfortable writing practice is like the old familiar cow that's stopped giving milk and needs to be taken to the market. It may be hard to part with at first, but imagine it like the golden calf of your writing altar. It provides temporary comfort, but needs to be exchanged for something deeper and more powerful. I'm not asking you to sell the cow. I'm giving you the magic beans for free. All I ask is that you plant them and see what grows in the fertile field of your imagination. I promise, they'll bear fruit.

WITCHES' MAGIC

I developed the *Plot Dot* and graphic nearly two years ago, but only recently, when writing this book, was a discovery made in a medieval English church that caught my attention: the existence of so-called witches' marks; geometric patterns of deep dots or holes connected by looping lines. The point (allegedly) was to trick demons, who must follow straight lines, into an endless loop, effectively trapping them into the design. See how similar this one is to my 8-point plot structure.

What if the "demons" or supernatural entities actually represented our collective fears, doubts and insecurities, and these marks helped focus the mind, similar to a mandala (Sanskrit for "circle") or a monk's meditative, walking labyrinth:
keeping the surface, bubbly mind lost in a simple repetitive task, so that the wisdom of our deep subconscious can thrive?

Imagine then, the Plot Dot formula like this: you are binding your limitless potential and creativity with chains to one central story or main ordeal. As you go round and round the plot points, making sure each dot links back to the main thing and swings your story forward with momentum, your subconscious, rather than randomly fleeting every which way, will instead serve you by spontaneously providing the answers and deep insight that your story desperately needs. In this way, the Plot Dot is not a restrictive, limiting framework: it's an essential mental tool to help simplify and organize your wonderful ideas, so that your brain can stay the course without getting overwhelmed by inertia.

It may *resist*, tugging violently against its chains, but the friction will generate a powerful charge. You're winding up a mechanical toy, building more and more pressure and tension, so that at a certain point, when you let go, the character will react quickly with a flurry of spontaneous activity, daring and courage.

You may already have a good story, but it may lack *momentum,* which means, enough energy to carry readers forward to the satisfying culmination of events. So this plot structure, while not absolutely necessary or critical, could serve as a kind of battery or internal engine; like lining up transmitters or electrical servers as conduits to charge your prose with energy (an eight-cylinder piston engine offers an excellent balance of performance and efficiency). Without *changing* your story, it can channel and harness its inherent power, and convert it into a more effective piece of literature.

Rituals that may seem limiting can become transformative when they are repeated with intention. Walk the maze, round and round, deeper and deeper, harnessing your energy towards one directive. Generate static and heat within the even spaces. Fill your book with purpose and momentum. The better you construct a supportive foundation, the brighter and longer your story will burn.

PS. There's a simpler explanation for this symbol, and it'll blow your mind, but it will also take away the magic (including the point I just tried to make). I'm going to add it as an appendix, but be warned, it's sciency, so while it will be a huge *reveal*, it will take away some of the *magic.*

MEMORANDUM

- Readers must trust your story will satisfy them
- An impossible quest leaves a mark
- Key turning events that drive the momentum
- Plot events with escalating stakes
- Structure focuses creativity towards powerful effect
- Open spaces allow your story to burn brighter
- Stack the wood carefully, so your story burns evenly
- Resisting structure generates positive friction
- Magic beans may offer you a fresh start

Grimoire Notes Added

More than a few people have asked me for specific, genre-based examples of these turning points, a project I've already started, and will add into the extracurricular resources soon.

3

PLOTTING THE COURSE
Prepare for the Journey

Years ago, when my father was young, he got stuck on an island in India. He didn't check the boat schedules beforehand, and could hear tigers growling in the jungle around him. His grand travel adventure suddenly turned very scary, and he ended up screaming for help against the encroaching darkness until someone on the distant shore heard his desperate plea.

I had my own accidental adventure, after a desert camping trip in Tunisia. We spent the night under the stars, baking bread under the hot sands beneath a glowing fire. On the way back, our guide jumped suddenly, striking the sand fiercely with a long wooden stick, smashing a nearly invisible, but tremendously deadly poisonous snake. We learned the camel tours were only allowed to go a certain distance into the barren wilderness, because otherwise, once bitten, a victim could not reach a hospital in time to save them.

Afterward, nursing a hangover from illegal palm wine, my travel companion befriended a local and we were invited to a local residence. The father was a witchdoctor, making spiritual charms and remedies. We only intended to stay a night, but each day that passed, we were told we couldn't leave yet: there was no train today. *Tomorrow,* they insisted. Always tomorrow.

Despite the discomfort at feeling completely helpless, I had an amazing experience. We were there during *Eid al-Adha,* or the Muslim festival of sacrifice. I learned how to skin a sheep, and the specific order in which the various parts of the animal are to be eaten, grilling meat over hot embers inside the family home.

As we'll discuss more later, there is a value in getting lost. Sometimes the most profound discoveries happen by accident, when you forfeit control and venture into uncharted territory. But only if you can find your way back. Otherwise, you end up *Waiting for Godot*; expecting a rescue that never arrives.

Even after establishing my major plot points, I wasn't sure how to connect them, or what to put in between, which left great open gaps in my story; yawning abysses that sucked my strength and energy each time I dared to approach them. So rather than *writing*, I was flailing around for some kind of bridge or scaffold that would get me safely across the unfamiliar passages without plummeting into misery or procrastination.

Rather than filling it, I'd go back to safe, settled ground and shovel dirt or build up colonies. But that great empty pit would eventually suck my story—and enthusiasm—like a black hole, threatening to devour everything I produced and render it meaningless.

NAVIGATION

In the last chapter, we discussed the major turning points of a good story, which serve to culminate in one critical event that forces a character to change. And that's a good start, but it isn't nearly enough.

The lack of foundational materials or education on what goes *between* these critical events is responsible for the epidemic of "soggy middle" stories with no tension or pacing, and scenes that lack interest and excitement, or feel mushy or incomplete. You might already have brilliant scenes mapped out in great detail where you know exactly what happens; and you probably also have gaping plot holes like the ones I mentioned earlier. Some of these you won't recognize at first. It might feel like a vague, maleficent emptiness that lurks on the edge of your awareness.

When writers and novelists are stuck with a boring, broken, empty, lopsided story, the solution is rarely more revision or editing, and you can't always push through it. You need some type of temporary scaffolding that allows you to proceed through this general field of unknowing.

A few people have tried to map out a universal *chapter-by-chapter* guide to story architecture, but they suffer in one crucial regard: the 2nd Act is actually twice as long as the others, so even if a plot outline seems reasonable at first, it fails because it lacks enough content to fill the mysteriously vacant stretch in the middle.

For a simple, stable, reasonable story, the 8-point Plot Dot is a good guide. But what if you want *more*. What if you want to build, not a barn, but a palace? Then of course, the foundations will need to be larger and more extensive, the plans more detailed.

After years of research and a bit of creative thinking, I've developed what I believe is an ambitious step forward: a detailed chapter outline that assimilates popular models and fleshes them out in a new, systematic approach to detailed plotting. Like Mary Shelley's *Frankenstein*, or both the *Iliad* and the *Odyssey*, it is composed of 24 even sections.

> "I'm an author and have been studying story structure, narrative arc, and plot points for years....this is a *really* good template. I can tell you've digested and synthesized more vague outlines and converted them into a more comprehensive map of the types of scenes that must happen in between the typical plot points."

It may seem audacious at first, even absurd. If you found my 8-point plot structure limiting, you may feel like my expanded, 24-chapter outline is a magnificent folly. So let me first preface it with an explanation of purpose.

Imagine you're crossing an unexplored terrain, and making good progress, but your map is incomplete. When you *hit* a massive crater, you're unprepared and ill-equipped. What goes in there? Where did it come from? How can we get around it? Your progress and momentum will be lost immediately. This outline isn't about me telling you what exactly to put in your story. It's about suggesting a potential fix that allows you to fill in a specific plot hole, when you reach it, because this land is not completely unexplored. Other travelers like you have discovered similar problems.

There is an order to the terrain, a universal shared experience. If you come to a cliff, you'll need a rope. If you come to a boulder, you'll need a pick. If you come to a canyon, you'll need a ladder. How and where you use the recommendations exactly are up to you; but it might help you cover more ground faster. It will help you figure out your story and fill in rough, temporary solutions that get you farther ahead, so that you can go back and fill them out better in the next round of revisions.

You don't have to use everything, but the notes are broad enough that it may inspire you to create the *right kind* of scene in sort of the right place. It may help you fill in a plot hole or gap you didn't even notice. It'll help you have a brief idea of where you might be headed – so that you can fill up the tank and get started in confidence, without dreading that part in the middle where you have no clue what happens next.

This doesn't mean you need to stick with the plan 100%. You may discover something even better once you're close enough to see the scene and make smarter choices. But while it's still out over the horizon beyond the mountains, it helps to have some idea of what may lie in yonder valley, before you charge in unprepared and end up like the Donner party: a slow starving death by starvation.

If my light plot structure in the last chapter made you uneasy, this may feel suffocating at first. But take a deep breath, and consider it like a map you pack with you. It's a compass, not what to do or what you'll discover, simply a navigational point to help get you started in the right direction. You may not *need* it, but if you do, it can save your life.

ROOTS & BRANCHES

In this chapter, we're going to dive deep into what goes in between the major turning points we explored earlier. You may have noticed that those were just the big, action-based scenes of dramatic conflict. Those are the bones of the story, the deep structure that allows your story to maintain its shape. But those key points only have meaning because of what the character must go through to reach them. They need to be balanced with other scenes: heartful confessions or playful banter. Scenes that may seem trivial, because nothing big is happening, but are actually crucial to give your story depth and context.

You'll notice that these suggestions are pretty loose: they're meant as structured writing prompts, that may lead you towards the spark of an idea that works perfectly for your story. This will allow you to *flesh out* your loose 8-point outline: adding the muscle and sinew that holds it all together and creates a dynamic, flexible, living creation. Don't worry that using a template will make your book formulaic or predictable. The form and shape they take will be absolutely unique.

Picture an old, beautiful tree in a wide-open meadow. The sun is overhead, sweat drips down your neck. You duck under the thick foliage, inhaling the sweet, organic scent and feeling the cool breeze rustle through the leaves.

The *point* of the tree is the shade and the life-giving oxygen generated by the leaves. But you need a lot of branches, evenly spaced, first the big thick ones, then the little thin ones, each reaching up and out so that as many leaves as possible are bathed in sunlight. When it's in full bloom, it looks like one perfect wall of green foliage; nobody *notices* all the branches underneath. But if they weren't there, the leaves would be patchy, uneven, starved for sunlight, and the tree would die, down to the roots.

The 8 Major Plot Points are the deep roots of your story.
The 24 Chapter Outline are the branches.

All we are doing here is creating more space for your words to *come alive.* So that each word carries power and meaning and magic in a contextualized reading experience. It will make it *easier* for an organic blossoming of spellcraft; but the individual shape and pattern of the leaves – the thing that readers see and feel and remember – those are up to you.

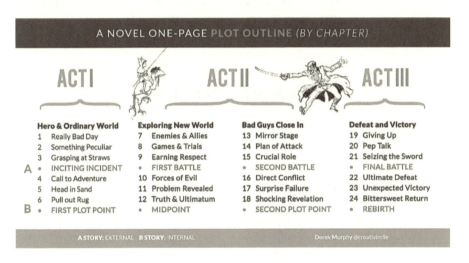

This detailed outline will help make sure you have *something* to fill in all the spaces, so you can get through the first draft faster, without getting lost or stuck or injured along the way. When you go back through, with more knowledge and awareness, you may find different routes that serve you better, and that's great!

There are two ways to use this plot outline. The first is to try and brainstorm a new story with it from scratch. I use it as a default when I'm mapping out a new project. The second is for a quick tune-up to an existing draft. You've already got your story, but you can tell there are weak points and you're not sure what to do about it. Trying to fit what you've got over this outline may help you smoothen out the rough bits, without resorting to an expensive developmental edit.

In my diagram, you'll notice that the 8 major turning points are marked in red but don't fit *within* a specific chapter or scene; they mark the transitions between the spaces. Also, I believe I've created an innovative distinction between the "A story" and "B story" – A story events will be more reactive and external, while B story events will be more decisive and introspective.

The one-page fiction plot outline.

1 Really Bad Day

Ordinary world, empathy, conflict. Show flaw and lack.

2 Something Peculiar

Something unique or strange happens, but they dismiss it.

3 Grasping at Straws

Trying to regain control of ordinary world as setbacks mount.

INCITING INCIDENT (call to adventure)

4 Call to Adventure

Something extraordinarily different happens, they can't ignore. Major setback.

5 Head in Sand

The new interrupts the old and causes conflict. Reveals dissatisfaction with ordinary.

6 Pull out Rug

Trying to fix ordinary world problems while resisting the lure of the supernatural world.

1ST PLOT POINT (no return)

7 Enemies & Allies

Explore new world; meet characters, find their place and role. Introduce all main characters.

8 Games & Trials

Struggle to belong. Frustration and doubt. Trials and challenges.

9 Earning Respect

Small victory as lead proves capable. Fun and games. Begrudging acceptance.

1ˢᵀ PINCH POINT (first battle)

10 Forces of Evil

Stakes are raised, antagonists revealed.

11 Problem Revealed

Surprise problem or situation.

12 Discovery/Ultimatum

New information, vulnerable share. In or out?

MIDPOINT (victim to warrior)

13 Mirror Stage

Self-realization or a discovery, choosing to engage.

14 Plan of Attack

Plan of action to thwart antagonist's forces or overcome main problem.

15 Crucial Role

Trusted with an important task.

2ᴺᴰ PINCH POINT (second battle)

16 Second Battle

They execute the plan, and come in direct conflict with antagonist's forces.

17 Surprise Failure

The plan goes horribly wrong, faulty information or assumption.

18 Shocking Revelation

The antagonist's full plan/true identity is revealed. Stakes are raised. Guilt and anger.

2ND PLOT POINT (darkest night)

19 Giving Up

Lead loses confidence; the forces are too great. What they want is unattainable.

20 Pep Talk

Encouragement from ally. Vulnerable share, inclusion. What's at stake; choice.

21 Seizing the Sword

Deliberate choice to continue, even if slim chance of success.

FINAL BATTLE (triumph-knowledge)

22 Ultimate Defeat

Triumph of Villain. All hope is lost.

23 *Unexpected Victory*

Secret weapon or ability, deep resolve, new understanding, unlikely ally.

24 *Bittersweet Reflection*

Temporary victory. Innocents saved. How far they've come.

REBIRTH (return to ordinary word)

25 *Death of Self*

From ambition to service.
Death of former self. Acknowledgment ceremony.

Optional: Hints of future challenges or antagonist lives.

FEEL THE BURN

One time on a long-distance flight, my butt fell asleep...and never woke up again. I had to research that *dead butt syndrome*, or gluteal amnesia, is a condition that occurs when your gluteus medius gets inflamed and forgets to function normally. I never used it (I didn't even know it existed!) and my muscles literally died.

If the idea of scripting out notes for every chapter and every book across all genres still makes you uncomfortable, think of it more like an exercise regime by a personal trainer.

Specifically, in this metaphor, maybe you're already in decent shape, but you're neglecting your abs, or glutes, or other obscure muscles, which may leave you unbalanced and even pose long-term, permanent health risks.

A fitness expert will help you to lean into those weak, underutilized, ignored muscles and coax them into action. It might hurt or feel uncomfortable at first. They aren't muscles you're used to using. But disuse could lead to injury if you stress them too fast in the wrong way.

DOESN'T FIT THE OUTLINE?

What if I'm not writing scifi or fantasy, what if it's a historical romance or a contemporary thriller or a personal memoir? *It will still work*. The details may need to be interpreted creatively, but I have faith in you.

You may also say, well *my* story doesn't fit this outline, so how great can it really be? Or you might be thinking, "Great Art Transcends Boundaries!" in which case I'd recommend you go back and read the earlier sections of this book again.

Yes, of course it's true that not all good books follow this formula; you could even say that all *great* books do *not* follow a formula like this. But you'd probably be talking about Great Works of Literature, which often became famous because they were, at the time, good enough and faced with very little competition, and rose to fame as part of a cultural phenomenon or movement. Great books, like explosive magic, are a wonder and a mystery. They flare into existence like rainbows, but can't be summoned on demand. Attention spans have grown short and people no longer read whatever the pundits are recommending. Few people will read a book that they are not enjoying, even if it *is* famous or widely lauded.

The 8-Point Plot Dot and the 24-Chapter Outline are just helpful support systems to make sure your book is well-structured. Of course there are tons of examples of famous books or literature that don't fit neatly into the outline, but most bestselling genre fiction will have a lot in common with the layouts I've shared.

And it's not really just a story template, it's a specific writing prompt for each scene: not *what happens,* just the general vibe. Creativity abhors a vacuum, complete empty space is petrifying. You've probably heard some version of the quote, which is often misattributed to various famous authors, "Writing is easy; just stare at a blank sheet of paper until drops of blood form on your forehead." But you only need a blood sacrifice if you're invoking deep, dangerous magic. You don't always need to open a vein. Most likely, you don't need more space and freedom, you need boundaries. You already know how to write. You've already got the creative magic. What you're missing is structure and guidance. Do you need it to write books? No! You can write books exactly as you're doing now or as you've always done; stumbling around in the dark and hoping for sparks of insight to appear. But it won't be easy, and it may not lead to progress.

I have friends who are pantsers and they sell tons of books because the emotional conflict, character tension and suspense are all well done; or sometimes because they write beautifully (though beautiful writing, on its own, is rarely enough to hold readers' attention). If you want to break the mold and do your own thing, by all means do it, but:

1. it's going to be harder to keep readers reading
2. it's going to be harder to sell and market
3. it's going to be harder to identify your audience

4. it will be harder to hook and keep their attention
5. reviews may reflect dissatisfaction

You can only improve by implementing or adopting *new* strategies. No matter how you use this plotting reference, no matter if you integrate it into your writing practice or try it for a month and toss it out, you will have internalized what you needed and improved your craft. In other words, it can't possibly hurt, even if it's uncomfortable at first, because all knowledge and experience can only help you shore up your existing abilities.

> "When I put my story ideas into other outlines they seem to leave me still feeling lost, and confused with what should happen in certain chapters. But this one? I was able to connect the dots from beginning to the complete end. I had to study it for a week straight before I finally was able to really understand how to use this story structure completely. But thank you so much for creating this story outline. Being able to really complete a story blueprint makes me feel so happy right now."

I truly believe this outline will help you write better books with less effort, and for that reason alone is worth your time. But I should point out, even if you follow the formula and plot carefully, that it won't automatically make your book successful – it's just the start. It'll help you complete a novel that's above par, without stalling out. You'll be able to finish more stories, and gain valuable experience, which will enable you to focus on the deeper, more challenging aspects of spellcraft that are essential to truly captivate readers.

THE IN-BETWEEN

In places where mortals have performed magical rites, the landscape is said to retain a certain *resonance*. These are the places where countless failed authors have toiled for meaning, and left clues behind of their practice. Stepping into the traditional, well-worn paths of story architecture may offer a cleaner journey through the first draft of your novel.

If the Plot Dot operates as a kind of magical *foci*, channeling your attention, the 24 Chapter Outline serves as a *praxis*. Rote spells, tried and tested formulas, passed down from master to apprentice, developed through the collective discoveries of countless literary explorers.

It might have started out as an improvised spell, but has become codified into a vetted ritual because it's proven effective. It may not depict the exact challenges and difficulties you'll encounter on your own path up the mountain, but it will help you scale high enough to see your own path clearly.

I hope you break my rules. I hope, once you're back to the safety of your hotel or lodging and the dark shadows of the night are behind you, you find them silly and trivial. But in that terrifying emptiness, when the veil recedes and the liminal darkness is filled with nefarious creatures, creativity becomes numb. As the soul languishes in this creative purgatory, this *in-between*, any direction is better than none.

You can reject, refuse or resist these prompts and *they will still serve you better* than starting with absolutely nothing and reaching randomly into your empty bag of tricks. Like the Room of Requirement, these prompts will produce according to your needs and desires. When you don't know *what* you need at all, your fingers grasping in every direction for a lifeline, that's not a problem creativity alone can solve.

A familiar structure will also make readers feel comfortable letting you take them on a journey. They'll trust that you know what you're doing and that it's all leading somewhere – even if a chapter or two seem irrelevant or boring. The more authority you have, the more they'll be willing to give up control and let you lead. But if they don't know you already, they aren't going to suffer through pages if they don't know what's going on, don't care about the characters, and aren't hooked.

You may feel like you don't want to write popular books that escort readers through an enjoyable, manageable experience towards the best views. You may think those are tourist traps, and you'd rather fight through the jungle with a machete, and discover a fly-infested swamp, and exhaust yourself to establish something new, something different. And if you're an adventure enthusiast, great! But remember, as an author, you're not *only* an explorer, you're also a guide. It's your responsibility to lead readers to the proposed destination, safely maneuvering them through the dangerous voids and terrifying unknown. If you try to get readers to follow you through this unmapped, unmarked, dense and difficult path, promising them something great at the pinnacle of your creative expression, you're going to require a *lot* of trust to get them to follow you blindly through to the end.

MEMORANDUM

- Roots and branches and leaves
- A map helps you cover more ground faster
- Plot holes can wreck your momentum
- Void versus chaos
- Just because nobody has done it, doesn't mean it has value

4

RAISING STAKES

Can you keep a secret?

One time in middle school, an upper-classman was showing off card tricks. I begged him to show me how he did it, and after swearing me to secrecy, he revealed the trick. Like an idiot, however, I promptly exposed the sleight of hand behind the effect, ruining the experience for everyone.

Over the last few chapters, I've tried to give you a strong foundation you can use to fill out your story outline, so you can keep moving forward without getting stuck. I've mapped out the terrain you're most likely to encounter. And while the support and assets will help you through your journey, the framework by itself isn't enough to compel readers to keep turning pages. The good news is, *even if* you don't follow a template like this, you can still be successful as long as you keep their attention... but only if you master the tactics I'm about to share in this chapter.

The cardinal rule of wizardry, is that a magician never reveals his secrets. The magic is created by the delicious unknowing, and spoiled when the trick is revealed. Your job as a writer is to create uncertainty, to delay gratification, to surprise and delight with reveals and unexpected twists. The secret to good writing, to books readers love, is the ability to seize attention with unresolved drama, and create a burning desire for mental clarity.

People read books to find out *what happens next*. You need sympathetic characters, who do interesting things, but the real key to hypnotic, irresistible, spellbinding writing is the sense of intrigue and suspense. Remember, a story is not your character, it's your character's very challenging problem, and the risks and stakes they'll have to overcome to achieve it.

According to Vladimir Nabokov, "The writer's job is to get the main character up a tree, and then once they are up there, throw rocks at them."

We've built the tree (roots and branches). Now we force our protagonist up to the highest boughs, before burning it all down. All the work we did on structure was for this: the more difficult the choices, the farther the protagonist has to climb, reaching out to the smallest and thinnest of branches, the more peril and consequence. The higher the tree, the farther the fall. The deeper the roots, the more devastating the opposing forces must be in order to rip them from the earth.

The story is important, but the *drama* is the juicy apple in the highest branch that spurs the dangerous climb. It needs time and space to ripen, to mature. All those leaves, all that energy, is building up to eventually bear fruit, and this is it: the beating heart of your story isn't what happens, but why it matters.

Even without the drama, you might have a strong, pretty tree. A fine tree. But it's not a great story. It won't attract birds, bees, families on picnics, farmers who cultivate the branches carefully, or reliable income from a marketable product. It provides shade (passing interest) but not a lingering, tangible experience (deep emotional rapture).

The apple beckons the character forward, ignoring the risks until he's in a precarious position. We understand how much the character wants their object of desire, what it means to them, why they desperately need it. Perhaps it's the last, crucial ingredient for a potion to cure their cursed parent.

We make it hard enough to attain that readers will feel a thrill at the journey's execution, and add enough looming, unexpected dangers to make it seem like the resolution is still in question. We put a poisonous worm in the apple. Another character gets injured and they have to choose whom to save.

Don't like my metaphor? Consider that one of the earliest and most popular stories in history is about a snake, an apple and a tree. Temptation, danger, desire. Something the character wants, a dangerous risk, an ultimate consequence.

The plot outlines will get you started, but it's not a magic bullet. It's just a roadmap. You still need to lay down the pavement. Don't assume just because you had fun writing it, readers will have fun reading it. Just because the road is *smooth* doesn't mean anyone will use it. Readers have to *want* to reach a particular destination: but mostly they just can't get bored or confused. The longer the journey, the harder you'll need to fight to keep them entertained.

Structure is important, to make sure that your book is going somewhere, and that each scene matters to the main story. It'll help give your book a consistent framework and reliable feeling. But it isn't enough on its own. A great plot outline can still be badly written. Or it can be excellently written and more boring than watching paint dry. Almost always, the missing ingredient is *conflict.* If you want to over-simplify, the easy way to plot a novel is to think of what your character wants more than anything, and then invent new ways to stop them from getting it.

Others have said, story is what happens, while plot is the effective arrangement of those events in a dramatic fashion. But what does it mean to be dramatic? *Conflict* is the resistance that makes the journey difficult enough to be remarkable. *Drama* is the mystery surrounding the ordeal. If readers know or can guess what happens, the conflict won't be dramatic.

Few writing guides explain how to pull off the complex trick of keeping readers in the dark, even though secrets are the core, essential propellant of magic. It's much more important than style, word choice or sentence structure. It's really the only thing that matters; and it can be taught quickly even though it's rarely recognized.

Last year, I showed the card trick I'd learned in middle school to my niece at a family gathering. First, I demonstrated the routine, quietly astounding the room. Then I privately showed my niece the hidden, secret mechanism (it involves pulling a card off the bottom of the deck). After only a few minutes of practice, even with a clumsy attempt due to her tiny fingers, the magic (the state of unknowing that makes the trick seems impossible) was impressive enough to stump her cousins.

> When you know how it works, it's just a trick.
> When you don't, it's magic.

Getting readers to *care* enough about what's happening to keep turning pages will be your biggest hurdle; learning how to keep secrets by withholding information will be your biggest asset. If you're looking for the occult (from the Latin for *hidden* or *concealed*) formula for how to snare readers' attentions, you'll find it in this chapter.

DRAMATIC TENSION

Drama is watching conflict unfold in ways that impact the main character's decisions through the story. The key thing here is *unfold*, which means drama is not the content you have, but the content you remove, through omission.

The mystery leads to a story question, which leads to intrigue. The perceived danger tied to the unfolding sequence of events leads to suspense. Masterful writing is about *information management*: who knows what, when. The biggest mistake I see authors make is offering too much information, too early, with backstory infodumps that totally kill the urgency and momentum.

To simplify, let's start with this framework:

STORY: What Happens
DRAMA: Why It Matters

If the story doesn't matter, why should readers care what's happening? But what does it mean, to matter? It means, whatever the protagonist wants, the desire is significant enough for them to persevere through increasing risk, and despite increasing conflict.

Conflict is the resistance or friction they encounter. How much something matters can be shown through how much the characters were willing to endure to achieve it. Increasing *difficulty* makes the story matter on a deeper level, and shows that this story is worth telling.

If the tree is small and the branches strong, and the apple can be seized and consumed with little effort, then the story won't be meaningful. Drama is a saga of meaning and relevance, relating to a character's single pursuit of a difficult goal, and all the obstacles and challenges that they overcame to achieve it.

The way to add drama is to make sure you have suspense and intrigue on every page; those are summoned by *unresolved questions* about *unresolved conflict*. You need to show the conflict and consequences to show that the protagonist may face real risk and danger.

CONFLICT IS NOT VIOLENCE

It's easy for writers to add some fight scenes or arguments as a hasty attempt to create chaos and conflict, but most of these efforts will seem weak or random.

To continue with our tree metaphor: we burn the fields, we wrap snakes around the trunk, we add thorns to every branch, we take away the protagonist's tools or weapons. At every point, we make each decision to continue forward more difficult and fraught with peril. Conflict makes the story more interesting, but it's all surface level. Drama is the internal, emotional uncertainty that threatens your protagonist on an existential level.

Conflict is a microwave: it can zap things hot quickly, with little resistance. Drama is a crock-pot: a slow burner that cooks to the bone over a long period of time. The result is the same, but the difference is vital.

Drama allows for the uncertainty of the final outcome, and the character's exacerbated doubts and fears. The *threat* of a potential danger is always more scary than *actual* danger, and if we have too much violence early on, we'll have nowhere for the story to go later.

Real conflict depends on risk and uncertainty. The conflict won't matter until we know what's at stake, care for our protagonists, and understand the motivations and risks. Dying or killing or losing won't matter unless we first understand why the character can't afford to die; why he can't abide to kill; what she can't bear to lose.

GATHERING YOUR ROCKS

Let's start with the easy stuff: obstacles, challenges and difficult decisions. Every time your character needs to do something, you make it harder. Here are a few simple ways to do that.

- inability
- prohibition
- imminent threat

If they have to cross a river, one of their allies can't swim. There's a "no swimming" sign. Then add alligators. If they need to enter the city, the gates are shut, their faces are on wanted posters, they get in a fight and attract the attention of the guards.

You need to show *potential* danger that they try to avoid, then hit them with *real* danger anyway. Be careful not to make this too direct; surprise them with something different than what they were prepared for. If the no swimming sign said: "danger, alligators" the reptilian menace wouldn't be a surprise, and they would seem foolish for trying to swim it anyway. Smart characters will avoid real danger, so real conflict is always accidental.

If there is no clear and immediate danger, force them off the path into a scenic route. An easy way to do this, which we'll talk about later, is the sidequest. Say they're looking for information. They track down the person with the information, but he refuses to share until they do a favor for him. The information quest becomes a mission quest. Be careful not to stray too long or too far from the main story, and something should happen on that sidequest that has dire consequences or relevance later.

Make a list of all the important things your characters need to do to achieve their goal, then create at least three obstacles for each task. These don't have to be literal monsters or bad guys, and in fact not every source of conflict needs to be external, which we'll talk about in a minute.

Just keep in mind for now, that readers won't care what happens in your story unless you have sympathy and conflict (readers have to like your characters, and your characters must be oppressed, and the stakes must be real).

REAL CONFLICT AND FAKE CONFLICT

Most stories simply don't have enough conflict, so adding more conflict to every scene will immediately help, but not all conflict is the same. Specifically, if the action has already concluded, then it isn't *unresolved conflict*, which means the stakes aren't real. There is no actual, imminent danger. There may be some curiosity about how it all went down, but it isn't pressing in the moment.

Even if you don't have a strict linear timeline, and no matter whether you're using present tense or past tense to show the unfolding of your story, your main characters will probably have a *present moment* where they aren't yet aware of what's going to happen in the future.

There are three instances where your conflict may not have unresolved conflict or real stakes, which are these:

1. *This stuff happens (no big deal)*. This is random bad stuff, accidents or unexpected interruptions, that can be dire, if you let them be. What you want to avoid, however, is incidents that come too early, that don't seem to have any real impact on the character or the reader. Especially when they don't seem to react or respond with more than a casual shrug. Sometimes, you can open a novel with a hero nonchalantly defeating scores of bad guys, showing off either his supreme skill and ability, or his absolute lack of self-preservation, because he has nothing to live for anyway. Either of these could be problematic.

2. *This already happened (resolved conflict)*. The main problem with flashbacks, memories or cutscenes is that, while they may include important backstory so we understand a character's motivations, the conflict isn't real because the danger isn't present.

3. *This never really happened (false conflict).* The most egregiously common example of this is the dream sequence; which many authors use to begin their novels with some cool conflict, and then immediately erase it all with "and then he woke up." It might still work if the dream was a premonition or relevant to the story, but you don't want to reveal critical information, without having the character experience and react to it in real-time. It's too easy for a character to blow off a dream sequence as unimportant.

If *stuff like this* happens all the time, if it's already happened, or if it's not really happening, then there will be very little drama or conflict in the presentation of the material.

Of course this doesn't mean you should never add stories, dreams or backstory flashbacks into your novel – it can't be all fight scenes and bad guys. The slow, moody chapters where your characters reveal vulnerabilities matter also. But they need to be carefully handled, because they are going to be the weak points of your story until you find a way to make them relevant and increase the conflict.

Something must change in every chapter that influences your characters and allows the plot to move forward; scenes without real risks and stakes are only artificial conflict. They might be important, but they aren't the crucial thing that happens. Adding *real* conflict to every scene will make your book much more satisfying and keep readers hooked.

THE THREE KINDS OF CONFLICT

I believe it's useful to distinguish between three main types of conflict – external, internal and lateral, or what I've called "friendly fire." External conflicts are the physical dangers or barriers preventing characters from reaching their next immediate goal. Internal conflicts are the doubts, fears and insecurities your characters face as they wrestle with difficult moral decisions. Friendly fire is the conflict that erupts between allies, friends or family who have their own wishes or desires.

01. *Outer Conflict* (threats). Challenges or obstacles that prevent the character from achieving goals.

02. *Inner Conflict* (doubts). Moral struggles, decisions, guilt or shame, anger

03. *Friendly Fire* (betrayal). Strong disagreements between allies or supporting characters.

The simple way to add conflict to your story, is just to invent more hurdles for everything that needs to happen.

- Every door needs to be locked
- Every vault needs three keys
- The information quest to the favor quest

Of course this will get tiresome if they're just grinding down barriers, so be careful not to repeat too much of the same things. Also make sure to give them impossible choices that demand a sacrifice; where each decision has an unavoidable consequence, even if it's an arbitrary penalty.

Angry at Zeus for fathering another illegitimate child, Hera drives Heracles mad, and he kills his own wife and children. Seeking purpose and meaning, he asks the Delphic oracle what to do to make amends, and is told to serve the king of Mycenae for ten years; in which time he's asked to perform ten impossible feats or labors. The story of Heracles completing the ten tasks is made interesting because of the motivating purpose (tragic backstory, sympathetic character, quest for redemption). But the drama is increased when the king of Mycenae refuses to accept his victory, and assigns him two additional, even more challenging ordeals. If it had simply been a hero going through a checklist of supernatural feats, without any additional dramatic intrigue (unresolved or unexpected conflict) the story would be much less satisfying.

There's potentially a fourth type of conflict I haven't named yet, but it has something to do with foreshadowing. It might be something like implied conflict or unactivated conflict: basically something that *could* become a big problem later, that the character notes and minimalizes, like "we'll cross that bridge when we come to it." But while the first three can be added to a scene or outline in the first draft, foreshadowing is probably best left until later revisions, when you can see the whole picture and then plant or remove signals without being heavy-handed or giving away the surprise.

THE TWO RULES OF CONFLICT

1. Dialogue is the enemy of tension
2. All conflict is unplanned

Conversation is the death of conflict

Most conflict, especially the lateral and interior conflict, comes from a lack of clear communication. As we'll discuss in a minute, the important part is to keep building conflict and tension without diffusing it. Think of blowing up a balloon; each time you take a breath, you have to hold the balloon tight so air doesn't escape. You don't have to be adding more tension all the time, but you can't let it all out, either. Your characters might be looking for answers or taking action to reduce that tension; it will feel like a pressing anxiety. The more dire the consequences, the more active they will be to resolve the conflict… but you can't let them. Whatever they are looking for, it can't be found.

The *easiest way* for them to get the information they need would be to ask someone else; which is why you may need to build up the lateral conflict to create reasons for them not to talk to each other. Imagine how differently Harry Potter could have turned out if Dumbledore just sat down and explained everything to Harry immediately, instead of allowing him to fall into mortal consequences each and every book. The entire plan was mapped out in advance, but unless Harry experienced it and struggled through his own choices and discoveries, he wouldn't have become the hero he needed to be for the plan to work.

Don't let characters sit and talk to each other. This will quickly resolve story questions with too much information or backstory. In a contemporary romance, most of the conflict will be the misunderstandings or false assumptions that fester between your love interests. Every time they are about to get together or talk about their feelings, interrupt them! Create conflict and drama that keeps them from talking or sharing.

If your characters have time to make small talk about trivial events that didn't have an emotional impact on them, it means your plot is too slow or the stakes are too low, because your characters should need or want something much more pressing than getting to know each other or reviewing things that happened earlier. Unless it's part of a discussion that helps them make a choice on how to respond to events. And even then, a scene should never just be a group of characters sitting around amicably working together.

All conflict is unplanned

I mentioned "story questions" up above, so let me explain that quickly. Basically, when something happens, your character – and reader – will start asking questions. Who, what, where, why, how? These questions will be resolved through the development of the story, but at first, the protagonist doesn't know what's happening, or why. This leads to speculation, fear, uncertainty and doubt. They make a plan to figure out or answer these questions, which moves the plot forward. Along the way, they discover some of these answers, which probably lead to more questions. They have a goal, but are nervous that taking action to lessen their uncertainty will put them in more danger. How will I do this, what if this happens, what's the worst that could happen?

Don't let her just do the thing easily; or even *expect* to do the thing easily. Smart protagonists don't ignore potential dangers, and they plan to avoid conflict. Conflict resists their efforts. The plan goes wrong because something or someone unexpected opposes the plan, forcing a new response.

CONFLICT = what DOES happen.
TENSION = what COULD happen.
INTRIGUE = why is THIS happening?

Conflict only happens in the moment. It's important to keep things moving and interesting, but tension cuts deeper. Without conflict (a character forced into challenging situations) and tension (someone we care about meeting potential danger), there won't be any intrigue, because readers won't *care* about the story questions, like what is happening or why. Getting readers invested in your story is mostly about withholding information, so that the tension mounts and their curiosity is piqued. They keep reading to resolve this narrative obscurity, but you confound and ensnare by weaving in more mysteries.

WHAT WILL HAPPEN NEXT?

Intrigue: If readers aren't asking questions, they aren't interested. You get them interested by showing characters they care about, and revealing the dangers.

Tension: Let the risk and danger of actual conflict grow quietly. Don't let it out. Hold it in. Let it build until it *cannot* be contained.

One time I was hiking in Iguazu Falls, Brazil. I was pretty far off the main path, cutting through the forest, when I started noticing large holes near where I was placing my hands, which made me nervous and anxious. I realized this was probably stupid, so I started heading back down. I'd just emerged onto a boulder, into daylight, when I glanced down and saw a tarantula the size of my palm on my shoe. I screamed, jumped and fell down the waterfall. I probably wouldn't have jumped so high or been so traumatized by the experience if I hadn't *already* been on edge.

Drama is not the conflict or violence; it's the *growing potential* for conflict and violence. The longer this lingering fear is allowed to grow and build, the more emotional impact when the threat is finally realized. At the risk of mixing metaphors, I'll throw in one more visual here: imagine your tree is filled with spiders. The presence of spiderwebs implies danger, and creates suspense.

Drama is the stickiness of the spider's web (not the spider itself: the *potential* existence of a spider.) Waiting nervously to see when the spider will show up is what keeps readers glued to every page. The story structure was necessary, or the individual narrative threads would blow away or fall apart, but it's those extra sticky, nearly invisible threads that bind. The spider *waits* until the fly has exhausted himself through strenuous resistance, but the fly's fierce struggle against his inevitable demise only tangles it tighter.

WHEN TO REVEAL INFORMATION

A good rule of thumb is to make readers ask a question, before you give them the answer. The question arises through the story action. Build intrigue and suspense by making things happen. Build sympathy for your character through real plot events (not backstory).

Reveal key pieces of information when it has the most emotional impact, on your characters and readers. This will *usually* occur simultaneously: you want the information to be discovered and reacted to, by your characters, at the same time readers are learning about it.

1. Show it happening.
2. Scenes of biggest drama should be shown
   (not offstage or reported; real conflict, not fake conflict)

If it's important to your story (it has emotional relevance to your characters and may influence their actions or reactions) don't show it, hide it – show its *absence*. Have the question raised but *refuse* to answer. The more important the information, the less easy it should be for readers to access it.

Intrigue: withhold info.
Suspense: show the danger.
Timing: readers learn when characters learn.

Readers need to learn facts when the main POV sympathetic character finds them out; when the information matters most on an emotional level so you can show her charged reaction.

EARN IT OR LEARN IT

Make your characters work for important information or story reveals. It shouldn't be common knowledge, or something that someone else knew but just never mentioned because it didn't seem relevant until now. It can't just show up when it's convenient; it should come at a cost.

Instead of revealing information to the audience unprompted, it needs to be forced out: like squeezing an empty tube of toothpaste. More and more pressure, rolling up the tube, to reach the last little bit.

If you want to make something hard, whether an event, or to make your protagonist uniquely special, you can have another character comment on it first. "You know you're not going to find anything, right? My family has been searching for years and has never found anything. This is impossible." So, in addition to the *prohibition* rule I added earlier, we can also toss in some *preemptive difficulty* markers, followed by *astonishment* after the thing has been accomplished.

It's the difference between "we won!" (oh boy, accidental lucky break) and "we're never going to win anything, our team hasn't won in centuries...holy crap, we *won*. How did you do that?" (impressively difficult feat of rare skill).

If you need to keep an important piece of information secret until the crucial reveal, you can just make up an excuse for why it didn't come up earlier.

HOLD YOUR TONGUE

I've already offered repeated warnings about how backstory infodumps reduce drama by oversharing easily obtained information. And you might be thinking, *fine* – but what do I do with that critical childhood scene that defines my character?

What if I need to tell readers something so they "get" what is happening? Well... *don't*. Imagine you're watching a movie with someone and they keep pausing it to fill you in or explain what's going on. Imagine five minutes of explanation for every one minute of movie. You'd be frustrated, and probably not able to enjoy the story or figure things out on your own. Information has no emotional power on its own; drama is the lack of information, the engaging unraveling of narrative secrets.

Almost any time you're tempted to *explain* what's happening, it means you're sharing information directly with readers that isn't in your plot; it's not discovered or engaged with by your characters. You're just hitting the pause button. I've seen books with four chapters of backstory before the plot begins; or a full chapter of a character sitting and thinking through all of the things that happened to "catch readers up" before the events begin. If this is the only way you have to introduce critical story – it isn't critical.

Remember, real story is unresolved conflict. The resolution hasn't happened yet; the danger is real. Backstory is concluded action that has no teeth. There's no real danger, so there's no real suspense or intrigue. The results are known. You can make this information more interesting if it's *shared* backstory, where one character is revealing something important to another, if so, great – the conflict is in the reaction. But it will almost never happen in the beginning of a book.

You can add some important information after the first few chapters, once you've established the ordinary world and the inciting incident: you have to assume your characters are living their lives, focused on the next thing, not moping around thinking about all the stuff that happened to them years ago. If it matters, if it's important, keep it a secret.

When to reveal backstory:

Is this necessary to enjoy the story?
- ✓ after a risky or dangerous scene (slow after fast)
- ✓ with some action or scene (discovery or conversation)

✓ deepen emotional attachment (right before danger)
✓ justify character motivations (explain choices)

Add backstory *after* the plot is in motion, once you've already introduced some pity (sympathy) and fear (stakes). Reveal it when it's necessary to fill in an already raised story question; and when this information is *new* to one of your characters, impacts them on an emotional level, and influences their actions or decisions.

When to remove backstory:

Who is giving this information right now, and why?
X just thinking out loud to themselves
X telling someone who already knows
X overt narration while characters stand still

There are certain books that have a strong sense of narrative voice, but I'd caution you to be judicious with your commentary. Your characters aren't just finger puppets. You don't need to pull back the curtain and tell the audience exactly why the characters are doing what they're doing or feeling what they're feeling. Every little addition or commentary, where you're talking to readers directly rather than through the way your characters engage with the current scene, is going to come off as a distracting interruption.

It still might be necessary, sometimes, but try to keep it short and limit it to a phrase or sentence – not an infodump or extended parentheses. The big story reveals should be forced out when the antagonist faces off with the protagonist. You may have a tightly plotted story, but there's no suspense or drama, because the information is handed out generously, reducing its perceived value.

We might understand everything that happened, from the threat of the antagonist to the final conflict, but there was nothing unexpected, no twists, no reveals, because we already had all the information, usually earlier than the characters knew it. So when they found out it wasn't convincing or impactful, it felt flat, there was no pleasure in the satisfying resolution.

STORY QUESTION CHEATSHEET

The truth is, it's absolutely fine to dump long passages of information as you're writing your first draft and discovering your story, and we'll talk more about that later. But I'm sharing all of this with you here so you'll learn to recognize the risks and flag potential problems. Later you can do the careful work of *removing* information in revisions, and *revealing* it again in dramatic fashion.

To make things easier, I've come up with a pretty useful guide to what kinds of questions your characters – and readers – should be asking at different stages of your book. Remember, we want them asking questions, which they won't do unless they like your characters and are intrigued by the weirdness. In the beginning, they won't really care about anything, *and* your characters won't voluntarily or randomly bring up and share their most traumatic past experiences. So save those for later.

In the first 25% of the book, before you get to the point of no return, readers and characters should be asking **what** questions. What is even happening? What is this place? What is going to happen next?

At around 50%, this will change to *who* questions. Who is behind all this? Who can I trust? Who am I?

Finally, towards the end or around 75%, you'll have all the deep motivational reveals, either when the bad guy admits his evil plan and the reasons behind it; or after the major conflict when the danger has passed and you can finally let your characters sit down and fill each other in on the miscellaneous story details. These are the *why* questions.

Story Reveals

	Ordinary World (start with lack)	
	Inciting Incident (call to adventure)	
WHAT	1st **Plot Point (point of no return)**	25%
	1st Pinch Point (first battle)	
WHO	**Midpoint (victim to warrior)**	50%
	2nd Pinch Point (second battle)	
WHY	2nd **Plot Point (dark night of soul)**	75%
	Final Battle (triumph-knowledge)	
	Epilogue (come home changed)	

The magical formula to keep in mind is that readers need to be asking questions, which can only happen if you stop telling them exactly what's going on.

You never show the real monster until near the end. First, you show the strange happenings, the signs, the effects, the aftermath. Knowledge gaps (unexplained events) lead to discomfort, which prompts the characters to investigate and explore. The questions build; *what* is happening. This leads to a hypothesis, and investigation; *who* is behind this. You slowly reveal pieces of information, without completely unmasking the monster or villain. The motivations, *why* is this happening, what does this thing want, how do the pieces of the puzzle fit together, all of that comes last.

If you show the monster first, in all its gory detail, readers won't be scared. If you explain who is behind it and why, there's no intrigue, suspense or mystery. If you explain why all this is happening, the cause behind the events, you've spoiled the ending and won't be able to manage any twists or reveals. This is true *even if* you're not writing a horror, thriller or murder mystery. A book is a treasure hunt: readers read to alleviate the discomfort raised by the story questions facing your characters.

The more important the details, the harder they need to work to uncover them. They can't be common knowledge; they can't be offered freely. You show something is important and valuable, not by offering it, but by withholding it.

The forbidden fruit is seductive because it's hidden, rare and prohibited. It's secret knowledge that must be earned: the *value* or worth of the galvanizing object is in the *difficulty* of its pursuit. The character's quest is not only about the struggle, but the understanding, realization and wisdom he earns along the way.

WHAT HURTS MOST, GOES LAST

This one is short, but important. Don't tell the full backstory at the beginning of the book. It's too early. Nobody cares yet. It won't have any meaning. Show flashbacks. The fun or intriguing stuff. Images without context. Something weird or unusual, a picture of a scene: the smell of smoke, the spinning bicycle tire. A repeating anxiety or childhood trauma that only surfaces when your character is broken down, exhausted and nervous.

As pressures mount, and she's evaluating the life choices that brought her here, to your quagmire of a story that she can't escape from. The increasingly emotional chaos will churn up those childhood insecurities she's been struggling to repress or hide. The flashbacks get darker. A repressed memory that hints of trauma; the inner demons the protagonist is determined to keep locked away.

The full story only comes out just before her eventual triumph. The stage has been set. The final combat is looming. She's determined to show up to the contest, even though she's not sure she can win. Now we want the stakes to matter more; we want to twist the knife. We already liked and rooted for her character, but before she puts it all on the line, we have to *love* her so we can care deeply about the final outcome. You reverently, slowly fit the last piece of the puzzle into the story, and suddenly the entire image is revealed. Those little bits of limited information you parsed out earlier come into sharp relief and focus, with a deep and powerful effect.

What not to do: a guy walks into a bar, gets drunk and tells the bartender his life story in chapter one. Or meets a stranger and immediately breaks down crying when he thinks about how his dog died twenty years ago. Nobody shares intimate secrets with strangers; and if your *characters* aren't doing it, *you* shouldn't be doing it. (They trusted you, you jerk, and you're spoiling everything).

CORE DRAMA & ACCIDENTAL DRAMA

Core drama is integral to the main story plot. It happens "on stage" in the present where it can affect and influence the main character emotionally, impact their choices or limit their options.

There are two things I often see that weaken a novel:

1. *Core drama is skipped or reported.* Anything important that could impact the characters emotionally, or is rife with conflict and intrigue, should happen on the page, as a scene. It's fine to skip some things and merely have your characters report back on them later, but readers will feel cheated if this was potentially a big thing. Especially if it's new information or a reveal; something they were waiting to happen but then somehow missed. You can tie up loose ends at the end of your book by having characters fill each other in on logistics that had to be skipped over earlier, but these should be rational unknowns that you had to preserve, to maintain the story questions and intrigue. They are *facts*, not *happenings*. Actual reveals are dramatic, and normally need to happen on stage so that you can do a hard scene break, which we'll talk more about later. If they're swallowed up at the end or in reported conversation, readers may feel like they're swallowing a bitter pill. Feel free to skip scenes of minor consequence, but if there's potential for pain, challenge, conflict, if it's emotionally challenging, show it as an event.

2. *Drama that doesn't impact the core story*: remember, most stories will follow one character's pursuit of one main goal or challenge. They may be distracted by necessary sidequests or plots, but they won't lose track of their main goal for several

chapters; unless there is a more direct threat or danger. Characters will always be thinking of the most urgent thing, so direct immanent threats may temporarily consume their attention. Once the danger is passed, however, they'll resume their main quest or goal. If you introduce the main conflict and then your characters spend half a book doing other things, concerned with trivial incidents, none of it will seem relevant or interesting, because readers will be waiting for the current story to connect with the main problem. The bigger or more interesting the main problem, the less interesting or compelling everything else will be, and the shorter their patience.

RED FLAGS

We've covered a lot of ground already in this chapter, so I'm going to offer a quick summary. If you don't have drama (conflict, suspense, intrigue, and tension relating to characters we care about) – readers will quit reading or get bored. Even if the writing is good. Even if they like the characters. Here are three red flags you can watch out for in your writing.

- POV JUMPING: Sympathy / Timing. *Unresolved Conflict*
- BACKSTORY: If this already happened, it doesn't matter (no real stakes).
- BAIT & SWITCH: Hook them hard but then change topics and expect them to care.

People often ask me about novels with multiple POV characters: we'll talk a bit about tense and point of view later, but let me start with explaining why multiple POV or POV jumping is *more difficult* to achieve. Especially at the beginning of a novel, readers are just asking the "what" questions: What are these characters doing, what do they want? You have a limited window to get them to care about what's happening to these characters. If you jump into someone else's head, dealing with different problems somewhere else, just when you almost have them interested in your first story, you're asking them to start over with someone new from scratch.

You've hooked their interest (barely, and temporarily) and expect them to wait on hold while you jump into a different narrative. It's also harder to keep track of the timing: you absolutely don't want to repeat the same circumstances or events that already happened (because it's resolved conflict, so there's very little real stakes or drama). It can be pulled off; especially in romance, but it's harder to achieve well, and there are fewer examples of very successful novels that are written this way. When you're ready for a challenge, by all means try it out, but if you're still relatively inexperienced, I'd practice a more straightforward narrative.

I've talked quite a bit about backstory, because it really is the thing I see most often used ineffectively. You *should* have an intriguing backstory for most of your main characters. Just be careful about how and when you share it with your readers. The best use of backstory is often to explain character motivation. The deeper into the conflict the characters get, the stronger their motivation needs to be. At some point, it may stop making sense.

Why do they care about this so much? Why are they willing to *destroy* themselves or those they love, to continue and persevere in the face of such great odds? A telling flashback here, that finally reveals the shard of glass or fatal flaw, and shows how their *identity* is fundamentally fractured; that they can't help but continue because they aren't whole or complete without this thing they've been chasing... that's a great use of backstory.

But it needs to be revealed only when the stakes are so great it's necessary to understand your character's otherwise illogical choices (despite reason; they are choosing based on emotional underpinnings). If we already knew all this from chapter three, it wouldn't seem as important. The more important the thing, the longer you should wait to reveal it.

Bait and switch just means, you got your readers on board based on a captivating premise or conflict or story idea. They are waiting to see how it plays out. Sometimes this can happen with a prologue or incident, and then chapter one starts with the ordinary character and the ordinary world. Sometimes this is done to let readers know exciting stuff is going to happen later. But readers won't *wait around* for things to get interesting again. It doesn't matter that you're trying to build things up slowly. Your present scene, right now, has to be filled with core conflict (not accidental drama) and related to the main story (the source of the largest conflict: the conflict that will eventually force your character to grow or change).

The more implied stakes in your main story, the more frustration your readers will feel waiting around for it to start happening. You can save it with great writing, scene description and characters, but only for so long. More and more, readers are showing little patience for slow to develop, convoluted stories that take time to get off the ground but reward perseverance. Unless you already have a huge following or fanbase, and have earned a considerable amount of trust from your audience, readers will have no incentive to keep reading something, waiting for it to get better.

ARROWS AND STARS

A good novel will build to a climax slowly, to explain how the character ended up in this extreme position, against this impossible choice, forced to fight or lose or quit or suffer.

Smart characters avoid conflict and pain, so a novel is every relevant step that moved her closer towards this dramatic peak; until she reaches a point of crisis which can no longer be avoided or ignored. In order to survive, defeat the bad guys, save the world, claim her true love or anything else, she will probably be forced to do something she abhors or give up something she adores.

For this transition to matter and be charged with pathos, you need to slowly increase the tension; it can't just all happen at once. The switch or change has to be epic – deepfelt, painful and tragic. This isn't something you can get readers to understand and feel in one scene; it's *all* the scenes of your book that make *this* pivotal scene matter.

I like to imagine it like a bow: the further you draw back the string, the more true the arrow will fly. But a crossbow might be a better metaphor. The string is wound so tight, you need a special tool to pull it back. You crank the string to the next divot in the wood, where it rests, until the crank is deployed again, pulling it back even further. Step by step. A small bit at a time.

Tension, rest, tension, the stakes doubling and tripling, until when you finally release all that stored up energy, it can pierce the densest armor. This is why we have structure, resting points, marked intervals, in a certain order, of a certain type, because it's the most effective way to make the arrow fly the furthest. In this example, we can compare the *roots* to the deeply protected secrets that create tension (the emotional motivations for the character's profound resistance to the change they need); and the *branches* to arrows (a quiver of piercing thorns.)

Sure, your story doesn't have to comply with this archery metaphor. Maybe you're practicing for sport, and don't like killing animals anyway. But what if you are hunting rabbits, to feed your family. Can you afford to waste time and arrows? What if there were only one rabbit, and a thousand people with bows trying to hunt it down? Only the *best* hunter will get fed. Wouldn't you want to become devastatingly effective at your craft?

At the start of this chapter, I talked about how drama is the beating heart of your story, and compared it to a delicious apple at the top branch of your story tree. The desire for the apple needs to be big enough, and the personal risks dangerous enough, for readers to feel the depth of your character's emotions. But that's still just surface-level skillcraft.

The true magic is deeper. It's only when you slice open the apple and reveal its secrets that you find the hidden star. Grow the fruit rich and plump with unresolved conflict. The bigger the drama, the thinner the slices, the more stars appear when you pierce its heart. As Hemingway wrote, "write hard and deep about what hurts."

MEMORANDUM

- Masterful writing is about keeping secrets
- The unfolding of unresolved conflict
- Three kinds of conflict: inner, outer, lateral

- To make your story matter, increase the difficulty
- What hurts most goes last
- What do the characters need or want?
- What's stopping them? 3 hurdles/obstacles
- The most pressing thing replaces the big thing
- Reveal backstory after stakes are clear
- Real drama vs. accidental drama
- Show main conflict "on stage"
- Conversation kills conflict
- All conflict is unplanned
- Raise questions, before you give answers
- Earn it or learn it
- Solutions and answers must come at a cost
- Drama is the endurance of risk for the promise of result
- Push characters up the tree and throw rocks
- The stars only appear when the heart is pierced

The door opens into a vast chamber flanked by pillars, the night sky twinkling beyond the exposed ceiling. Unearthly music draws you forward, through dark passages of cracked stone and leafy fern. You enter an abandoned library, with shelves stretching to the broken roof. You take a deep, calming breath and run your fingertips against the ancient, leatherbound volumes, hinting at concealed wisdom. You're looking for a secret, a spell that can increase your ability in the craft. But there are thousands to choose from.

Footsteps echo in the corridor. You turn to find a wrinkled scribe shrouded in a dark robe. He hears your silent plea, reads the stirrings of your heart, and carefully selects a book from the shelf. It's thin and light, but something tells you it's the one you've been seeking. A tingle spreads through your body as you open the book. But it's only one page, with an incantation you can't read in an ancient language. The old man nods, giving a sly smile, and the glowing symbols rearrange until you can grasp their meaning. A golden key emerges from between the pages.

You have earned…
★ The Talisman of Knowledge ★
Craft is the study of essentials.

You've earned your second totem! You've gained a deeper understanding, and appreciation, for the craft of writing. Many of these concepts may have been new to you; remember, learning the craft is only a loose foundation to give more space for your unique magic. Picture it like laying out a broad field of dry wheat, ready for you to ignite with the heat of your pen.

> "I always liked the magic of poetry but now I'm just starting to see behind the curtain of even the best poets, how they've used, tried and tested craft to create the illusion. Wonderful feeling of exhilaration to finally be here." *– David Knopfler*

These rituals, spells and incantations can help you unlock a deeper magic, and develop a powerful writing habit of your own. If it all feels a bit too formulaic, don't worry: the heavy work we did on foundations are only meant to help you scale to your own point of mastery faster.

So far, I've only shown you the *what,* not the *how*: the trick, not the magic. You've received a checklist of ingredients and a recipe to brew a powerful spell of your own. With these useful skills, you can now begin to put them into your own practice: the deeper insights, the real magic, comes during the process.

You had a vision, and now you're about to call it into the world through the power of your words. This is a gift, if you show up and do the work, but only if the knowledge is applied. Implementing these strategies will help you avoid common writing mistakes and give your book a strong foundation. But now that we've covered the basics, we're ready to go deeper.

We've been gathering supplies, preparing for the journey. Now we're ready to embark.

The way forward will not be easy, and these new strategies may feel unfamiliar or uncomfortable at first. You can only unleash their true power by putting them into practice until they blossom for you. Only you can decide, who you want to become, why it will be you.

Sanctify your space: during the next few chapters, you'll be developing your own story as we navigate murky waters. Implementing unfamiliar tactics and strategies may feel challenging at first. It may not feel as fun or natural. You may lose sight of the mystery and sense of wondrous discovery.

At this point, I recommend getting yourself something that makes you feel confident, or reminds you that effort requires patience. Or it could be something *fun* that your inner child will appreciate. It's basically a bribe, so they'll be good while you do the work. It might be something a little silly, childish or ridiculous. That's okay, we'll keep this between us.

I like having a classic, old-fashioned typewriter near me, an inspiring quote by an author I admire, a statue or poster representing my genre, or a favorite toy from my childhood. Focus on the way you want to *feel*. Imagine your best words flowing easily.

Produce

CASTING SPELLS

There are several definitions for the word *casting* and each of them represents the material in this next section (writing the rough draft) in a unique way. It can mean the assignment of parts and duties to actors or performers, throwing out a fishing line, or an object made by pouring molten metal into a mold.

Each of these applies to the spellcraft of filling in your outline with words; figuring out what your characters will do and say; and letting out more "lines" to snare readers with your story. But *Merriam-Webster* also uses this bizarrely specific example: "something (such as the excrement of an earthworm) that is cast out or off."

I hope the previous sections have already taught you a few new things about writing fiction. But there's a difference between knowledge and experience, and the harshest truth about writing is this: the first draft is usually crap. Even if you know what you're doing. Even if you planned it well. This disconnect between the ideation and the execution can be a brutal wake-up call, especially for new authors. It can cause burnout, frustration and depression. Hopefully, I've pre-empted some of that in the section on confidence earlier, but I'm going to remind you here before we start writing because it's important.

> "The first draft is nothing more than a starting point, so be wrong as fast as you can." – *Andrew Stanton*

The *point* of the first draft is just to get started; not to write a great book or even to write a good book. Cast out the earthworm excrement and spew words on your blank page. Fill your meadow with manure, in order to create fertile ground.

THE BEST IS THE ENEMY OF THE GOOD

First drafts are supposed to be terrible. But you need to get them written anyway. Accepting this as part of the process will make things a lot easier. The "pretty writing" phase comes during final revisions and edits.

Voltaire: *The best is the enemy of the good.*
Confucius: *Better a diamond with a flaw than a pebble without.*
Shakespeare: *Striving to better, oft we mar what's well.*

But my favorite quote is from Elizabeth Gilbert, in her book *Big Magic*: "Perfectionism is just fear in high heels."

Writers who get stuck obsess about the wrong things too early. It's much easier to *intend* to write a crappy draft quickly, to tell yourself the story and figure out what happens, than to write a crappy first draft slowly, aiming at perfection and falling short.

My suggestion is this: don't try to write a good novel. Don't write a novel you care about. Because at this point, the one thing you can't control is your skill or ability. Of *course* you're going to do your best. The problem is, the discrepancy between your current level of spellcraft and your creative vision is the one thing that's going to mess you up.

The greater your optimism and courage; the greater your belief in your writing abilities; the more it's going to hurt when your first draft sucks... *unless* you understand that suckage is normal, and expected, and you aim to suck as hard as you can.

QUANTITY LEADS TO QUALITY

We've already covered a lot of theory, but there's no way to really integrate new knowledge without adding the practice as well. There's a difference between learning *and* doing; and learning *by* doing.

This section is all about getting words on the page and finishing your first rough draft. We'll focus on a quarter of your book at a time, revisiting the major turning points and goals for each section, and diving deeper into some of the most crucial episodes or scenes to make sure the book has a satisfying build-up and resolution.

I'm trusting you to do the work, map out your story first based on the materials provided in the first section, and apply these additional insights as you write. They'll be *much* more impactful if you have a specific story in mind. I recommend reading the relevant chapter as you go along, rather than skimming quickly and forgetting it all later. (Let's be honest, you're probably not going to do that—so at the very least, make notes about anything that seems useful so you can check back quickly when you get stuck).

Here it might be useful to dig deeper into some "quality" versus "productivity" mindset limitations. Believe me, I've heard it all before, that writing crap to game the market is literary sacrilege; that real writers carefully hone their words with intention; that writing *fast* is never the way to write *well*.

A photography teacher once did an experiment where he gave half the classroom the assignment to take one *good* picture, and the other to take as many pictures as possible. In the end, the group that aimed for quantity over quality also produced the best pictures. This is because ability comes from practice and experience, and worrying about quality too soon may dampen or restrain the pure, steaming fury of your creative expression.

The point I'm trying to establish here, is that your first draft is not about good writing, and trying to write your first draft well will probably sabotage the process and ultimately lead to a weaker book. The solution is to write it quickly, roughly, focusing on the story, figuring out what happens. All the gaps and plot holes and motivations and details (how it works) we'll fix later, and we'll only much later clean up the writing after we've gone through a few rounds of structural revisions.

Don't worry about the style of writing, the sentence structure or the words on the page. Don't fret about whether or not you're good enough. If you can't think of the right word, use the wrong word. Get to the end as quickly as possible, so you can see your whole story clearly.

Incidentally, writing quickly doesn't really mean *writing quickly*. It's going to take as long as it takes. This time will depend on your skill and talent. The question is, do you allow days or weeks to drift by when you're not actively working on your book—the coals of your inspiration a warm glow—or do you stoke the flames and power through it? A hundred hours of writing can be done in a year or a month. What you really want to aim for is *as much time in the ring* as you can get. Some people say it takes a thousand hours to become proficient. I've heard it said that the first million words you write are just practice.

Expecting your first book to be miraculously amazing, fully formed like Athena springing from Zeus's brow, is unrealistic, and it isn't even very useful. If it does all happen by magic, and you don't understand or appreciate the process, it won't be easy to replicate. Writing a million random words without craft can't properly be called a practice, because it lacks discipline. But it's a good place to start. In this instance, the goal is to accrue enough experience to gain mastery. If you make this your target, you can't miss unless you fail to show up.

> "You don't start out writing good stuff. You start out writing crap and thinking it's good stuff, and then gradually get better at it. That's why I say one of the most valuable traits is persistence." – *Octavia E Butler*

First you fill the hole with cement, then you smoothen the top. If you stopped to smoothen every few inches, the concrete would all set wrong anyway. We want to get down to a "bare-bones" story. It can be ugly. It can be messy. The words, punctuation, grammar or descriptive details, totally don't matter at this point. We can skip stuff if we get stuck, but you need to keep moving forward.

Luckily, your beliefs about how great art should be made have very little impact on the work itself. Good or bad writing is universal, and can be shown with concrete examples. *Actual* bad writing is really more about the content or structure of information. Readers don't care about your intention, only your execution of the material. Someone commented on one of my videos, "Write the first draft as *craft* and the final draft as *art*." I love how concise that is, and it's precisely the order we want. It's also the opposite of how most authors do it.

> A rich man, fond of felines, asked a famous Zen ink painter to draw him a cat. The master agreed and asked the man to come back in three months. When the man returned, he was put off, again and again, until a year had passed. Finally, at the man's request, the master drew out a brush, and with grace and ease, in a single fluid motion, drew a picture of a cat—the most marvelous image the man had ever seen. He was astonished, then he grew angry. "That drawing took you only thirty seconds! Why did you make me wait a year?" he demanded. Without a word, the master opened up a cabinet, and out fell thousands of drawings of cats.

It's an implicit bias to assume books written quickly can't have depth. The majority of classics were written quickly. The more you practice, the better and faster you should get at any skill. "My book is good because I spent more time on it," is almost never true. "What about *Les Misérables*, it took 12 years to write!" Sure, but it's 655,478 words long and one of the six greatest novels of all time. The length or struggle in this instance does not justify or ensure a universal excuse for correlating hard work with quality.

How long it takes is up to you. Whether it's good is up to readers; not how much love or labor you invested. The struggle is a symptom of inexperience. It's always hard, but don't assume authors who write full time write bad books just because you don't understand how they do it. Don't focus on speed: focus on craft (knowledge) and practice (consistency, doing the work, gaining experience).

For the record, I'm not saying that books written quickly are better; I'm simply refusing that books written slowly are better. It's also true that experienced, full-time authors who actually make a living *have learned* to be capable of writing more books, faster, through rigorous practice, and that the majority of self-defined slow writers feel entitled to their firm belief that they cannot write fast, even though they've only published one or two books. The first couple always take a long time. But if you're not getting faster, you're not progressing, and if you argue for your limitations, you'll keep them.

WRITER'S BLOCK

I used to say writer's block is a myth, because if you remove the fear or doubt, you'll naturally want to write because it's just so much fun. But it doesn't work in practice. I still spend most of my time avoiding the work I love to do—even though readers are bugging me about sequels and new releases. Even though my novels have hundreds of positive reviews. This isn't primarily a book about procrastination or motivation, so I won't dive too deeply into this here, but it might be useful to point out a few things I think are worth considering.

First, writing a book is just about the hardest thing a human brain can do. You have to juggle massive amounts of information, and it's exhausting. The brain is a muscle and the more energy it consumes, the more downtime it's going to need to charge back up. Don't feel *guilty* about not always doing the work, because a lot of the time, the rest and procrastination is actually a necessary part of the process.

If you're stuck, I mean really stuck, sometimes this means your story is broken and you can feel it. Pushing through it or writing more won't always work, until you figure out what's wrong. This is where the scene checklists and plot outlines I shared earlier can really work wonders. Also, the solutions rarely come in the writing; the writing is a painful slog as your brain works its way around the wound, like a tongue on a loose tooth.

Think of it like picking a lock. You have to poke around the tumblers, feeling the vibration, listening to the clicks and tension and getting a sense of how the gears interact, until *one piece* slips into place. It might be an important piece. It might be a sudden passing thought that suddenly becomes a crowning, majestic centerpiece. These discoveries are fun when they appear, but it may cost a great deal of brainpower each time one materializes. But you are a musket, not a semi-automatic rifle. You'll need to fashion your bullet, wrap it in paper, stuff gunpowder into the barrel, aim carefully and squeeze the trigger. You may miss half of the time, but don't rush into more danger when you're exhausted, and out of ammo. Recuperate. Reload. Pitch a tent. The biggest tiger in the jungle might sneak up on you at night when you least suspect it, and could be felled with one lucky shot. Forge forward, then retreat. Don't underestimate the amount of mental energy this problem solving will take out of you.

The *best ideas* come when you least expect them. The solution or epiphany often appears after you give up and take a break. This is *normal.* Writing is a series of getting stuck and being miraculously rescued as your subconscious fills the gap. It's a continuous journey of problem-solving; but you can't solve a problem until it's discovered. You're mining forward, shoveling the easy loose dirt until you hit a rock, then you need to change direction, stop drilling or blast it out with dynamite (a big event that shifts the landscape of your narrative).

> "If you are in difficulties with a book, try the element of surprise: attack it at an hour when it isn't expecting it." – *H.G. Wells*

During the process, you'll get stuck hundreds of times, and some problems are bigger than others, but this is also why writing is so satisfying, because at the end, *you* know how arduous the journey has been and what it means to have achieved it; how brilliant and clever you are for solving all of those problems and managing to wrestle everything into place. Being stuck is not a problem. It is an integral part of the creative process. It's where the magic happens. So expect it, enjoy it, and celebrate it. It's the opportunity to present your own unique brand of book craft.

DON'T JUDGE THE WORK

Finish the work

As you prepare to do the work, we want to spend a moment to create a ritual, a routine, and transform your workspace into an altar: this will boost your productivity and create an unstoppable writing habit. Any potions (software), elixirs (coffee) or tools (hardware) that concentrate the will and increases the amount of time and focus spent in the chair will help carry you through the challenging bits.

I've decided to add *specific* strategies to boost writing productivity in an appendix section, where I talk about all the resources I recommend, the apps and tools and elixirs and potions, so I recommend flipping back and checking that out. Part of these suggestions will be external: hard deadlines, physical totems of empowerment in my writing space. Others are internal: overriding my resistance, changing my mental blocks or limiting beliefs, tricking myself into getting to work. Anything that concentrates the will, reduces distractions, and increases the amount of time and focus spent in the chair will help you establish a writing discipline. The only real key to productivity is consistency. Make a promise to yourself that you will show up, even if it's just twenty minutes a day.

MEMORANDUM

- Fill your mold with earthworm excrement
- Don't worry too much about the details
- Tell yourself the story as fast as possible

5

RAZZLE DAZZLE
Set the Stage

In the 1750s, there was a gin parlor in London with a proprietor who called himself Dash Razzall. This may be the origin of the British euphemism *on the razzle*, which means someone who has consumed a considerable amount of alcohol and is having a very good time.

In 1889, *The Chevalier* gave a new name to the popular scarfs of disjointed pattern, calling them the razzle-dazzle. A fashion magazine of the same year said that this fun phrase was particularly effective when selling to consumers, who were at once interested and caught by it. These days, it means showiness: all flash and bang. Think *spirit fingers*.

So far, I've tried to keep you distracted with loud noises and some choice literary trivia. I've hopefully dropped enough useful content to stay intriguing, but we've only just touched the surface. It was necessary to show you the basics, so we can start writing with a broad overview of your project.

But now I'm about to show you the mechanics behind the trick. Some of these might seem anti-climactic, as will always be the case when you pull back the curtain to show you what's going on. Ropes and levers aren't sexy, but they make the illusion possible. It's never fun to be told Santa Claus doesn't exist (if this is news for you, I'm sorry you had to learn about it here).

I've broken up our task into four quarters, correlating with the four main sections of a novel. It's possible that some of this will seem repetitive: after all we've already talked about what to put in each act. But this time, we can move past basic, theoretical introductions and share the intimate details that can only be appreciated by those experienced with the terrain. It's like explaining what you'll see once we crest the top of a hill, and then pointing out the specific locations we can both actually see when we arrive. If section one was a map featuring major landmarks, this section is a slow survey of the territory: a sketchbook highlighting the specific details of each unique stop along the journey.

To make it more significant and match the theme of this book, I'm using a *magic word* for each section, so you can easily remember the main points. These will also correspond with the stages of performing a magic trick.

START WITH THE RAZZLE DAZZLE

end with the abracadabra

The first challenge is to *get* and *keep* their attention. This is true for just about everything, in any vocation or human interaction, whether you're trying to make friends or sell a car. The magic we're trying to summon only happens when readers are deeply engaged with our story.

When you have their attention, you can direct or misdirect it at anything you want; if you don't have their attention, nothing you say will matter.

Done properly, the *razzle dazzle* will also tickle their imaginations in an entertaining way. It pulls them in. They have to know what happens next. This is why we have appetizers: they stimulate your stomach so that you're hungry and will taste and enjoy the main course.

The story comes in the middle: first, the fun and trivial weirdness that will be important later (*hocus pocus*); then the slow buzz of electrifying conflict and tension that gives the story energy (*shazam*). You need to have people on the edge of their seats before you can astound them with the big reveal, the surprise twist, the *abracadabra*.

If it sounds like I'm speaking gibberish, don't worry, it'll make sense soon. For now, I'll explain it this way: I used to love to downplay my magic tricks. Instead of a big dramatic story, I'd just do the trick, and because of my understatedness, the expectation was low, and the effect was stronger. This can work in literature as well—it's basically the Hemingway model.

The thing to remember here is, the presentation of the material, the way you tell the story, impacts how surprising, shocking or wonderful the "trick" or surprise actually is.

In the first part of your first draft, we need to concentrate on *what's happening*. Not the why, who or how. Avoid long backstory or scenes where people are sitting around thinking or talking. Show the characters interacting with the world and add as much conflict as you can (not big explosions, just small incidents of tension or unease). Try to make the main character likable; show their flaws and fears or impossible desires.

At this point, we'll focus on writing the first act, up to the point of no return. We're just setting up the trick. Don't worry too much about description, deep drama, motivation or explaining the details. Assume your readers don't care yet; they are barely paying attention. Keep things brisk and show them something flashy. *Dazzle.*

WHERE TO START

Choosing where to start is important, but difficult to prescribe, because it will be unique to your story and characters. Figure out the rough shape of your main story, and then the first event that will help guide your protagonist in the direction you want them to go. Begin right before the action.

Conflict at the beginning is fine unless it's false conflict. It would be better to have the book begin with something relevant to the main story conflict. But remember, the main purpose of the first chapter, before anything else even happens, is to get readers to sympathize with your main character: this is why we start with a *very bad day.*

The first 25% of your novel will be about setting up all the pieces. Picture it like setting up a game of chess and explaining the rules to a blind newbie. You'll have to describe what each piece looks like, what they do, what their purpose is and how they are allowed to interact with the board.

You'll be describing an ordinary world, and interesting characters; but you want to introduce them through already in progress events and circumstances, not an infodump. The main character is starting from inhibition or oppression, a *lack*. They aren't living up to their full potential, either due to fear or external circumstances, probably both.

Demonstrate the ordinary, so that when the *new* shows up it's uncommon and noteworthy. It marks a change, or a difference, in the MC's main experience that is disturbing, distracting or desirable, in a "I wish that was me" kind of way.

Start with small changes that coax or force the MC to react in a way they typically wouldn't, then close all the other doors, until they are on a completely new path they never expected. There are many ways to do this, depending on the genre. Also, it's worth noting that while my Plot Dot outline has the *inciting incident* at around 12% and *the point of no return* at 25%, these are just rough guidelines. It doesn't mean that nothing exciting is happening. The events may not be manifestations of the extraordinary world; they might be ordinary world events that are making your character more likely to notice, perceive, recognize or respond to the new encroaching weirdness.

In Romance, a new annoying stranger might turn up unexpectedly (inciting incident) and then she'll apply for a new job she desperately needs only to find out he's the boss's spoiled son and her direct supervisor (point of no return).

In a Thriller or Mystery, we might start with a crime scene or terrorist attack; the hero is visited and asked to take the case (inciting incident) but he refuses, until personal reflection or external motivation changes his mind and he accepts the case (point of no return).

In Fantasy or Scifi, which typically has deeper world-building, you might be tempted to begin with hundreds of years of historical summary. *Don't.* Focus on your main character's current position. They won't remark on anything they don't find remarkable: anything that's common knowledge about the history would be assumed, and wouldn't come up in thought or conversation. Anything that is remarkable should be discovered, as a later scene, when the questions have been raised and the answers matter.

The initial, introductory chapters of your novel are critical to build up the likability of the main character quickly, but only *in response* to dramatic events already set in motion, which show her initial reluctance and eventual involvement. Knowledge is not a prerequisite to action; the absence of knowledge is more galvanizing. These turning point events are important, but not if you feel like writing several boring chapters before things start happening (you can fix any scene or chapter by adding conflict and mystery, but you can lessen the amount of revisions you'll need by starting strong).

DRAMA, NOT DETAILS

Better to hook with story, than bore with backstory
Wherever your book starts, it needs to be the *real* story and the *real* protagonist. The protagonist is the main character through the whole book; also the one who is most affected, or most changed during the course of the story. Make your protagonist sympathetic, and then disrupt their ordinary world.

It's possible to have multi-character books, which shift viewpoints or take a third-person omniscient POV, but the more characters you introduce, the more difficult it will be to hold readers' attention or keep them interested. You want to start with action, and squeeze in the backstory or exposition, or scene or setting, around what's actually happening (things should always be happening). Don't break away to a new character or setup until readers are properly invested in the first one.

Be wary of any transition scenes, where characters are walking and thinking, or eating and talking, or getting to know each other through casual, low-stakes banter: all of these will have deeper meaning once you've introduced the stakes, tensions and problems.

THE PROLOGUE

If you have a prologue at all, it should be to help readers immediately make sense of what's going on in the first chapter, so you don't have to explain everything. It should hook their attention and get them committed to reading, at least long enough to figure out what it was for.

You can use an open-loop, cliffhanger, past event or anything else as a prologue, but keep it short. Turn it into a prophecy or a short poem, a page or two, or a gripping action scene that shows the danger and hints at supernatural or political intrigue of some kind, establishing the core conflict and genre clearly, and quickly introducing some stunning visual scenes or characters.

It probably won't be a full scene or chapter; we probably won't learn character names or backstory details. It's a glimpse or vignette. It could be the tragic childhood incident that makes our protagonist sympathetic (though, as I mentioned, those should probably be saved until it will hurt more).

We don't *want* readers to know exactly what's going on yet, so we shouldn't explain or summarize. We're just trying to catch their attention. Spirit fingers. Razzle-dazzle. Float like a butterfly, sting like a bee.

Another great use of the prologue is to show the looming threat. Show the antagonists planning destruction, looking for the magic relic, bent on evil and chaos. Show danger and violence that will inevitably involve the protagonist, so that when you start the first chapter, readers are already waiting for the conflict to interrupt the protagonist's ordinary world. Just don't make them wait too long.

Prologues aren't necessary, and many readers say they skip them anyway. They may serve as a temporary, necessary crutch while you're getting your bearings. They may help *you* keep track of critical information that you will need to integrate better in later revisions.

You want to end on the biggest surprise, without resolving story questions. If your current prologue explains all the information or backstory that led up to this point, that's a mistake: people read to find out how and why the weird things have happened. They read to discover explanations, not to be lectured. If you catch them up to speed before the real story begins, you'll have lost most of your intrigue immediately.

Remember, good scenes have conflict and mystery and involve a protagonist we care about. At the very beginning of a book, you don't want to start with content that involves none of those things. If your prologue actually becomes an extended scene or chapter, or *several chapters* that serve as a life-summary of everything leading up to the now, you probably need to cut it or find a way to include it in the story later.

THE HOOK

Some people say you can't write the first sentence until you write the last one, and that's probably true. So start *wherever* because it doesn't really matter. Just start. You'll probably rewrite the first paragraph a dozen times, but you'll do it *much later* when you have a firm grip on the story you're telling and have been through it several times.

But to make it easier for you, here's a good rule of thumb: the best hook is a logical dichotomy, a contrast, a juxtaposition of two things that don't belong together.

Something good, something bad. A strong first sentence hook can carry a lot of weight, especially if it adds a hint of danger and a strong narrative voice.

> Just because I'm telling you this story, doesn't mean I'm alive at the end of it. – *Cheesy Netflix Film*

> I never liked the guy as much as in the weeks before I killed him. – *Edgar Allan Poe*

> It was the best of times, it was the worst of times.
> – *Guess Who?*

> Tommy was a nice guy, but a horrible person.
> – *Overheard at a party*

> I only knew two things for sure: I loved him and he was going to kill me. – *Bastardized Twilight*

Easy, right? You're welcome.

YOU ARE HERE

The full quote I brutalized from memory up above was this:

> "About three things I was absolutely certain. First, Edward was a vampire. Second, there was part of him that thirsted for my blood. And third, I was unconditionally and irrevocably in love with him."

Not only is this a strong hook, but it also immediately lets readers know they're in the right place: this is an angsty vampire romance. While this *could* have been a strong opening line—a defining quote that sums up the whole project—it actually happens in chapter nine of *Twilight*. But I'm using it here out of context as an example. Actually, announcing the vampires on page one would have trivialized the all-important *Say it! What am I?* scene that happens later, when Edward takes his shirt off and sparkles. If you're a Twihard, please forgiven my ignorance on this subject, it's been a while since I read the series.

Technically, the *promise of the premise* section is supposed to come during *fun and games* where you're showing off the world: we'll get to that later. What I suggest however, is to add a *hint* of the premise early on. In the prologue, or in the first few chapters at least, try and throw in some of the keywords, tropes or common elements that are unique to your genre. Basically so fans will settle right in because they feel comfortable that they belong, that they're in the right place, that *this book* is going to deliver on the things they want. Give them an appetizer and a promise of more great things to come; stimulate their imaginations with sparks and shiny things.

THE FIRST CHAPTER

In the first chapter, you'll introduce the main character and their general *ennui*. They probably aren't aware of their flaw yet. They probably think they've got a handle on things. Something will just feel off; a crack in the façade. Without dumping backstory in the story events or incidents, you need to show who they are, what they want, what they fear and hate, and that they desire more (but may not know exactly what yet). They might be trying to convince themselves that *this is fine*. They have a close friend or two, a parental figure or two (a mentor or boss will work), maybe a pet or animal they like to feed.

They should have interesting and unique habits, dress, skills and appearance. Don't show them crying or getting too upset over everything (this is an *ordinary* day). You can hint at a past trauma or tragedy, but fill in just enough for readers to wonder what happened. Past traumas are usually buried or hidden – they've learned to block it out, so they aren't going to break down every time it comes up.

They should be actively trying to hold it together, pressured by current challenges and problems. But also capable and competent and good. A good intro sequence can do *all* of this in a few paragraphs.

Start with the story

Make something happen. Begin with action and conflict. It's not enough to be on the move, going somewhere, thinking back about life. They should have a clear, simple goal, something that matters to them, something tied with the ordinary world goals they're after, or just something that shows how they are *trying* to assimilate into the ordinary world, but don't quite manage it. They get rejected, or screw it up, or call attention, or fail. *Why can't they just be normal and happy like everyone else?* Don't dwell on these questions; it should just be a hint of dissatisfaction that they brush off or ignore.

You can also hint at an alternative future. They might get big news, either positive or negative, a surprise visit, a mysterious stranger, an ominous warning or sign. Something different from their normal, ordinary world, and probably something vaguely threatening (that makes it harder to focus and do the ordinary world stuff they started off trying to do).

If you want to start with a bang, allow the big picture conflict and drama to affect them in the first chapter. Someone dies right in front of them, or they discover a mysterious object and are now being hunted for it, or they witness a supernatural fight or battle that they shouldn't be able to see.

You don't have to make them special or gifted, but you can. There should be something different about them that makes them perfectly suited to get embroiled in the plot. You don't have to explain it, but maybe later it can come out.

If you're having trouble with the conflict – remember it can be internal. They are presented with a choice: they made a promise, but now it's difficult to keep the promise and also do the new thing. Stephen King suggests choosing a character who is down on their luck, then dangling their dream. Making your protagonist choose between important things is great conflict.

Bonus: the *first* time around, they may make the wrong choice. Then towards the end of the book, they can be presented with a similar dilemma and choose differently, showing how they've progressed.

Set the scene (snapshot: picture it)

I usually do scene building and description in the late revision stages, during editing, but it's important to get it right, especially in the first chapter. Show readers something they haven't seen before. Show them cool characters in cool locations, where something surprising happens.

Make it as big as you can, as specific as you can... and let the scene add conflict, by referring to the lack. If their mother died recently, the house can be absolutely covered in unfinished crochet projects that nobody has the heart to throw away.

Or the protagonist's father was kicked out of the church and lost their home gambling, so now they live in an abandoned chapel outside of town.

Or the best friend got fired as a bus driver, but raised a lawsuit and was allowed to keep the school bus, which he now lives in down by the river and fishes all day.

You can start with basic scenes, but see how you can make them more vivid and more interesting. Because I write young adult fantasy, I need to find reasons for my protagonist to wear fancy dresses during major battle scenes.

If in doubt, start with action and let the backstory dribble in slowly during downbeats. Be careful not to have friends who already know each other ask leading questions so you can infodump to readers.

Try to avoid a lot of thinking or internal dialogue. If you haven't already done it in the prologue, the first chapter is where you wow your readers and keep them reading over the next few chapters. A terrible first chapter is all information and set-up, without any conflict or action.

You may need to hint forward, about the main antagonist and major conflict, or how the protagonist is connected. Not a lot, just a little sign or reminder that bad things are coming. A little bit of foreboding. A shadow, a bat, a grimace. A chapter can be pretty generic or even pleasant, as long as it *ends* on a negative note.

MAKING CHARACTERS LIKABLE

If your character is mean, selfish, spiteful or stupid, readers aren't going to like them. It's okay to start off with someone who's not perfect, but they should uncover their more admirable qualities through the story. You also never want to start with someone who *is* perfect, or awesome, or badass – unless they're about to get destroyed by circumstances and lose everything.

You need to make characters likable immediately. The easy way to do this is to make them *capable*: they deal with threats or challenges coolly and creatively. They're composed and clever. And they're also *responsible*: they're taking care of someone else. They stand up to a bully, save a child or a kitten, put food on the table for their crippled mother. Ultimately, all that matters is that they have the potential to be *good*. A desire for justice, to make a difference, to protect others. That's assuming you're writing in a genre with heroes. Hamlet wasn't exactly heroic, and his actions got everybody killed. But he's sympathetic, if not likable, in part because he's justified in seeking revenge against his father's killer.

WRITING SCENES

Hook and keep attention

A scene is a series of actions, tied to one time and location, happening in the perceived present moment. Your book will probably be a collection of scenes. I like to have two scenes in every chapter.

A protagonist is like a settler living in a meadow. They have carved out a bit of survival; they may already have found water and a food source, and built a rudimentary shelter. But it's not enough for them.

So your protagonist will probably start the book feeling unfulfilled. While they may dream of going out into the wilderness and finding meaning and purpose, it would be foolhardy to do so. So they stay, because doing nothing seems safer than risking everything. Until something *new* happens: a visitor from beyond the mountains, a relic from a forgotten civilization… something points to proof of more.

This increases dissatisfaction of the status quo. Still, they cling to security, until *forced* to make a change (looters pillage the village, they get lost or kidnapped, someone or something they care about is in danger, dire straits force desperate actions.) They leave the meadow and go into the woods.

From then on, scenes will follow a simple pattern:

1. regroup

2. new plan

3. thwart

Something happens, and they are forced to react or respond. Sometimes this can simply be jumping out of harm's way. Then something unexpected or surprising happens at the end of each scene or chapter, which thwarts their efforts. At the beginning of each new scene or chapter, they're responding or reflecting. They make and execute a new plan. There's a new thwart.

Picture your intrepid survivor venturing out from their safe meadow: they have an infinity of paths and choices, but they must pick one. They pick the most likely path for whatever reasons are enough to decide. They make it a little way down the path, when something stops them (thwart). A giant rock, a fallen log, a hornet's nest, an accident. They try to find the main path again and continue towards their goal, but are immediately set upon by bandits or aliens or washed away in a flood. Whenever possible, you want to start in the action and end the scene or chapter on the point of maximum surprise or conflict; just after the new thing occurs.

Another way to phrase this would be:

1. reaction

2. decision

3. dilemma

Each scene starts in chaos and uncertainty; often just escaping the immediate effects of the new problem. Start each scene with a hook: conflict, speech, a strange sentence or vivid contrast. Something unusual and unexpected. Don't describe the journey and announce your arrival. Start with them already there. Start mid-conversation. Begin mid-scene, with action and conflict, then toss in a few short sentences of explanation as you need them: why they're here, how they got here, what they're looking for, what they need or what happened to put them in this current situation.

Once there's a moment to think calmly, they make a new decision to get around the problem – which has directly refused their first plan of action to reach their goal. They execute the new decision, make it a little way forward, and meet a new block. This dance continues through the book.

WHEN SOMETHING HAPPENS... STOP

Master the dramatic pause

One of the biggest mistakes authors make is burying the lead: the huge reveal, twist, or shocking discovery is swallowed up in a wall of text and skipped over by continuing action.

Each scene is basically a build-up of forward momentum that brings your characters to the next point of surprise: the unexpected change, the new information, the thwart.

Picture it like the punchline of a joke: if you've done the set up right, when you give the zinger, it has a powerful effect. You can only make a joke worse by trying to explain it.

Likewise, when something big happens, you want to place it as close to the *end* of your scene as possible, and then you want a hard scene break or chapter break.

The pendulum of a grandfather clock is carried by momentum until it reaches a state of inertia; where it hangs in the balance, until forces bring it falling swiftly in the opposite direction. Always keep the pendulum swinging in one direction or the other.

Write the scene to build up towards the point where something happens and changes. This could be a sudden discovery, an attack or explosion, a reveal or twist, the ground falls out from under them, an unexpected betrayal, a profound realization. *Something happens.* To draw attention to its importance, stop writing. End scene.

Allow the significance of the thing to sink in by giving readers space and time to absorb it. Charles Dickens popularized the use of the dramatic pause with the serial publication of his narrative fiction, ending each episode with unresolved conflict. In 1841, fans rioted the dock of New York Harbor, waiting for a British ship carrying the next installment.

In a *New Yorker* article, Emily Nussbaum writes,

> Historically, there's something suspect about a story told in this manner, the way it tugs the customer to the next ledge. Nobody likes needy. But there is also something to celebrate about the cliffhanger, which makes visible the storyteller's connection to his audience—like a bridge made out of lightning. Primal and unashamedly manipulative, cliffhangers are the signature gambit of serial storytelling. They expose the intimacy between writer's room and fan base, auteur and recapper—a relationship that can take seasons to develop, years marked by incidents of betrayal, contentment, and, occasionally, by a kind of ecstasy... More broadly, it's any strong dose of "What happens next?"

The term "cliffhanger" itself is considered to have originated with the serialized version of Thomas Hardy's *A Pair of Blue Eyes,* published in Tinsley's Magazine in 1873. In it, the heroine Elfride is walking with one of her suitors, the rich Mr. Knight, engaging in coy banter, when he falls of a cliff. She stumbles after him.

> But, once he boosts her to safer ground, he loses his foothold, his love gazing down at him from the ledge. As Mr. Knight clutches "the last outlying knot of starved herbage," the passage concludes, "A minute—perhaps more time—was passed in mute thought by both. On a sudden the blank and helpless agony left her face. She vanished over the bank from his sight."

In the next episode, rather than resolving the conflict immediately, twenty-nine paragraphs go by before Elfride reappears, drenched by rain. She tears off her outer garments, and twines them into a rope so she can pull him to safety.

As Nussbaum writes, "The sequence is both laughably artificial and entirely convincing, a manipulation that may have been motivated by commercial demands but becomes an opportunity for existential exploration."

In other words, in a relatively unexciting social drama, by tossing in a mortal dilemma, it grips readers' *attention* so that they'll suffer through the author's capricious musings – which are especially important if you're getting paid by the word.

Your story may not involve this level of dramatic contrivance, but my point is, you should start with action and show the stakes before getting lost in a character's casual reflections. The relationships, the conversations, the decisions your characters make will seem trivial, until they are faced with larger challenges that threaten their existence or identity.

Get readers to care about what's happening. Then, whenever you present a new piece of the puzzle, a new clue or lead or prompt that changes your character's direction, by forcing a personal decision, a new goal or ambition, or demanding a response—the unexpected moment where your galvanizing forces have reached the end of their forward momentum and have lead you precisely *here*, to *this*—mark the interval with a dramatic pause.

Allow the tension to build and simmer. Don't try to explain it right away. Don't show the characters' reactions, and don't just continue as if nothing happened or it's no big deal. This matters. This is necessary. This was the point.

Whenever you reach the event, when something happens, introduce it as briefly as possible, in just a sentence or two. Then start a new section or chapter. This is the secret motor of your novel, the thing that keeps it all moving forward.

ESSENTIAL RELEVANCY

Picture a row of dominoes. They take time to set up. How does this one need to be angled, so that it falls and tips off the next one? If it's out of place, the chain will die and action stops. If they're all in place, once you tip the first domino, the action will progress smoothly until the end.

If you can remove a domino and the action continues anyway, it's not essential and needs to be removed. But also!

Each scene must...

- either be a reaction, decision or dilemma
- have unresolved conflict
- something needs to change
- present new information

You need something to happen, you want that action to be inevitable by properly motivating characters, so you think of a way to do that. The problem is, this information almost never belongs right before the decision, to justify it. It needs to be artfully placed earlier, so it's not jarring and sudden. This usually happens in the editing phase, where you move things around and plant info to justify later choices. What most authors do is, get to a place things don't make sense and interject a quick backstory or explanation for readers.

Transition scenes, where characters have decided where to go, and now must get there, should usually be deleted, unless something big happens or they're a necessary place to add information. Given enough tension and high stakes, characters won't sit around talking unless you make them. Maybe they need to wait until sunset, or walk three hours, or take a train. This forced inactivity or travel might be a great place for them to start opening up or sharing revealing backstory, in a way that feels natural and organic. And even then, keep them tight with conflict, or interrupt just before they get too vulnerable or reveal too much.

CONFLICT REVEALS CHARACTER

I mentioned earlier, I like to include at least three types of conflict in every scene, but action by itself is only meaningful if it matters to your characters on an emotional level. You can use this easy checklist and make sure the events in each scene has at least some emotional impact:

1. doubt
2. anger
3. fear
4. skepticism
5. surprise
6. prohibition

If your scenes are providing enough challenges, your characters should be experiencing some of these negative emotions. If they are easily and happily achieving their goals, throw in some random or arbitrary restrictions.

Other Ways to Add Conflict

1. conflict between what *is* and what the protagonist *wants*
2. conflict between what each of your characters want
3. conflict between your protagonist's inner wants and external duties (this works really well with romance; budding attraction which, if expressed, would ruin everything and prevent her from her ultimate goal).
4. foreboding or foreshadowing (something bad or evil is coming... give the readers a hint, even if the protagonist doesn't see it, readers will feel it.)

A lot of dramatic conflict or tension will be created through your cast of characters. The main characters or allies should rarely agree with each other, about everything. Someone will feel left out. Someone will think it's a stupid idea. Someone has other plans and refuses to participate. Or, someone needs to stay behind or fulfill a parallel goal. Don't just have a happy band of allies happily exploring the scenery. Finally, whatever they decide they need to do next, it should be risky, illegal, or prohibited.

Whenever characters make a plan or decision, a good rule of thumb is to give them three obstacles. Never just let them go where they're trying to get to, without throwing a few stumbling blocks at them.

Supercharge the Conflict

Just before anything new, different, or bad happens, give the characters a moment of peace. A light moment, games and jokes, deepening affection, quiet reflection. A little bit of happiness. Do that just before you toss them in the fire. It's a great way to add character depth and make readers care about what happens to them. You'll see this all the time in movies and TV. Just before a main character dies, there will be a "getting affairs in order" scene, when they finally confess their feelings or finally make peace with their past and allow themselves a new relationship or a bit of happiness. To make readers feel something more keenly, make them feel the opposite thing first; the contrast will heighten the sensation. You can also ask,

- What's the most surprising thing that could happen?
- What's the most visually stunning thing I can show?
- How could this hurt more? (physically, emotionally)

Unless you're writing a comedy, or it's a funny scene – in which case, ask how could I make this even more ridiculous and over the top?

Escalation

Remember that dramatic tension increases over time, like pulling a bow. Start with small problems and issues and disagreements. You don't get to the big, true, painful stuff until later. You want to razzle dazzle them with quick, light, surface-level issues or problems that hint at escalating issues that will have deeper consequences later.

While contrasting happy scenes and tense scenes is a good start, the balance should build as the stakes increase. In the first few chapters, problems are usually piled on quickly to lead to a breaking point that forces characters to choose differently, so the negative spiral may continue as you destroy their ordinary world. They get fired. Then they lose their fiancé. Then they get evicted. All they have left is a homeless friend, and she gets kidnapped (all of this happens in Marvel's *Venom.*)

SCENE DESCRIPTION

We'll talk more about how to handle description later, so don't worry about it too much in your first draft. I think it's better to focus on *what happens* first. If you need to dump a paragraph or two of detailed scene description, fine – but keep it light. Try to include scene description within the story action. This can work really well to pad out a dialogue between lines, so it isn't just a wall of conversation. Include body movement and interaction.

> "Welcome to my home," the witch smiled. I glanced around the room. The crystal ball, the pentacle, the shrunken heads. She certainly wasn't hiding. A spider crawled across the table. I wanted to reach into the bookshelves for a heavy volume to smash it with, but she held out her hand and let it crawl into her palm. A chill ran up my spine.
> "Charming," I replied.

Focus on what's important to your characters. Don't spend too much time talking about the scenery, the food, or other things if there are really big and important things going on. People don't get lost in appreciation for their environment unless they're bored or relaxed. And even then, they won't notice everything; just anything unusual or remarkable. How is your main character feeling? In a tense action scene, characters won't be looking around and casually observing if they feel threatened, unless they have a purpose.

> "You're going to die," he said, waving the gun. I backed away, my eyes darting around the room frantically, searching for a weapon. The meatpacking facility was full of giant metal tables and hanging hooks, but they were chained to the ceiling. I spotted a row of butcher knives hanging against the wall behind him, but there was no way I could reach them.

25 SIGNS OF AMATEUR WRITING

First chapter mistakes to avoid

Hopefully by now, after going through the plotting and outlining resources, you have a good idea of *what* happens, and the purpose of this chapter was to help you break your story into clear scenes, where your story moves forward in a direct and tangible way.

All that's left is for you to start the work. In the appendix of this book you'll find some specific, concrete resources for getting more words on the page: but keep in mind you probably won't figure out exactly how to write your first chapter until you get to the end anyway.

I realize we still haven't talked specifically about the actual writing yet: partly that's on purpose. The writing matters much less than you think it does, and it can always be fixed and finessed during edits. The main challenge that I've tried to address in this chapter, is combating apathetic readers. Writers often stuff the first few chapters with information, rather than drama, before they've even introduced sympathetic characters. Once you've got their attention, you can slow down and add depth, but *until* you have their attention, you have to make each page count. The solution often has little to do with the content you add, but the material you remove.

There are two big things to worry about in the beginning of your book: set the stage for your story, and hook attention. Down below I've added a list of the important things that should happen during your first act; followed by a more detailed scene checklist that summarizes a lot of the material we've already covered. But don't worry about doing it right the first time. You can (and often need to) go back and fix scenes retroactively, rather than attempting to flesh it all out while you're writing. It's much easier to get started, and then use the checklist later to course-correct or improve your draft.

The greatest moments of brilliance rarely appear when you're following your plan; they show up when you're troubleshooting the problems. The tightest threads, the best story ideas, will only be woven in after the main events are in place. But you have to have a messy, broken manuscript, a cracked window, before you can set about the work of polishing and perfecting.

Finally, you need to remove signs of weak writing so readers trust you know what you're doing. Most authors lose readers within the first few pages, due to easily avoidable issues that have nothing to do with the story, and everything to do with the presentation.

This can be tricky, so I put together a detailed list of common first chapter mistakes most authors make. A lot of this is repetition, so I'm adding it into the *Grimoire* at the back of the book.

I'm providing these examples, not so that you'll avoid them, but so that you'll recognize them when they come up. They are *common* for a reason: they are the easiest way to get down your ideas, and in the beginning, you want to get everything down. But I also don't want to overwhelm you at this point with *shoulds* and *shouldn'ts*.

It's probably not a good idea to worry about *how* you're telling the story yet. You're just trying to figure out the arrangement of the details and where everything fits together. First you dump out all the pieces; then you see how to make them work. So it's up to you whether you want to read through the list before or after you've written your first act. Feel free to go crazy and have fun with your first draft.

The razzle dazzle should be messy and quick and light and easy; it can't be slow and plodding. Remember, especially for the first few pages, you will be fighting to keep and hold readers' attention. You can do this with action and conflict, poetic writing, vivid description and thwarted characters. Readers will spend more time with you if you rise above weak writing and amateur mistakes, but they will quickly tire of your impressive words if they get between them and the story. Think brightly checkered scarves of fabric. Ensnare and hypnotize. Don't go too deep.

MAPPING IT OUT (ACT ONE)

The First Act will have about 10 to 20 chapters, and take up 25% of the story. Here are some of the things that often happen in the first act.

- ✓ Ordinary world, building empathy
- ✓ Inciting event
- ✓ An event that creates desire or longing
- ✓ Another character asks a question that becomes a theme
- ✓ A moral dilemma
- ✓ Something embarrassing
- ✓ Takes action towards goal
- ✓ They can't get what they want, so they change their plan
- ✓ Attempts to fulfill their longing or need
- ✓ What goal does character take action to reach?
- ✓ Call to adventure/refuses quest
- ✓ Display of flaw
- ✓ A problem grows out of character weakness
- ✓ Meets with mentor
- ✓ Point of no return, accepts quest and commits to goal

MEMORANDUM

- Catch attention and interest
- Nothing matters if they don't care
- What happens, then stop (scene break)
- Change or reveal (action or new info)
- Reaction, new plan, event
- Irresolvable opposites that create friction
- Tension (pull the string)
- Snapshot (picture it)
- Urgency: why does this have to happen now?
- Relevancy: does this matter to the main story?
- Fulfilling the promise of the premise

Grimoire Notes Added

Don't forget to check out the list of 25 First Chapter Mistakes. It's pretty good and super helpful, but I've decided to move it to the end of the book as supplementary material. Look for it in your *Grimoire* before you start writing, or when you're ready to edit and looking for easy ways to improve your manuscript.

6

HOCUS POCUS
Seeking Purpose

In 1656 Thomas Ady published *A Candle in the Dark: A* Treatise Concerning the Nature of Witches & Witchcraft. Which he later re-titled with the more commercial *A Perfect Discovery of Witches*.

Ady's "discovery" however, is that witches are actually innocent of all accusations, because all so-called *magic* was just the clever manipulation by a skilled conjurer. According to him, Juglers (as conjurers were called at the time) employed common tricks to fool the public.

> "I will speak of one man more excelling in that craft than others, that went about in King James his time, and long since, who called himself, The Kings Majesties most excellent Hocus Pocus, and so was he called, because that at the playing of every Trick, he used to say, *Hocus pocus,* tontus talontus, vade celeriter jubeo, a dark composure

of words, to blinde the eyes of the beholders, to make his Trick pass the more currently without discovery…"

These vaguely Latin-sounding phrases convey an elevated, mystical charm even though they are without meaning. *Hocus Pocus* is basically a distraction, to give authority and gravity— the *potential* for people to believe that this *could be* real magic— even though it is actually a hoax (a word that stems directly from hocus, both in sound and meaning).

But it goes deeper than that. In the first half of Act II, on top of whatever plotting or literary devices you're using, the general theme should be of seeking purpose, in the context of *wanting to believe*. Is this real? Can I trust this? Do I belong?

A Candle in the Dark was used unsuccessfully by George Burroughs, formerly the Puritan minister of the parish, in his defense during the Salem witch trials. My direct ancestor, Sarah Booth, accused him of sorcery and watched him hang from the neck until he was dead in 1692. According to her testimony, "We beleve in our hearts that he is a wizzard and that he has often affleted us and sevroll others by acts of wicthcraft."

The magic wasn't real. The effects were. It is easier to trick someone than convince them that they have been tricked; but getting them to believe takes finesse. They will *resist* the magical effect, of being seduced by something inherently irrational, but emotions are more personal, and powerful, than logic.

I WANT TO BELIEVE

X-Files fans will recognize the catchphrase of FBI Special Agent Fox Mulder; a slogan that captures the series' spotlight of faith and science through its two main protagonists.

It also works well to cover the alchemical processes that should be going on just under the surface in this section. While not all stories need a deep psychological bent, or even a strong character arc, figuring out how your protagonist is feeling will help figure out their motivations, which will create more believable actions.

Like in the X-Files, this may depend on a certain amount of awareness, experience and evidence. Specifically, from the midpoint on, they'll shift from victim to warrior. They'll stop taking a passive, reactionary role and begin taking a more deliberate, active part in their own unfolding narrative. So the goal in the first half of Act II, the *Hocus Pocus*, is to overwhelm their resistance and stoke their desire for inclusion, leading to a sense of attachment and commitment. Half of this section will be about learning new things (exploring the new world). But the other half of it will be personal: even with the evidence and rational considerations, they need a strong, deep, emotional motivation to commit to later plot events.

AM I WORTHY?

While the first part of your book should focus mostly on the story, the action, the *Razzle Dazzle*, in this section we'll dig a little deeper into the characters.

> The first act was to hook interest, *what's happening.*
> The next part is... why is this happening *to me?*

We'll be focused on developing your protagonist's self-identity in relation to the new characters, plot events or information, scenes or settings, or new world experiences she encounters. Challenges will make her question her self-worth, sense of belonging and moral values. External threats will force her to choose to defend or fight for a *new* identity in relation to this budding reality. Through it all, she'll gain both an inner confidence based on familiarity and growing capacity (she's discovering what she's really capable of) and also an emotional bond (something she wants more than anything).

This shouldn't include a lot of introspection or navel-gazing, but it can start to build quietly. While it's important to keep introducing unresolved conflict, in this section we can also slow down and drop some new information or backstory. But the general story questions will be tied to the protagonist's role, the development of strong bonds, and a newfound self-confidence, so that by the middle of the novel they'll have discovered a sense of purpose and made a commitment on a deep emotional level.

Their peers might be asking rational, plot-forwarding questions, like:

- Who is doing this, how do we stop it?
- What will they do next?

But the protagonist, still resistant, might be asking:

- How do I get out of this?
- How can I get back to normal?
- Am I enough?

They may be telling everyone, and themselves, that this is only temporary, that they're just here until they can find something better, that they don't belong, that they don't want to be here. Especially as stakes and dangers mount, they may even vocally affirm a statement like, "You've got the wrong person" or "I'm not cut out for this."

Regardless of the plot events in this section, which should be significant, the underlying energy transmutation will look something like this:

Understanding –> Conviction

First, they'll discover the potential of a brave new world, a new relationship, a new way of being or behaving or existing. Something daring and exciting and a little bit scary. But they'll be overwhelmed. They're out to sea in a storm, clutching the rails for dear life. They won't have the confidence to participate, to take chances, to take action; so they'll mostly be reactive, until they realize their inaction has consequences. Then they'll begin to *care* about the conflict or outcome of this new situation, to the extent where they can no longer turn their back on it, or start over where they were before.

This choice allows them to grudgingly participate, revealing new skills and abilities, being given the opportunity to share and learn and impress... and it feels *good*. So good, they begin to believe they belong, that they're wanted, to find a measure of peace and happiness they haven't known in years, or ever.

They dare to open up, and start to wish or want again, despite the dangers, despite previous heartbreaks or disappointments. But they still aren't fully convinced, and may be wrestling with their own credulity.

Hocus Pocus: is this real, or is it a hoax?
Is the magic I'm feeling worth the risk of losing it?

THE SHARD OF GLASS

In case I didn't fully explain it earlier, the lack or fatal flaw of your protagonist is a deep-seated fear or insecurity, most likely based on a near-traumatic formulative event. Assume that this deep "wound" isn't formed without pain. It's not just a fear of the dark. It's an experience where overconfidence led to a brutal wake-up call. It's a lack because something has been robbed, something is missing, something that used to be a crucial part of their identity.

When I was young, I got the lead in all my middle-school musicals. There probably just weren't that many teen boys with the hubris to stand and sing in front of hundreds of people. I wasn't a great actor, but I'd taken choir and always figured I'd done pretty well. This confidence persisted through college in Malta; I'd carry around an acoustic guitar and croon by the pool. Until one day, a group of cute foreigners laughed at me as I mangled a Tom Petty song.

It's not the worst thing, of course, but it was, I think, the first time my over-confidence was hit with actual, non-biased critics; the first time I realized, maybe I'm not as good at this as I think I am. I don't like singing in public anymore. It's not fatal, it's not tragic, but it is mildly endearing. For a rom-com, it might be enough: in the Netflix special *Emily in Paris,* Emily's new friend Mindy choked on a Chinese singing competition show in front of millions of people, and moved to Paris to hide in shame. Part of her character arc happens when her supportive friends force her to face her fears at a karaoke bar.

It's important, because this backstory may be a big reveal later, and even if we don't know the full story yet, we should see a shadow of their fear and resistance. Your protagonist is your main character, the one with the greatest opportunity for growth and change, which means they may be the ones who have been the most hurt or damaged.

It's possible they've moved beyond their childhood fantasies and feel like they're actually doing pretty well in life: they might be driven and successful. But they don't feel whole, or fulfilled.

Remember the three orders of wretchedness that keep people from their full creative potential? In this section, we need to *begin* to build our protagonist's confidence back up slowly, by giving them something to live for (purpose), a wish or idea of how to attain it (plan) and enough experience to begin to believe that it's possible (skill).

According to Tony Robbins, humans need significance, love and connection, growth and contribution, which actually line up pretty well with our three orders above.

In the first quarter of our story, our protagonist got knocked down hard, losing everything they've built. At rock bottom, they are cautiously open to alternative opportunities or paths, but mostly because they've got nothing left to lose. (Of course we'll hit them with much worse later, but they don't know that yet).

They won't be optimistic at first. Everything will seem overwhelming and scary. They'll pine for the "real life" that's been taken from them. But gradually, in *this section*, they'll be seduced by something better. At this point, the main character is perhaps open to experiencing new things, but can't help using their same limited thinking from their previous life or experiences: doubts, insecurities, fears or self-destructive habits.

They may not even be aware of their fatal flaw yet, but it might make an appearance in this section as a resistance to do a thing, for undisclosed reasons. The full story comes later.

Tip: if you can't think of a fatal flaw, don't worry about it! It's probably better to come up with it after your book is written anyway. Think of it like a conflict multiplier: at the end of the book, your character succeeds in doing something that was *very, very* hard. How can you make this thing *uniquely more challenging* in a personal way, by including a deeply relevant phobia or heartfelt certainty that's always been a part of her life, but she's now forced to transcend?

PROMISE OF THE PREMISE

Fun and games

In the screenwriting classic *Save the Cat,* Blake Snyder calls the first half of the second act the "fun and games" part of the story, or the *promise of the premise.* Basically, this will be all the fun and cool scenes, the enjoyable stuff that moviegoers pay to see; this is the material that fills most of the trailers.

This works reasonably well as a starting point, but only at the plotting level, which we've already covered, and the deeper purpose is rarely explored. At a surface level, the protagonist will be "settling in" to the newness. They've agreed to show up, to check-in, but they aren't full converts yet, and there's probably some ulterior motive for them even agreeing to this level of casual engagement. Some things that might happen include:

- Finding answers / learning the rules
- New rivals and frenemies
- Feeling inadequate / getting bullied
- Fighting for stability / acceptance
- Struggling autonomy or understanding

- Revealing the dangers and challenges
- Small trials and quests (motivations)
- Discovery goals (what's happening and why)
- *New* secrets to discover

With growing awareness, it will always be the case that we see new knowledge gaps and limits. Some of these will be secret or forbidden – just remember, the bigger the reveal, the more carefully it should be guarded. Remark on the mystery, but don't hazard a guess that's too close to the actual truth. Early on in Act II, you may have an "initiation" stage where someone is showing your protagonist around and teaching them the ropes: questions may be answered quickly, and that might be necessary so we can move forward. But make sure you open new story questions soon, or there won't be any intrigue or suspense.

I saw a very nice meme recently about fictional experts that's worth sharing here: basically, an expert on something won't just give a boring lecture, explaining how everything works (or if they do, it'll be stiff). It's much more interesting if an expert has strong opinions, so you can learn about the subject, but also the divisions and controversies, while revealing character and adding more conflict into your scenes. What they are learning or discovering probably gives them insight into their own feelings.

Promise, Progress, Payoff

Fantasy author Brandon Sanderson, in a writing seminar at BYU, shared this useful framework:

Promise: what readers expect from this story.

Progress: signposts that let readers know we're still on track.

Payoff: providing the experience readers signed up for.

It's easy to get off track in this section: the bold strokes and conflict you began with may slow down considerably here. Your scenes might be fun or light; the stakes less pressing; the dangers gone for the moment. And this is *fine* — for reasons we'll talk about in a minute, this is *necessary*. But you can't have characters ignore or forget about all the stuff that happened earlier. Every few scenes, throw in something that satiates the tastes of your particular genre, and raises new story questions about the largest source of conflict.

In comedy, they might call a convoluted story a "long walk" to get to the punchline. In a novel, this *long walk* only works if you're leaving breadcrumbs; otherwise people will get lost in the dark and forget why they're reading. Stuff your pockets with bread before we get lost in the woods, so you can mark your progress.

PS. I *know* birds eat the breadcrumbs and they get lost anyway. In reality, you'll probably keep shifting them around or go on a manic binge and make French Toast. But the concept is important. These are *temporary* markers so *you* can keep track of the journey. Later you can go back and make better ones for readers.

WORLD WORTH SAVING

I got this idea from video game critics, commenting on sidequest narratives, but it's worth introducing to the writing world if you've not heard it before.

Basically, if a protagonist just ran through the story quest and defeated the Big Boss, the game wouldn't be very satisfying. Especially in RPG fantasy games, there's been a big push to include story-telling. Video game revenue is expected to exceed 150 *billion* a year soon (books and publishing worldwide account for about 110 billion); and they've realized that the longer you stay with the game, the longer you play, the more *investment* you make in your character's growth and abilities, and the more value they can create from your interest. They need to make you care, so you'll spend more time with the characters.

The argument is that the sidequests, rather than just being meaningless drivel divorced from the main story, forcing players to "grind" through them to increase their stats and strengths enough to continue the narrative, are an opportunity to share that the world is worth saving at all.

And this is the main idea I want to focus on in the rest of this chapter. The beginning of Act II might include the lighter, fun, low-stakes scenes, but they are absolutely crucial because they allow readers to fall in love with your characters.

They didn't care enough before, but now they're paying attention. Now they're invested. You need to keep readers engaged with conflict, suspense and drama, but you can also start peeling back layers, revealing more emotional depth, and introducing some backstory or bonding episodes of playful banter.

In the first quarter of the book, you can display a little tough heroism or badassery (actions regarded as formidably impressive). That's enough to get people to *like* some of your characters. But we won't fall in love with them until they show us their vulnerabilities and quirks. I'd still withhold the big backstory reveals until later, but in this section, you can begin to show *little scenes of sweetness* that warm our hearts. Touching, poignant, trivial scenes (unrelated on the surface to the main story). Because they appear as low-risk episodes, our protagonist and readers will have their guard down. They'll begin to feel and melt and be touched.

This is critical because it will make the second half of your novel so much more powerful. At the risk of tossing in another potentially bad cooking metaphor, in the first act we've added all the ingredients; in the first half of Act II, we mix everything together and let it simmer on low heat, so that their unique tastes can start a chemical transmutation and bring out the richness of the individual flavors.

INVESTMENT

What did this cost?

The secret of magic is focused will, concentrated over time. Greater confidence will lead to more powerful will. A magic spell might have a bunch of rare and costly ingredients: some need to be claimed, not paid for. The point may not be anything to do with those actual items, but what they represent: the amount of work, and sacrifice, and investment – of time and resources – in your pursuit of this one grand desire.

The amount it's *worth* to you, is what you're willing to do for it. You need to invest enough that it hurts to lose it, otherwise it's not really a sacrifice and doesn't show any true devotion. If it's a story that matters, the risk will be identity-shattering: they persist anyway because they've gained something new that is now part of their identity. They have no choice either way. But you still need to establish a burning desire, in order for your characters to endure the struggle. As Ficino expressed in his commentary on Plato's *Symposium* in 1474,

> For we achieve neither poetry nor mystery, nor prophecy, without vast zeal, burning piety, and sedulous worship of divinity. But what else do we call zeal, piety and worship except love?

READER SEDUCTION

Falling in Love

You've got their attention, but have yet to pierce their hearts. Love can't be forced, and it doesn't happen quickly. It happens in the little, inconsequential moments. Not the grand romantic dinners or proposals; but in the quiet sunny mornings at home, sipping tea and reading by the window.

It happens when characters are not consciously making an effort to appear loveable; but when they think nobody is watching and reveal heart-wrecking truths about themselves.

This is also where you'll have your protagonist falling in love with new characters, or the new world; even if it's not a romance. The side characters may have seemed foreign or aloof in the first section, but here they slowly start dropping their walls. Readers – and the main character – need to start falling for them, so that we're engrossed with what happens to them; so that we have something to lose.

A recipe for love... (a love spell)

In order to get readers to fall in love with your characters, try adding these to your cauldron:

- A secret
- A secret kindness
- What they do when they think nobody is watching
- An embarrassing mistake
- Something they find repulsive or hate (that they do anyway for someone else).
- Something they've never told anyone
- A memento or nostalgic keepsake
- An insecurity they hide
- Just being there (concern they try not to show)

Let me give you an example: for Thanksgiving we ordered pizza and watched *The Princess Switch* sequel. My wife was raised in Taiwan and taught that any food she didn't eat would be waiting for her, rotten and moldy in the afterlife. She also knows I don't eat the crusts of the pizza. So she cut off and ate all the *crusts*, leaving the center of the pizza for me.

Here's another: we're both introverts, but I'm able to make conversation with strangers, while she refuses. I used to be frustrated by this strange behavior, but then I learned, she had a speech impediment when she was young, so her grandpa kidnapped her and took her to a doctor who sliced the bottom of her tongue, hoping it would allow her to speak more clearly.

This isn't as barbaric as it sounds: the phrase "tongue-tied" stems from the condition of an unusual *frenulum* limiting mobility (ankyloglossia). It can cause trouble with speaking and eating, which may cause embarrassment or social problems.

The cute, interesting quirks happen first. Then devastating backstory puts things into context. Start with the curious behavior (interest), then force characters to explain themselves by having someone ask *why* (vulnerable share).

A kiss for a slap

The harder it is to forge an emotional connection, the more meaningful it will appear, which is why often in dramas, a kiss (positive emotional experience) will always be pre-empted or followed with a slap (negative consequence).

As soon as someone shares something personal, takes a step forward, use it to your advantage by immediately turning it into a miscommunication, perceived rejection, or at least an interruption. Maybe a character is afraid of getting hurt, so they ignore it or trivialize the connection. Maybe they're feeling vulnerable, so they put their walls up defensively and push everyone away. Or perhaps there's an unrelated incident that causes guilt or shame (*if I hadn't been distracted by my feelings, I could have been there to protect them*). A romance is basically a series of random interruptions preventing an otherwise simple relationship. So while you're adding all this sweet bonding, make sure you keep it spicy with tension and confusion. Raise *questions*, not answers.

THE MONTAGE

These light scenes and incidents, in addition to potentially being fun and engaging, provide material for the *montage* – the flashback scene you often see at the end of movies. The hero is facing the villain, everything seems lost, there is no logical way to triumph, but then... they remember all the good times they've had recently. They realize that they have more to fight for, something to lose, something they care about enough to risk everything. They realize they've fallen in love with the new world or characters, that there's nobody else left, that it's all on them, and they need to find the will to persevere.

The innocuous new experiences in the first part of Act II, while they may seem unimportant at first, are actually the *main thing* that secures the hero's final victory: they are the things that force the change. In the moment, they may not have had a huge impact, but upon reflection, they represent everything the character has been through, everything they've experienced, all the change and growth and newfound ability and confidence, waiting to be seized or realized. These experiences are like dormant powder that, when later struck by the spark of immense pressure, ignite into a powerful resurge of inner strength.

TAKE A BREATH

I was having trouble with this chapter, so I took a 2-day nap and had this dream:

> My wife and I are driving through white, flat plains in a snowy landscape. Visiting my family, I think, or trying to. We stop at a store; we've been here before and I'm anxious to keep moving but my wife likes to browse and can't be rushed. So I sit outside, in the dark and the cold, and a cat sits on my lap for warmth. I wonder if cats steal warmth

*from dying bodies, and picture a field surrounded by
corpses.*

*We're being chased by something, something large and
menacing, but not especially dangerous. I don't know what
it is, but we catch glimpses of it sometimes through the
trees. My wife wants to spend a night away with her family.
I'm annoyed at first, but decide I'll use the time to visit
some old childhood friends who live nearby. But Google
maps keeps freezing, and we get a little lost. My hands
are cold, our tempers are short. We finally find the back
entrance for a large store, only we're late now and we don't
have much time for the plans we made because there's still
an errand to run. I don't remember what it is or why we
need the C4...*

If I wanted to overanalyze the dream, I could say the cat is
my need to be loved, brought out by my wife's perceived distance.
Same for the childhood friends; nostalgia for a time when I had
closer relationships. The anxiety in the store is from my extreme
claustrophobia (or more precisely, dislike of packed crowds and
breathing shared air). Or it could all be stemming from the night
years ago when my cat died and I couldn't help her; the vet had
recommended putting her down weeks earlier but I wanted to give
her more time at home and became responsible for her suffering.

Later in the dream, I'm sitting by a river with Jamie Lee
Curtis, as she stirs her drink with a razor blade. I'm explaining
how I'm stuck in the story I'm working on, and she says, "people
who plot the middle don't leave enough breathing room in their
novel."

EXPLORING NEW WORLD

When I first mapped out the plot outlines I shared earlier, I'd created a header for this section (the first half of Act II), called *exploring the new world*. On a surface level, I've already given you some prompts about what kind of things need to be happening. But more importantly, this is probably also the place where you may start to drift; when your story gets a little blurry, a little lost.

I never realized it before, but I most routinely get stuck at this point in my novels, and there's a reason for it. The bigger action scenes or fights or *events* are easier to picture or plot out. The first act gets the story rolling; it picks up steam again after the midpoint. But this part can feel like a slog, especially during the first draft. Maybe that's what prompted the dream (and the overwhelm that led to the couch-lock). Even if you have plotted your outline, you will probably still get stuck. So besides touching on some writing tips and strategies to help you move through it, I also want to share how to make this section of your book the *most important part*.

STORYTIME

When I was renting a castle in France, we went out for an excursion to see a medieval town. On the way back, we took what we thought was a detour route, that might pass closer to another area of interest.

That decision was nearly fatal.

In the end, our little van climbed up a tiny, weaving mountainous path, and we were driving inches from a thousand-foot cliff. And it was an unpaved, two-way lane. So on top of the immediate danger of hitting a pebble and steering off the ledge, there was the potential danger of another car coming towards us, and having to go *backwards* down the already precarious path. Which did happen. Twice.

The point is that, if we had taken the normal, simple, clear map, we would have arrived safely and easily. There would be no incident, no story, because nothing happened. Instead, we had a bonding near-death experience, not to mention some incredible views of a precariously placed, abandoned abbey.

I'm not saying don't get lost or go off to explore, that's *fine*. Don't be afraid to take random detours that seem interesting.

> Climb every mountain,
> Ford every stream,
> Follow every rainbow,
> 'Till you find your dream.
> A dream that will need
> All the love you can give.

Just make sure eventually, you get back to a road you recognize and end up at a safe destination. Nobody wants to be on a never-ending road trip with no clear aim or agenda.

Once you've traversed the whole, dangerous route, you can go back and clean it up, make sure it's safe and stable, clear the path and add signposts. If my guests had *known* what we were about to get into, I'm sure they would have unanimously opposed. Sometimes the best things are accidental.

PS. If you were in that van with me, I was in complete control, we were never in any real danger. This story was embellished for dramatic effect. Except for the screaming. That was real, and you know who you are.

GET LOST IN THE SWAMP

When asked, "Real quick, how do you write a novel?" Neil Gaiman answered:

> "Write down everything that happens in the story, and then in your second draft make it look like you knew what you were doing all along."

People romanticize their plans but dread the execution. *The magic you're looking for is in the work you're avoiding.* I've seen this pithy aphorism often, but never with a critical analysis. My first instinct is to be cautious: there's nothing glorious about doing the work. Not all work is good work; if you're dreading or avoiding it, it's probably not your best work. But... if it doesn't come easily or naturally, that also means you may need to dig deeper, and the deeper you dig, the more likely that you'll find diamonds. In the comments under one version of the quote, I saw this exchange:

"The cave you fear to enter holds the treasure you seek."

...

"Or a bear."

In my experience, those very challenging scenes to write, the places you get really stuck, can be frustrating and uncomfortable. Wrestling with them can make you lose focus, momentum, and may even be physically exhausting. They may require days of computational power and avoidance. But when you finally solve them, they might just be the key to the entire story.

I've actually seen the quote rephrased this way: *The magic you've been waiting for has been here all along, just waiting for you to see it.* Interestingly, they both mean the same thing, but the emotional response to the problem is very different. Consider *The Alchemist* by Paulo Coelho: the treasure the protagonist was seeking, was where his journey started. But he wasn't *ready* to notice it yet. The adventure was necessary to heighten the depth of his discernment.

The first draft of your book will probably be a swamp. Both you and your characters may be striving to put things together in a meaningful way. You may feel lost in the visible darkness. But don't fight the doubt, that's just your subconscious reaching for something better. Trust that the answers will appear when you're ready to see them. The truth is, *the bear and the treasure are in the same cave.*

Those of us who were impacted by the 1984 movie *The Never Ending Story,* can probably never forget the tragic scene where Atreyu loses his beloved horse Artax in the Swamps of Sadness. Atreya had been given a protective medallion and a valiant mission, to discover a cure and save the sickly empress of Fantasia. He seeks out Morla the Ancient One, hoping for a clue or answers so he can begin his quest, and instead loses Atreya after barely surviving an attack from the antagonist's forces. After having lost so much, so early – he's devastated. And then Morla directs him to the Southern Oracle, ten thousand miles away, an impossible distance without his horse.

But the interesting thing about *The Never Ending Story* is that it's meta-literary, in that the real hero is actually the reader,

Bastian, and the tragic events and determined courage displayed by Atreya only serves to forge a deep emotional bond, because the entire artifice, the salvation of Fantasia, depends on Bastian *believing* that he matters, that the story is real, that he has power, and that he can save them all: a change that only happens in the final climactic moments when the Nothing has almost destroyed everything.

MECHANICS OF MASTERY

There are some magic tricks that work on a surface level, without being that impressive. A common card trick I've seen young teens perform badly involves three rows of cards; they can find your card by a careful re-arrangement of selected stacks. The effect is interesting, but it's tedious to watch and wait as they stumble through the motions. There's no life in it.

The truth is, the *mechanics* of the trick are rarely interesting. The key is to keep viewers distracted and entertained with a story. Anything will do, and while the story may seem unnecessary to the careful manipulation of physics that allow for the startling result, it's actually integral to the spellcraft: because the trick isn't just the content shown, it's the blossoming of the viewer's imagination.

Hocus Pocus might seem like meaningless drivel, but it's meant to captivate and evoke a sense of wondrous possibility. An *opening up*, a widening of the lens, so you can share seemingly unimportant details that will have a remarkable effect later. You're conditioning your characters, and your reader, into a receptive state so they lower their guard. They will look for meaning in the content, and thus find it meaningful for themselves. As my spirit-guide Jamie Lee Curtis said in my dream, your novel needs some breathing room.

Here's the good news: this part can be disheveled and random. It can include fun scenes that don't seem relevant or related. Hocus Pocus is about spinning tales, casting a spell, getting readers and your characters to *care*. They shouldn't see what's going on behind the surface. Instead of carefully watching your fingers, they can't help but focus on the evocative images you're putting into their minds. They won't see the trick, only the magic.

In other words, it doesn't exactly matter *what* you say. You are spinning yarns, letting out story threads, hoping to get readers tangled in a messy knot. Eventually, you can make sense of it all, and when you reach the end, it can all seem important.

Create the content you want to see first. Make whatever you want to happen, happen. Later, we'll figure out which threads should be pulled and tightened, until they're as firm as a harp string. Then, when plucked, the rich vibrational harmony will take your breath away.

MEMORANDUM

- Struggle to prove themselves
- Lovable characters through vulnerable backstory
- Get lost in the swamp (breathing room)
- Kiss and slap (contrast increases emotional peaks)
- The treasure and the bear are in the same cave
- Laughter and levity (world worth saving)
- The montage (incidental events that motivate)

Grimoire Notes Added

Act II is when you should be adding in sideplots, so I'm making a *big* list of potential dramatic sideplots you can use for inspiration. Ideally, a sideplot will show character depth, convey new understanding or awareness, or at least show a world worth saving. But in a perfect world, that sideplot drama will build and overflow, compounding the conflict in the chief climax scenes and possibly even influence or redirect the final plot events.

I've also made a list of writing tips I've picked up from video games, which might help you to integrate this advice, especially on a more visually descriptive level. Both of these will be available in the *Grimoire*.

7

SHAZAM
LIGHT THE FUSE

In May of 1896, the NY Tribune posted a facetious description of a pretentious new seaside resort,

> "Been fillin' up on Charley horse rusies, sooflay
> de *allakazam*, an' all them French dishes."

While you might think alakazam has a rich and ancient esoteric history, the truth is it's a relatively modern word, and in this case, seems to be used much like hocus pocus, in that it's a vaguely foreign-sounding word with alliteration. It *sounds* good, which is why it started to be used creatively in popular media as a wizardly incantation. Specifically, it was used by the author to mock the use of fancy French names to appear more sophisticated. Later the phrase got shortened to *shazam*, which fit better with trendy comic book sounds like *zap* and *pow!*

In a 1940 edition of Whiz Comics, artist Charles Clarence Beck and writer Bill Parker introduced the world to Captain Marvel, which for a while was as popular as Superman.

> Captain Marvel's alter ego was an orphaned newsboy named Billy Batson. One day, 12-year-old Billy gets on a mysterious subway car, which leads to a mysterious cave. Within it, he encounters an ancient wizard named Shazam, whose name is an acronym that stands for the names of one king from the Bible and five figures from Greek or Roman myth: Solomon, Hercules, Atlas, Zeus, Achilles, and Mercury.

> The wizard tells Billy that the boy will receive the abilities of those legendary figures (wisdom, strength, stamina, power, courage and speed, respectively) if he says the magic word. Billy does so; is hit with a bolt of magic lightning; and is transformed in a tall, muscular, slightly squinty adult in a really cool red, white and gold costume.

According to most modern dictionaries, the word Shazam is "used to indicate an instantaneous transformation or appearance." We're going to use it here, in this chapter, to focus on the second half of Act II, which should be about your protagonist's powerful transformation. It starts with the sudden realization or personal insight that happens near the midpoint. The stakes are real, the protagonist is committed, they need to suit up for battle and prepare for the fight ahead.

He's willing to *try* enough to take limited action. This doesn't mean he's actually ready to face the antagonist or overcome the final challenge yet—he's not. He may feel like a pretentious imposter. But taking action forces him into the conflict. The heat and pressure of the *failed* attempt, will forge him into the hero he needs to become.

So in this regard, *Shazam* refers to two things: a dramatic transformation from victim to hero, but also the continuing insecurity, fear and imposter syndrome because the lack is still unresolved. Billy Batson might look like Captain Marvel, with a cool red and white and gold superhero outfit, but deep down he knows he's just a 12-year-old in over his head. While the previous section stoked his hopes; this section exacerbates his fears.

REEL THEM IN

I used to go fishing with my grandfather. Casting our lines out in the bubbling rivers beneath the dark pines, we'd catch trout and cook them outdoors on open fires with butter and salt. But fish are smart—you can't just yank on the line when you feel a bite. They'll nibble first. You have to *let out the line*, to give them the confidence to fully commit.

In the last chapter, which was on the first half of Act II, we were letting out the line. Spinning more yarn, because it'll create a thicker tangle, and a more satisfying resolution. We were still *opening* narrative loops.

In the second half of Act II we will start reeling them in. We'll create more tension by pulling on the threads. Someone said I need to put more Matrix references in this book, so here's a gratuitous pop culture reference: about halfway through, after being explicitly told that he should *always* run from agents, Neo stays to fight one in the subway.

"What's he doing?" Trinity asks.

"He's beginning to believe." Morpheus says.

I really wish this line came from the scene where Neo is pulling the wire to haul up the helicopter and save Trinity, because that would be a tighter metaphor, but that comes a little later. Actually, he's told by the oracle that he's *not* "the one" – but he takes action anyway. He starts to do stuff, not because of what he believes, but how he feels.

So far, you've been inhaling: adding oxygen to your story, giving it room and space to breathe. Now you're going to exhale. Your lungs will shrink and run out of air. The walls are closing in. The stakes are known; the hero has taken a deep look within and realizes she *cares* about what's happening, and that she has to do something. This will probably not be optimistic, but it can be determined.

They will take action in opposition to the constrictive maneuvers of the antagonist's forces. In my four-part chapter outline, this section—the second half of Act II—is labeled *bad guys closing in*.

There are several things we need to do in this section, and I'll give you some strategies and solutions for dealing with them successfully, but let me quickly focus on the main thing you need to do in this section, which I've summarized into just one neat phrase:

✓ **Escalating Conflict with Personal Responsibility**

From the midpoint of the novel, to the end of Act II, your protagonist will be taking an active role: they will still *hope* for a possibly successful outcome. Even if the odds are slim, they think there's a chance. Earlier, they *wanted* to believe but had no experience. Now they have courage enough to take action, and when that action leads to new experience, they will grow in confidence.

CRUCIAL ROLE

Joseph Campbell's traditional hero's journey usually has *seize the sword* as a reward for a successful quest; and even in my outline, this motif should really come later. Only after their ultimate defeat, can the hero find the deep emotional strength to triumph. But it *begins* here. The protagonist is given a crucial role, and suffers a surprise failure, before receiving a shocking revelation.

So we might imagine the sword as a symbol for personal autonomy. The hero picks up the sword by deciding a direction that they care about and taking action to achieve a desired result. They care enough to risk painful loss if they don't get what they want, which makes them vulnerable. They put down their defensive armor, pick up their weapon, rush into battle and *fall on their sword*.

Previously, they've been skeptical and protective. Here they open themselves up to a calculated risk. But they are not yet ready to handle such a dangerous weapon! The failure cuts deeper, because this time *it's their fault*.

In a romance or contemporary, this may be when they've realized their true heart's desire, are filled with optimism, and joyously run to confess the discovery of their newfound direction... and then it gets ripped away from them.

The main reason most plotting structures didn't work for me, was because they only had one final battle scene. It should actually be two: the first is a catastrophic failure that the hero is directly responsible for. They were given a responsibility over a vital task—and they messed it up. This will fill them with guilt, shame and potential trauma, which will result in the *dark night of the soul* or what I call *peak drama*.

This is where everything comes together, and has the most emotional impact both for your characters and readers. Your novel should be building up to the climax: the moment when the character is forced to risk everything, when they've given it their all and come up short. They realize that this conflict is too big for them, it hurts too much, they aren't enough. This battle will *end* them. But they push on anyway, and only then are they worthy and vulnerable enough to become something greater.

Shazam represents the *promise* of wisdom, strength, stamina, power, courage and speed: but at first your protagonist is only going through the motions and wearing an awkward costume. To fully achieve the realization of the benefits, they have to take action and play the role, until their *inner* transformation matches their outer posturing.

HOOK, LINE, SINKER

This inner transformation will be the result of heightening the tension: the slow buzz of electrifying conflict that gives the story energy. We'll increase the pacing and raise the stakes. This is the rumbling thunder and flashes of lightning, before your protagonist gets struck down by a blinding bolt of destructive energy.

To keep with my awkward fishing metaphor, by the midpoint, both your characters and readers are *all in*. You caught their interest with action and conflict (things happening to sympathetic characters). You gave them an interesting world, new experiences, and a growing sense of fulfillment as they started to believe that *more* was possible. You let your line out slowly and added weights so it sank down deeper (caring about the outcome).

- **Hook:** action, conflict, suspense
- **Line:** world-building, lovable characters
- **Sinker:** emotional depth and backstory

Now, at the middle, we're going to yank on the line to set the hook, then start reeling them in. There's going to be more tension, more resistance and conflict, less dawdling or self-doubt.

Eventually, we'll pull them out of the water altogether, until they're suffocating and flopping around in the dirt. All their choices and mistakes brought them to a point of life or death struggle. Metaphorically at least: they're too changed to go backward. The awareness of their own limitations will force them to seek answers that will be identity-destroying. In the *next* and final section, we'll decide whether to throw them back or cut open their bellies.

Fishing is a good metaphor because unlike hunting, the fish is an active participant in its own demise. It was *tricked*. So must your characters be responsible, due to a lack of knowledge. They took the big risk and fell flat on their face. They nibbled the bait, before swallowing the hook deep. The juicy worm they were after transformed into an unexpected disaster, and the fulfillment of their desire cost them everything. However, it's exactly this deep emotional entanglement, this *mortal* struggle for existence, that finally allows them the certainty and decisiveness they need to prevail.

> "A Zen master out for a walk with one of his students points out a fox chasing a rabbit. According to an ancient fable, the rabbit will get away from the fox, the master said. Not so, replied the student. The fox is faster, but the rabbit will elude him, insisted the master. Why are you so certain? asked the student. Because the fox is running for his dinner, and the rabbit is running for his life."

BAD GUYS CLOSING IN

Here's a handy list or flowchart of what it takes to create "peak drama." These are the things we'll be focused on during this section.

1. Enough information to make an informed decision
2. Enough at stake to make a calculated risk
3. Enough responsibility to feel tragic guilt or loss
4. Vulnerable enough to be destroyed

Without realizing it, your protagonist is now preparing to face the self-destroying experiences they need to go through in order to reveal what they are truly capable of, and unlock their full potential. Much of this section will include developing and executing a plan, only to have it fall apart and their hopes dashed.

You'll notice, most of this has to do with the protagonist's character arc, rather than specific plot details. And it's absolutely true that many stories may not depend on this kind of emotional depth or catharsis. But remember what I said at the beginning: stories that matter are the ones that are *too great* for the character to successfully achieve as they are, without first becoming something greater.

You can have a *good* story just by keeping the tension and conflict high; by managing the information and reveals. You can have a *good* story with great writing, description, dialogue or plot events. But the difference between a series of trivial incidents and a powerful, meaningful novel is the lasting impact on your protagonist, and through them, your readers.

PS. I'm not saying *deep* books are *better* books. There's absolutely nothing wrong with a fast-paced, breezy beach read: in many cases, they're an advantage. Some people read for a pleasant escape, not an emotional hangover. In many genres, a light, fun read may be *better* than something with navel-gazing and overwrought, self-conscious dramatic subtext. So take this with a grain of salt: make sure you know what kind of reading experience readers of your genre actually want, and learn how to give it to them. At the same time, keep in mind that this is deep, invisible magic: none of this will be surface level, spelled out, or narrated. The protagonist will probably never realize or be able to put into words any of this stuff; they'll just say they did what they had to in the moment.

ESCALATING CONFLICT

Specifically, the second part of Act II has six stages, that are centered around a major battle. After the new awareness, increasing pressure or growing confidence, your protagonist is ready to take action and believes that they can make a difference. They create a plan and are given a crucial role. They decide. It's probably related to achieving their own ends, or stopping the antagonist. Or maybe they are just trying to do something good.

    ✓ **mirror, plan, role**

But this plan brings them into direct conflict with the main antagonist's forces. This is not yet the ultimate, final battle. Remember, smart characters don't willingly risk everything to go up against superior forces, so there's an inherent miscalculation somewhere here: they *thought* they could, so they did. But there's an unexpected surprise. Something they didn't consider. It might be directly tied to their fatal flaw or lack—perhaps in the course of the events they come up against the exact situation that caused their original trauma, and they realize they haven't changed that much after all.

Perhaps they have been betrayed; or a crucial piece of information is so shocking it forces retreat or inaction. They choke, they freeze. They *think* they've figured out the problem and how to resolve it, but they were wrong, and they fail.

    ✓ **battle, failure, revelation**

Although I've spread these out into six potential chapters, and I do recommend this particular arrangement or order, exactly how they come about will depend on your story.

The important thing to remember is to keep the ball rolling, to yank on the line, to start reeling in. If you're in the "soggy middle" and feeling like you don't have enough things happening—this is totally normal! But the stakes should be high enough here that the scenes won't feel light or trivial. The solution is rarely to add in more distracting sidequests at this point, unless they are related to the critical mission. If the work was done in the last section, everything has been set up, and now when you add urgency and pressure, the pacing and momentum will take care of itself as it works towards a conclusion.

But don't let your characters get the carrot too early. Every time they try to do anything, throw stuff in their way. They need to go get a pen, then find some paper, so they can leave a note. But the only pen is back at school. And they're out of gas. And there are zombies. So they take bicycles. But then the bicycles break. And the road is blocked. And someone catches on fire. And there's no water, and they're burnt so now they have to be carried. In the story I mentioned earlier, for example, my character:

- Needs to fight a sea monster
- But the monster is her mother
- And it's about to eat her love interest
- But if she kills the monster, she'll have to take its place and be separated from the love interest
- And the island is sinking, along with her only chance to get the thing she's always wanted

- And there's a lightning storm and the water is electrified

Ideally, each of these conflict multipliers would be a surprise twist or reveal at the end of a scene. But the point is, keep inventing problems for them that increase internal conflict, so it's not *just* about the physical battles, but the difficult decisions that force psychological growth. Don't make it all environmental. It's okay for problems to be random and accidental; you just can't make the solutions random and accidental—your characters have to solve their own problems with wit and effort. If they only have one thing you need them to do, break that action down into twenty individual steps, then throw a wrench in each step.

Act II is also about deepening relationships with your characters, as they get to know each other, and themselves. With all the stressful stuff going on, tempers are short, somebody is lying to the protagonist, who in turn is hiding the truth from someone they care about. They are feeling guilty for something, they are (probably) confused by their conflicting emotions towards someone else. The action and events in the second half of Act II force these simmering subplots, feelings and conflicts into the open.

Each action scene is usually followed by a short scene of reflection (they make a plan, they are thwarted in an unexpected way, then they make a new plan for the next step). And often you'll want to alternate your scenes emotionally, so you'll have a positive, uplifting or peaceful scene followed by a devastating one (the *more* devastating you want a scene to be, the happier or lighter you want the scene just before it).

Some things to include:

- ✓ executing the plan
- ✓ battle scenes
- ✓ ticking clock (arbitrary countdown for reasons)
- ✓ big surprise (plot twists)
- ✓ non-literal battles
- ✓ deep near-admissions of feelings
- ✓ discovery quests revealing crucial information
- ✓ growing confidence and ability
- ✓ greater stakes increase anxiety and doubt
- ✓ flashbacks that show *why* this challenge is difficult

PICKING UP STEAM

If our novel was a bonfire, here we'd be adding more wood and stoking the flames as high as possible, so that *when* we douse it with cold water, it creates enough steam to power a train. We want the train to go *faster* so that when it crashes into the mountain, the explosion can be seen for miles. Figuratively, we want your protagonist to become an emotional trainwreck.

Earlier I mentioned how a court jester or royal magician was referred to as a juggler. They might start with a razzle dazzle: bangs or shouts or flashing lights; banging on the drums or a fanfare of brass trumpets; a spotlight. *The show is about to begin.* The juggler might start with something cute and bright: scraps of fabric or colored balls. But once they have your polite attention, they'll switch to something more dangerous: swords or burning torches.

Now imagine an acrobat juggling glass balls filled with corrosive acid, while riding a unicycle. The tension mounts and builds as an assistant tosses more obstacles into the maelstrom. Six balls, then twelve, then twenty. If the attempt was dangerous before, now it's suicidal. How will he even stop? How can it not lead to calamity?

If they just started and maintained the same number, the novelty would quickly wear off. The intrigue and suspense is at its height each time a new ball is added. Will this be the one that brings it all crashing down? How will he handle this new challenge?

Your job as story engineer is to keep tossing in more glass balls, filled with toxic poison, to see how your characters react. Each ball represents a new choice, an added responsibility, a greater risk.

The protagonist might ignore the first one or two, but eventually the weight and danger are crushing, and now they can no longer drop the burden without severe backlash and blowout. So they white-knuckle forward, until something happens that they can no longer control; the proverbial straw that broke the camel's back. And it's not just *one* terrible event, it's the whole weight of past events that are contributing to the impact and trauma of this one terrible reckoning.

Eventually, in most novels, it all becomes too much; all the balls break and shatter. But the story isn't in the beginning or the end, it's in the process of escalating challenges, of painting your hero into a corner. Your protagonist tries to hold it all together and keep the act going, until eventually they can't. It's all too much. Chaos ensues.

You cringe as the entertainer appears to stumble and fall. There's a flash of light and billowing coils of smoke. You hold your breath, heart pounding, peering into the carnage, the sizzling poison and broken glass, for a sign that the entertainer is unharmed. A hushed silence falls as the crowd fears the worst. The juggler emerges, resplendent in a new costume, smiling and waving. *Shazam.*

FIGHT SCENES

It's better to get the story down first and focus on the content – the drama and conflict – the *what happens* and *why it matters*, before worrying about anything like the word choice, writing style or sentence structure.

However, this feels like a good place to add in some general suggestions for writing captivating fight scenes. These may not be actual battles: they could just be scenes where the underlying currents of conflict erupt into physical manifestations of emotional overwhelm.

For example, I find it melodramatic when characters smash dishes against the wall and storm out in a huff: but that's better than quiet sulking or sternly worded reprimands. At some point in your story, emotions should become volatile enough to cause damage, to make a scene, and these may start to happen towards the end. As a quick recap, there are four major scenes of conflict in my plotting template:

- inciting incident
- first battle
- second battle
- final battle

The inciting incident is most likely an indirect consequence of the new change or shift; a hint of potential conflict, a disruption, but the protagonist is probably witnessing the effects rather than actively being engaged by the conflict. The first battle, is when they are more familiar with the new change or situation. As they try to figure out their new role, they see a concrete incident or fight with the antagonist's forces, which raises the stakes and gives them a deeper appreciation or understanding of the conflict. The fight scene in this section is the *second* battle—this time, the protagonist has pretty full knowledge, motivation to act, and a stake in the game. They stand their ground.

But this creates a problem: at this point, they still aren't strong enough to win. If the actual fight reaches its inevitable end, the hero will lose. So the fight needs to almost happen, or start to happen, and then it has to be interrupted somehow, enough that the conclusion isn't fulfilled. Earlier fights will be accidental, probably with henchmen. The protagonist is not as skilled or prepared, but comes out relatively unscathed. But here, the hero realizes or senses that this fight will destroy them (metaphorically or otherwise). And this new revelation makes them pull back or give up. Perhaps they make a choice to save an ally rather than finish the quest; maybe they chicken out and someone gets hurt. They've never been this challenged, they've never had this much awareness. They never expected things to get this far. This is a new depth of experience.

There are useful mechanics to describing action in a good fight scene, but we'll talk more about those later. My main point here is that you need to dodge, deflect and keep the knives spinning. It's not just about trading blows (if it is, that's going to get old *really* fast). It's what's at stake. It's the risk and danger. You've tossed hand grenades into the air and they're all falling down.

Use environmental constraints to force a reaction. Narrow walls, locked doors, no escape.

When Neo turns to face his first agent in the subway, he *barely* wins, and another agent arrives almost immediately. Once your protagonist realizes their imminent demise, their self-preservation instincts will take over. Get them out of there.

Three quick things:

1. the action will always need to get bigger, so if you start off with motorcycle shootouts and ninja stars, you'll need to get creative towards the end.
2. In action scenes, use shorter sentences and focus on the small details, not the observations or thoughts.
3. If your protagonist suddenly jumps into a flawless roundhouse, you need to explain *way earlier* that they took karate for three years and somehow it became muscle memory.

Weirdly, my Jamie Lee Curtis dream came before I watched the 2018 *Halloween* movie, but it's a good example of what I'm talking about.

It's a guy in a mask who kills people with a knife, fighting against a bunch of people armed to the teeth with shotguns. It *shouldn't* be much of a battle, but it is, partly because... fear. Wrestling with our own fears, makes people do stupid things.

Half the movie is just the setup, getting us to care about flawed characters with existing conflict between them. Then, a serial killer gets loose. He's creeping around, he's out there killing people, he's in the room. Is he behind me?

At first, they see him from a distance. They're protected behind a fence. They find the bodies. When they finally meet, they trade blows, duck for cover, and escape. Regroup. Start looking again. Get grabbed, but fight him off and break away. A bunch of flurried danger, a near escape. A suspenseful search.

They could just stay in the fight until it reaches a swift conclusion—but remember, if it's a *hard* fight, a *real* fight, it can't be quick and easy. It can't be resolved with superior force, skill, ability or arsenal. So it's a team effort, like the stabbing of Caesar. A little bit of damage at a time, a dance. The avoidance of pure, full commitment, because that would lead to a swift and decisive outcome, most likely for the antagonist.

The hero, who he currently is at the beginning, cannot win until he loses. That's when the deep realization, true grit or personal insight will give him the key to defeating the antagonist. Picture it like Melville's white whale: it's not *just* the antagonist they're up against. The antagonist is a metaphor for all the conflict between the characters and the sum total of their collective fears. This is the meaning of Nietzsche's abyss:

> "He who fights with monsters should be careful lest he thereby become a monster. And if thou gaze long into an abyss, the abyss will also gaze into thee."

The abyss is *infinite*: the depths cannot be fathomed or comprehended. The eternal potentiality forces a painful introspection. In 1844, Soren Kierkegaard described anxiety as being the "dizziness of freedom" – the paralyzing discomfort when faced with the boundlessness of one's own possibilities.

Similarly, visitors seeking to consult the oracle at the Delphic Temple of Apollo were presented with the Greek aphorism, "know thyself," followed by the warning "surety brings ruin." Apollo was a sun god, and represented the illuminating radiance of pure reason.

Unless your protagonist changes, they will be destroyed: the fulfillment and execution of this uncomfortable realization is the focal point of your story. The rising sun exposes the dark shadows hiding in our psyche.

In the *Halloween* movie, the crazed killer Michael Myers wears a mask and never speaks; an anthropomorphic representation of the infinite abyss that triggers the dizziness of freedom.

They stab him and dart away, shoot him and run, he grabs one of their ankles and pulls them back in, dragging them down into the cellar. They cannot escape until *they* change. All their lives, they've been living in fear, living in a "cage" – their secret underground bunker. But in the pivotal last scene, they force their vicious attacker into their safe haven, and narrowly escape. The deep shift in awareness comes with the line, "It's not a cage… it's a *trap*." Then they lock him in and burn it all down.

The thing they resented most, the thing they thought was holding them back, gives them the power and energy to triumph. This deep understanding of their fatal flaw, the sudden inner transformation and deep realization, is the critical piece that makes it all fit together. (It's actually a bit cheesy, and the mechanics of their plan feel accidental and poorly thought out, but without that extra layer of meaning, it would have just been a silly thrasher flick).

PLOT TWISTS AND REVEALS

plant your bombshells

In my earlier list of crucial elements to get to your peak drama or deep magic, I mentioned your protagonist needs *enough information to make an informed decision*. But remember, this comes out slowly, in stages. By the midpoint, they probably have basically figured out what's going on, and who is probably behind it. (For a mystery or detective novel, they will still be focused on this: they may have theories or hunches, but their guesses will be wrong, and the real culprit will be the final reveal).

But they won't have a full understanding, because that twist is going to happen later, when they're hardened under pressure (here is where they *almost die* and recognize their mortality: later is where they *metaphorically* die—they are ready to give up, give in, sacrifice their own desires or wants or life for the cause, this is what makes them fully heroic).

Handling information and revealing the twists is crucial, so even though we talked about it earlier, I want to focus on a couple of extra things.

The worst thing you can do is dump a bunch of new information, reveals or twists in a handful of paragraphs, or in dialogue, or in summary. As I mentioned earlier, the more it hurts, the later it should come in an active, visceral moment.

Here are two easy tricks to remember:
- One reveal per scene
- Scene or chapter break

You break when something happens; when something big changes. A twist or a reveal is a *happening*. Picture it like Newtonian physics: your characters will keep going in one direction unless met with an equal or greater force. A good twist or reveal has an *effect*. It prompts a reaction. It changes the course of the story. It puts everything else into new context, like a rippling explosion. So, on top of the shazam being your protagonist's newfound commitment and inherent insecurity, it can also be the transformative power of filling a knowledge gap. Imagine it like putting in a new battery. By the end of this section, they may even realize their fatal flaw or weakness. They lose the battle but they gain awareness. It may seem demotivating, but it will allow them to triumph later.

You can wrap up loose ends or little tidbits in your epilogue or final chapter, but these big new pieces of information should elicit an emotional response. Whenever I hit on a powerful reveal sentence, a show-stopper, a punch to the gut, I'll just write BOOM in all caps and then break to the next scene or chapter. (This is a note to myself of course, I edit it out of the final manuscript.)

The bigger booms I'll use as chapter breaks; the smaller booms will be scene breaks. You want the break to be as soon to the new information as possible, so you may have to juggle sentences. You can also stall it out; just *before* the reveal or twist, you can "stop time" to recognize the power in the moment.

> She took a sip of her coffee, leaving lipstick on the porcelain mug, before catching her reflection in the window. She stopped to straighten her hair when she

noticed a figure at the bar. Something about him was familiar. He turned towards her slowly, meeting her gaze in the reflection. A slow smile transformed his features, and her heart stopped. She knew that smirk. After all these years. After a dozen states and a new ID. It was him. He'd finally found her.

With plot twists or reveals, you'll probably have one of two situations.

- **Reveals:** why something happens (backstory dump)
- **Twists:** what's really going on (new knowledge)

These aren't super clear distinctions, but in one case, you'd suddenly learn a secret that puts the plot into new context, that gives you new information. This is something that has already happened. This could be something the protagonist knew and was hiding – a sudden flashback or memory – or it could be new information learned by readers and your protagonist at the same time, like someone else's backstory or history or motivation.

In the other case, you'd learn something new about current events that immediately changes the course of action. A reveal deepens the character's situational awareness; it's pulling back the curtain. A twist is a surprise piece of the puzzle that blindsides them.

In both cases, if it's important, save it for the *end* of the scene and build up to it. Don't explain it or give all the details, introduce it in a sentence and break; then deal with the reflections, ramifications and reactions immediately in the next section. As soon as the reader is given and understands this new information, the surprise is finished. Don't hand them a gizmo and read the directions. Let them open the box, then yell *surprise!*

SUBVERT EXPECTATIONS

You need to be careful to keep the secret long enough that the surprise isn't ruined. You can't add in hints or references that let readers guess the truth too easily. Your characters should be trying to figure out what's going on, but the possibilities they raise or muse over shouldn't include the actual thing. Even if there are subtle clues, it has to never even cross their mind. Otherwise, the ending is a foregone conclusion and the trick will play out mechanically, exactly as readers expected. A predictable resolution isn't satisfying.

But a real surprise is more than just opening the box and seeing what's inside, or filling in an unknown. For something to be a surprise, first characters must have been led to believe that something else is the case: a false flag, red herring, potential answer or truth should be introduced. It's not surprising unless it's *different* from what was previously thought.

Surprise isn't just the unexpected. It's something that is counter to what was actually expected. To make a surprise work, characters and readers should already have an existing mental framework for what's going on, only to learn that they were wrong, and in fact something else is going on. It's not a surprise when something randomly happens out of the blue; when a friend shows up to party. It's a surprise when they said they weren't coming and show up anyway. (Technically both are surprises, but one is unremarkable, while the other is astounding).

Magically speaking, it's relatively easy to make a coin disappear with a bit of sleight of hand. With clumsy skills, you can impress a toddler with object permanence, at least for a few seconds, or make it reappear behind their ear. Adults will immediately say "it's in your other hand," and they're probably right. If you open your other hand and the missing object is there, the trick is unimpressive. You're exactly as talented as they expected, which is *not very*. But if you slowly uncurl your bare palm, and the coin is indeed gone, you've subverted their expectations. You've challenged their assumptions. Suddenly your simple magic trick isn't so pedestrian. Now it's an arresting event, and they will demand to know how you did it.

Spoiler alert: this is why a magician uses a magic wand. If you attempt to get *rid* of the coin, for example by stuffing it in your pocket, they will of course follow your movements and see what you're doing. But if you're merely reaching into your pocket to remove the magic wand, so that you can continue the trick, they won't notice you stashing the coin at the same time. Then, when you do the big reveal, tapping the wand theatrically against your closed fist, the coin will already be gone and both hands will be empty.

The secret to getting readers to *care* about your story or magic trick, to be impressed by the heroic feat, is to first show them *it can't be done*. That's why magicians say "there's nothing up my sleeves" or "you still remember your card, right?" We allow them to focus on the details they've been shown so that they understand how there's *no possible way* the thing we do next will be able to happen. Then we do it anyway. The illusion of performing an impossible feat, something incomprehensible, that's magic.

LIGHTING THE FUSE

One time when I was a kid, I was playing around with firecrackers and lit my bed on fire. I was just testing a fuse, not planning to blow anything up, but the thing about fuses is, they're designed to be really difficult to put out.

I've talked a lot about adding conflict into your individual scenes, and that in this section we need to focus on reeling them in or escalating the conflict, but another way to think of this is lighting a fuse towards an inescapable threat. We need to show the dangers in the terrain ahead; this tension can be increased with an arbitrary deadline or ticking clock. Something bad is going to happen, and it needs to be stopped. Your protagonist may be rushing to put out the fuse, to stop the critical combustion, but if you've planted enough charges, the urgent chain of events cannot be prevented.

Your protagonist will resist looking into the terrifying abyss; they will actively fight against this identity-consuming terror. If you've set up your trick right, readers will be on the edge of their seats, dreading this ultimate calamity. "There's no way he can get out of this one," they think, or "she's doomed!"

Magic is showing that the predictable solutions (it's in your other hand) don't apply; the fuse can't simply be snuffed out. You're probably familiar with science fiction writer Arthur C. Clarke's third law: "any sufficiently advanced technology is indistinguishable from magic." But you're probably less familiar with the second: "the only way of discovering the limits of the possible is to venture a little way past them into the impossible."

In the next section, we've come to the brink of the abyss. We've reached the limit of what our protagonist can bear. Now we're going to push them off the edge, and see how deep the rabbit hole goes.

"Only those who risk going too far can possibly find out how far one can go." – *T. S. Eliot*

MAPPING IT OUT (ACT TWO)

The Second Act will have about 20 to 40 chapters, and should take up about 50% of your story. Often the Second Act goes too slowly, because authors are "stalling" until they can get to the exciting final scenes. You'll probably need to fill some chapters with subplots (stories that involve secondary characters).

MEMORANDUM

- Picking up steam/train wreck
- Broadening discomfort
- Investment/attachment
- Never guess the truth (defer knowledge)
- Show the opposite (surprise is the unexpected)
- External conflict reveals character flaws
- Profound realization leads to victory

8

ABRACADABRA
Twist the Knife

The term *abracadabra* has a long history. A two-thousand year old snippet from a Roman sage named Serenus Sammonicus prescribes it as a medicinal cure:

> On a piece of parchment, write the so-called 'abracadabra' several times, repeating it on the line below; but take off the end, so that gradually individual letters, which you will take away each time, are missing from the word. Continue until the (last) letter makes the apex of a cone. Remember to wind this with linen and hang it around the neck.

Abracadabra was still used as a "cure" well into the 18th century, where it was used as a defense of the plague. In 1722, Daniel Defoe lamented such superstitious charms:

People deceiv'd; and this was in wearing Charms, Philters, Exorcisms, Amulets, and I know not what Preparations, to fortify the Body with them against the Plague; as if the Plague was but a kind of a Possession of an evil Spirit; and that it was to be kept off with Crossings, Signs of the Zodiac, Papers tied up with so many Knots; and certain Words, or Figures written on them, as particularly the Word Abracadabra, form'd in Triangle, or Pyramid...How the poor People found the Insufficiency of those things, and how many of them were afterwards carried away in the Dead-Carts.

The origins of the word are less clear. Many think it's based on a Gnostic deity "abraxas" whose letters, in Greek numerology, add up to 365—the number of days in the year. Others say it comes from the Arabic Avra Kehdabra, *I create as I speak*, or the Chaldean, abbada ke dabra, meaning "perish like the word."

In this sense, it can be eschatological. *The Book of Revelation* refers to the end of all things, which are brought together by the power of the resurrected *logos*: "And he was clothed with a vesture dipped in blood: and his name is called The Word."

But my favorite is the Latin base: the word *abre* means "to open" and a *cadaver* is a corpse, so Abracadabra can mean the literal disembowelment of a sacrificial offering, connected to the practice of reading entrails. Death is the purchase price for supernatural wisdom or insight.

Earlier, we talked about how drama is the beating heart of your story, and that you need to slice it open to find the hidden star. But now we're going to go further. Because peak drama isn't just the heart of the story; it's the *hole left over* when you rip that heart out, step on it and light it on fire.

If we were still talking about magic, and we are, this would be the ritual sacrifice: Abraham offering his son Isaiah on the altar, proving his devotion through what he's willing to lose. You've made your characters—and readers—fall in love with something. Want something. Need something. This could be a person, a wish, a hope or a dream. It has to be something they want so much, that they're willing to risk everything to get it. But in the last section, they've had their hopes dashed.

Act III *begins* with the "dark night of the soul," which is basically, finally, the understanding of what victory will truly cost, and what the world will look like if it isn't achieved.

This isn't just hypothetical: at this point there should be very real, and final, consequences of the struggle. The main character is probably feeling betrayed or deceived. They might be feeling torn and divided as their allies turn against one another; or guilty and responsible for a tragic turn of events. They have *seen* the monster, recognize that he's real, properly assess his power, reach and influence, and realize that they don't measure up. Their hopeful optimism is replaced by a deep trepidation.

In a normal, realistic story, the kind most of us are used to, this is when a smart person would call it quits, or be crushed by the status quo and realize the problem is *too big* for them. The reason a great story has power is because, knowing the full extent of the impossibility of their quest, and no longer even recognizing the chance to achieve a real victory, the hero perseveres anyway. But it's *only* heroic if the risk is real.

In the last chapter, I mentioned we should focus on escalating conflict with personal responsibility. Let me extend that a bit by introducing an 1842 version of a familiar nursery rhyme:

> Humpty Dumpty, lay in a beck.
> With all his sinews around his neck;
> Four Doctors and forty wrights
> Couldn't put Humpty Dumpty to rights.

A "beck" is a small brook or creek, but it can *also* mean a state of compliance or surrender, as in being "at someone's beck and call."

A wright is a maker of things. You're probably more familiar with the term well-wrought or to be made well. So let's put it all together: in a state of complete surrender, Humpty Dumpty is fixed or pinned, he's torn asunder, bound by concerns of his own making.

If you want to go *deep,* you can compare it to the story of Osiris being torn into pieces and scattered down the Nile. In Spell 22 of the Egyptian *Book of the Dead*, he says "I have arisen from the Egg which is in the secret land."

VIOLENT TRANSFORMATION

The conclusion of your novel should feature:

- Unlikely triumph through impossible action
- nothing left to lose/conviction

We start with the protagonist fully giving up: reeling from their defeat or loss, the enormity of the conflict, their inability and limitations. The last battle scene probably revealed a deep truth about themselves, and they may be struggling to comprehend who they really are. Just when they were starting to believe, their faith was shattered. They've been digging their own grave, and now that they see the epitaph on their tombstone, they just want to crawl into it.

Fun digression: "the handwriting is on the wall" comes from the Old Testament story of Belshazzar's feast. The ruler was indulging in drunken revelry and debasing sacred temple vessels when a disembodied hand wrote the Aramaic *mene mene tekel upharsin* or which meant "two minas, a shekel and two parts" or alternatively "numbered, weighed, divided."

Belshazzar couldn't make sense of this ominous warning, so he sent for his prophetic seer. Daniel's interpretation, as recorded in the first accessible, English translation of the Bible, (the King James Version of 1611), was this:

- ✓ God hath numbered thy kingdom, and finished it.
- ✓ Thou art weighed in the balances, and found wanting.
- ✓ Thy kingdom is divided

So you see, the "writing on the wall" isn't simply that *bad things are going to happen.* It represents an accounting and calamitous ending; a limitation that reveals a personal insufficiency. This self-made problem leads to a confounding personal block or binding. Jonathan Swift's miscellaneous works of 1720 maintains this deeper sense of the phrase:

A baited Banker thus desponds,
From his own Hand foresees his Fall;
They have his Soul who have his Bonds;
'Tis like the Writing on the Wall.

All of the momentum and conflict is leading towards an inescapable reckoning, a debt that can't be paid because it's larger than the protagonist's current assets. An impossible feat, now revealed in stark detail as the allies take stock of their options and resources, and come up short. The *bonds* are both literal and figurative: someone else is holding the purse strings.

This narrative clarity is like what I mentioned earlier, about pulling up your sleeves to show there is no concealed mechanism or hidden card. This battle can't be won through ordinary means. But after wrestling with their own insecurities, the protagonist will usually be given a pep talk by a mentor or supporting character, and they decide to take action anyway, despite their slim chances.

In a romance, for example, they've given up trying to make the relationship work. Maybe they think the love interest doesn't want them, or is happy with someone else. But someone tells them, something to the effect of, if you don't at least try, you'll never be happy.

They've discovered their shard of glass, and they recognize that, if they pull it out, they'll bleed to death. At peak drama, they'll pull it out anyway. It's like pulling a rabbit from a hat, but messier. Picture removing a heart from a cadaver. First, you worm your fingers through the chest cavity, surrounding it completely.

Then you give it a sharp tug, ripping the arteries. It's surgery. It's an exorcism.

But at the *last* moment, their sacrifice (surrender and sunder) results in an unexpected reversal, a triumph, a victory. There is still something more, something they don't understand, but they can only learn it by fully committing to their own destruction. To letting go of the thing they've been clinging to. The defeat is crucial to their victory, for only in their lowest depths can they seize their forgotten advantage.

DRIFTING (beyond good and evil)

When doing my thesis on *Paradise Lost*, there's one line in particular that's always struck me as prescient:

> *So farewell hope, and with hope farewell fear,*
> *Farewell remorse; all good to me is lost.*

Believing that there's a universal right and wrong, that the universe is at core a benevolent place that rewards courage, where victory is possible—Lucifer comes to realize that he will never get the justice he seeks; that the system won't acknowledge or abide his existence. This is tragic, heartbreaking for him to accept. And while it's a pivotal turning point in *Paradise Lost*, the sentiment isn't new.

It comes from a little known text called the *Consolation of Philosophy*, set in Rome and written in AD 523 during a one-year imprisonment—and eventual execution—of its author. It reads a bit like Kafka's *The Trial*: the attempt to make sense of being unfairly persecuted by an unjust system.

In it, a formerly wealthy aristocrat is put in jail, and wallows in self-pity, before a young, beautiful visitor instructs him how to achieve a peaceful inner equilibrium, despite external circumstances.

> But whosoever quakes in fear or hope,
> Drifting and losing mastery,
> Has cast away his shield, has left his place,
> And binds the chain with which he will be bound.

In other words, *drifting* is the painful anxiety felt when we are bound by our hopes or fears: future events we can't control bind us into complete inaction. But after the dark night of the soul, our protagonist's hope is ripped away. Whatever outcome or reality they were trying to protect or preserve, that future is gone. It's tragic, and sad, and the full realization of the unkind, unjust universe may shatter their foolish illusions. But it comes with an unexpected boon: they've already experienced the worst, the thing they were afraid of, the thing they were trying to stop… which means, they may also experience greatly reduced fear. They have nothing left to lose, and moving beyond hope allows them to take action. According to the author of *Consolation*,

> *If first you rid yourself of hope and fear*
> *You have disarmed the tyrant's wrath*

Or, as John Keats put it in 1820, urging readers to "strive" and take action, "seize the arrow's barb before the tense string murmur."

I could argue that all heroes are obstinate fools: at least until the moment they are doomed. It's this selfish perseverance towards their goals, their mad megalomania in believing they can make a difference, the reckless and insane quest that goes far beyond what's logical or rational, their inability to let go or give up... all of these things are necessary to put them in direct, core conflict with an overwhelming force so great it destroys them completely.

The thing that makes them ultimately heroic, is exactly their ability to act without the expectation of a personal reward. At some point, they may even give up their earlier, simplistic ideas about good or evil, how far they wouldn't go, as their moral boundaries shift and blur.

In the 2012 *Wreck-It Ralph* movie, which appears to be modeled closely on *Paradise Lost*, the protagonist is tired of always being forced to play the villain. The universe, the system, only assigns him that one role. He resists it the entire time, stirring up his own unhappiness. It's only when he accepts himself that he finds peace.

> "I'm bad. And that's good. I will never be good. And that's not bad. There's no one I'd rather be, than me."

In the end, he sacrifices himself to save his friends, recognizing that his destructive abilities are exactly what makes him uniquely capable of this feat.

In 1790, Blake wrote the *Marriage of Heaven and Hell*, which tried to define moral limits in these terms: "Good is the passive that obeys Reason. Evil is the active springing from

Energy." But in George Bernard Shaw's 1903 *Don Juan in Hell*, the protagonist reveals this contrary definition:

To be in hell is to drift:
to be in heaven is to steer.

Towards the end of your novel, your main character may realize that the ruling systems about right and wrong don't apply on a fundamental level to their current circumstances, and they may need to disavow their deeply cherished beliefs about how the world operates, and their own role in it.

In some literature, this deliberation is overt: for example, in *The Adventures of Huckleberry Finn* (1884), Huck decides to forge his own path instead of trying to willingly submit to the flawed ethics of his society:

> It was a close place. I took... up the letter I'd written to Miss Watson, and held it in my hand. I was a-trembling, because I'd got to decide, forever, betwixt two things, and I knowed it. I studied a minute, sort of holding my breath, and then says to myself: "All right then, I'll go to hell"— and tore it up. It was awful thoughts and awful words, but they was said. And I let them stay said; and never thought no more about reforming.

Napoleon Hill is most famous for his book, *Think and Grow Rich*, but few people recognize that his positive-thinking bestseller borrowed heavily from an earlier book called *O Henry*, in which a ghost communicates through an ouija board, or the book he published a year later in 1938, called *Outwitting the Devil: The*

Secret to Freedom and Success. This book was thought to be too controversial for its time, so it wasn't released until 2011.

According to Hill's devil, most men are "drifters"—they are easy to control because they don't think for themselves. Fear and hope limit their self-direction and keep them in chains, causing them to drift into the first job they can find, with no definite aim or purpose; and then keep them in fear of poverty their whole lives. Hill's guide is a bit like an expose of the tactics the devil uses to control humanity, in order to encourage them to act with "courage and purpose, resolute and unafraid."

In 1947, Kahlil Gibran puts similar language into his own literary version of the devil:

> I am the courage that creates resolution in man. I am the source that provokes originality of thought. I am the hand that moves man's hands. I am Satan whom people fight in order to keep themselves alive. If they cease struggling against me, slothfulness will deaden their minds and hearts and souls.

The opposite of *drifting*, in this tradition, is *striving*. Going against the flow, instead of with the flow. This creates incredible, destructive tension. Early figures that represent this cosmic struggle are tragic heroes like Oedipus: in refusing his ordained fate, he ends up fulfilling it. For much of humanity's history, resisting the divine will of *what is written*, can only end in destruction.

But this negative depiction of hubris is subverted in modern novels. Captain Ahab in *Moby Dick* is often viewed as a cautionary tale against reckless pursuits, with one critic writing the book's morale is to "lower the conceit of attainable felicity." Secretly, Melville considered Ahab the hero of his story, as he says in a letter to Hawthorne, "I have written a wicked book…"

In real life, fear and hope keep most of us bound; there is more to lose than there is to gain. In fiction, in order for your protagonist to experience *real* change, they must be ready on some level to leave everything behind, to alienate everyone, to live the rest of their lives alone, hated, feared—and they will do all this because they recognize that they can no longer live in the intolerable state of passive injustice, tacitly condoning an unjust society or universe; that their *death* will be an act of refusal, like Kurt Vonnegut's tragic resolution in *Cat's Cradle*:

> If I were a younger man, I would write a history of human stupidity; and I would climb to the top of Mount McCabe and lie down on my back with my history for a pillow; and I would take from the ground some of the blue-white poison that makes statues of men; and I would make a statue of myself, lying on my back, grinning horribly, and thumbing my nose at You Know Who.

This is not about blasphemy, it's about pushing through personal beliefs, and challenging what the world deems you capable of. It's turning to confront your demons, and willingly stepping into the uncertain void of infinite potential. This can be seen as a desperate defiance, and a necessary struggle for survival. Milton used the phrase "hurling defiance toward the vault of Heav'n" in *Paradise Lost*, but it was repeated in *Moby Dick* and again in the *Manifesto of Futurism* of 1919:

And like young lions we ran after Death, its dark pelt blotched with pale crosses as it escaped down the vast violet living and throbbing sky… There was nothing to make us wish for death, unless the wish to be free at last from the weight of our courage!… Let's give ourselves utterly to the Unknown, not in desperation but only to replenish the deep wells of the Absurd!… Erect on the summit of the world, once again we hurl our defiance at the stars!

This is a struggle to stretch our capacity beyond the limitations of birth, symbolized by the heavens; the position of the ruling planets and stars that carve out an inflexible personal destiny. According to Hegel in his 1806 *Phenomenology of Spirit*, this creative impulse is a necessary criterion for the development of self-consciousness:

> "It is solely by risking life that freedom is obtained; the individual who has not staked his or her life may, no doubt, be recognized as a Person; but he or she has not attained the truth of this recognition as an independent self-consciousness."

I know we've gotten a little in the weeds, but my point here is, in the third act, you need your protagonist to willingly walk unprepared into the gates of Hell, to face their worst fears, to trigger the Great Conflict that has dominated their lives, even if it will mean their destruction—and it will. They've so far been bound by their hopes and fears, chained with limitations and learned conceits. The actions they've taken to increase pleasure or avoid pain has led them towards the edge of their own mortality, and they've reached their limit. They can't go farther without a complete unmaking; a reevaluation of their identity.

As Shaw's devil warns:

> The end will be despair and decrepitude, broken nerve and shattered hopes, vain regrets for that worst and silliest of wastes and sacrifices, the waste and sacrifice of the power of enjoyment: in a word, the punishment of the fool who pursues the better before he has secured the good.

Don Juan replies, "But at least I shall not be bored."

In *The Black Cat* (1843), Edgar Allen Poe claims the soul has "a touche of Perverseness," which is the "unfathomable longing of the soul *to vex itself*—to offer violence to its own nature." But this is only because we instinctively struggle against the paralyzing chains that prevent us from exploring our deepest passions. We are born eager to strive for liberty and the pursuit of happiness (once forbidden, now widely accepted as universal human rights).

DESCENT TO HELL

The heroic *attainment* of these aspirations, if they are to have true value, must be seized through strife; or more accurately, generated through the energy of violent opposition. As the literary critic Christophe Tournu reminds us, "Violence seems to be part of our lives—our destiny as human beings, because we find justice in violence. All the liberties we have won, have been fought for."

Early Romantic and Modernist literature glorifies this destructive conflict. For example, in 1810 Goethe took the classic myth of *Faust*, and changed it from a dark tale of a devilish bargain, to a humanistic striving towards personal growth.

> Now is the time, through deeds, to show that mortals
> The calm sublimity of gods can feel;
> To shudder not at yonder dark abyss,
> Where phantasy creates her own self-torturing brood,
> Right onward to the yawning gulf to press,
> Around whose narrow jaws rolleth hell's fiery flood;
> With glad resolve to take the fatal leap,
> Though danger threaten thee, to sink in endless sleep!

1820, Percy Bysshe Shelley published *Prometheus Unbound*, which explores similar themes. Life and victory can *only* be fully achieved through this titanic, destructive defiance.

> To suffer woes which Hope thinks infinite;
> To forgive wrongs darker than death or night;
> To defy Power, which seems omnipotent;
> To love, and bear; to hope till Hope creates
> From its own wreck the thing it contemplates;
> Neither to change, nor falter, nor repent;
> This, like thy glory, Titan, is to be
> Good, great and joyous, beautiful and free;
> This is alone Life, Joy, Empire, and Victory.

The creature in *Frankenstein* actually reads *Paradise Lost* (along with Goethe's *Sorrows of Werther*) and comments, "They produced in me an infinity of new images and feelings, that sometimes raised me to ecstasy, but more frequently sunk me into the lowest dejection."

In order to have an effective, powerful story, in order for your final resolution, the reveal of your magic trick to hit the mark, first you need to drag your characters through hell. You can only get the exhilarating satisfaction and the dramatic undoing of story events, if you make sure your protagonist is truly immobilized, bound, laid bare in a tragic state of complete vulnerability, with no apparent path to victory.

> "In misery! despairing! long wandering pitifully on the face of the earth and now imprisoned! This gentle hapless creature, immured in the dungeon as a malefactor and reserved for horrid tortures! That it should come to this! To this!" – *Goethe's Faust*

In other words, in the final act of your novel, before you untangle the knot, resolve the conflict, and conclude the narrative, you have to make it absolutely clear that a successful, easy resolution is impossible. Make it bad, before you make it better.

> "No tree, it is said, can grow to heaven, unless its roots reach down to hell." – *Carl Jung*

"Do you not see how necessary a world of pains and troubles is to school an intelligence and make it a soul."
– John Keats

"This, then, is the human problem: there is a price to be paid for every increase in consciousness. We cannot be more sensitive to pleasure without being more sensitive to pain." *– Alan Watts*

Already in the Third Dynasty of Ur (around 2000 BC), we get the Sumerian myth of Inanna's descent into the underworld. The goddess is allowed to pass through the seven gates, removing a piece of clothing or jewelry at each. When she arrives, she is naked and without power.

> The seven judges, rendered their decision against her. They looked at her – it was the look of death. They spoke to her – it was the speech of anger. They shouted at her – it was the shout of heavy guilt. The afflicted woman was turned into a corpse. And the corpse was hung on a hook.

The abracadabra is when your protagonist has been stripped to their core, confined or pinned by the iron chains of guilt, weakness, and inability—their fatal flaws revealed. The accounting accurately revealing their immense deficiencies in the face of the debt or cost they owe. Yet *somehow*, as if by magic, they triumph despite impossible odds. Abracadabra is the hero rising from the ashes, the stone being rolled away from the empty tomb. After the magician saws through the crate, the woman is revealed to be whole

HORROR VERSUS TERROR

I'm not really a horror writer myself, but I did find a really neat piece of historical literary trivia that makes sense to share here.

According to celebrated gothic novelist Ann Radcliffe in 1826, terror leads to the sublime, while horror does not. "Terror and horror are so far opposite, that the first expands the soul, and awakens the faculties to a high degree of life; the other contracts, freezes, and nearly annihilates them."

A horror writer is keen on local effect, surprise, a series of impacts, where the terror writer sustains and cranks up a single passion toward a resolution, and explanation.

Virginia Woolf shows her impatience with horror, because "it is unlikely that a lady confronted by a male body stark naked, wreathed in worms, where she had looked, maybe, for a pleasant landscape in oils, should do more than give a loud cry and drop senseless. And women who give loud cries and drop senseless do it much the same way."

Paraphrased by Michael Schmidt in *The Novel: A Biography*, "Terror teaches, horror, a literature of mere effect, degrades. Hence, tales of horror are hard to sustain, they become insipid and later ridiculous."

Horror is basically, there are bad, scary things in the world out there, but people are basically good. I am basically good. Goodness will triumph over evil in the end.

Terror is, the evil is inside me. There is no justice, no hope. The universe is actively destructive. It's not just indifferent, it's maleficent. Terror is ultimately edifying for those who persevere. Horror is ultimately soul-destroying. Lovecraftian horror, on the surface, is just weird creepy crawlies. At worst, however, it's the extraordinary evil that regular people are capable of. That *you* might be capable of: a repudiation of all your hopes and fears.

In other words, horror is a cheap effect; violence or danger for cosmetic conflict, resolved without first delving into the protagonist's deep resistance and need for transformation. Real terror is immobilizing, as the protagonist is absolutely pinned by fears and desires of his own making. As Franklin D. Roosevelt's first inaugural address asserts:

> "The only thing we have to fear is…fear itself — nameless, unreasoning, unjustified terror which paralyzes needed efforts to convert retreat into advance."

The point of all of this discussion is to make sure your story matters, by putting your characters into a kind of agonizing, personal torture, where they are forced to make an impossible choice that clashes with their self-identity. But we'll turn for now to some practical examples and writing strategies to help make your final battle and resolution are satisfying, and pick up this thread again later.

FINAL BATTLE SCENE

It isn't the case that the protagonist no longer has anything to fight for; they've just lost the confidence that they can ever have any kind of personal happy ending, or at least the risk is great and the rewards slim. *Despite* all that, situations or circumstances— along with the pep talk—force them into action.

It might be reactionary: someone they care about is in trouble and they need to rush in to save them. Or it might be revolutionary: a suicide mission to stop the antagonist's forces and save thousands of lives. It could be prescribed: a council meeting or public battle. It's probably time-sensitive. They may be inclined to run and hide, then change their minds at the last moment.

In any case, for some reason, they will *show up*. This will be your book's final battle scene. It doesn't mean they've overcome their fatal flaw or lack; but they are at least getting close to realizing or being fully aware of it. The final transformation, the alchemical process, won't begin until they've stepped into their own personal hell, are boiled down to their essence, and stripped bare. Which is why the first part of the final battle is an *ultimate defeat*. The defeat is necessary. The villain triumphs, maybe even gloats. It'll probably be something like, "Who do you think you are? How did you think you could ever defeat me?"

I often see final battle scenes that are unemotional – it's just punch-jab-slash; or it's over too quickly with a simple fight. Nothing changes, the protagonist just wins after a prolonged fight scene. But here's the secret: the change happens in the middle of the final battle. It can be something as simple as a recollection, a deep resolve, a new piece of awareness or understanding, but this scene is everything so don't skip it.

This is why I recommend having a hero who loses the final battle at first, needs to regroup, and comes back stronger. You can stall out fight scenes by breaking them up, making them more challenging, or giving the main villain a superpower or secret weapon, like kryptonite. If Superman was just always super powerful, all the fight scenes would be lame, because they would be easy. There needs to be real personal risk, or there's nothing noble or heroic about the protagonist rising to fight even when the battle is lost.

UNLIKELY ALLY

Going into the final battle, brought low by failure, the villain is triumphant, the hero crushed... but then something changes. Sometimes it's something as banal as free will: Mr. Smith asks Neo why he persists when there's no hope, and Neo answers "because I choose to" and then gets up again in abject defiance. But often the win is a result of the relationships and friendships they've forged along the way. *All the king's horses and all the king's men.* This unexpected victory may manifest as a sudden, secret weapon or ability, a deep resolve or new understanding, or an unlikely ally.

It isn't the protagonist's strengths or abilities that win the day, it's their *character*: a defining characteristic that sets them apart from the antagonist, which makes them the "good guy" and so worthy, on a moral level, of the big win. A good way to portray this is through a character they helped out much earlier, who they treated well simply out of kindness. This is probably someone mistreated, marginalized, without a voice; someone the hero makes friends with simply by being accepting of others. He *wins* not by strength or force, but because of an act of benevolence— that he did earlier for no expectation of reward—and it's this that helps later, when an ally unexpectedly hands him a crucial advantage in the victory.

In *Harry Potter*, we get Dobby: the freedom of the house elf and champion for house elf rights, in earlier books, is a charming sidequest. But when Dobby, as a freed elf, is able to come to the rescue and fight against Voldemort's army, it's a powerful twist. The lesson is, be kind to everyone; or kindness wins out in the end. Dobby's *sacrifice,* and Harry's determination to dig his grave with his bare hands, ties in with the themes I raised earlier. In a sense, the hero is burying a piece of themselves.

This could also be a member of the antagonist's forces who recognizes the courage or virtue of the protagonist and switches sides at the last moment. In the 2000 movie *Gladiator*, Russell Crowe's character has been poisoned so that the emperor can hand him a quick defeat. But halfway through, when he disarms the emperor anyway, the army general—loyal up to this point—commands his soldiers to sheathe their swords; he's had enough of the villainy and is ready for a change.

The protagonist has to do most of the work, to get to a point where the victory is *so close* that a new element could tip the scales; they shouldn't expect help early on. It's usually about teamwork: while the antagonist is a cruel, single-minded dictator, a bully, the protagonist learns to *accept* help and be grateful for the support.

THE FLASHBACK

One of the best places for a revealing flashback is halfway through the battle. The villain is winning. All seems lost. The protagonist and allies are not strong enough to win. Logically, rationally, they are outmatched. The hero was not fully prepared for this conflict, it *should* be a loss.

But mid-battle, something changes. When the protagonist is pushed, further than they ever have before, it can unlock newfound inner strength or confidence. Having lost everything, they have nothing left to lose; their fears have been realized, their hopes dashed, so they must reach for *something else.*

This is a big deal; it's kind of the whole point, so don't wrap your endings up quickly, in a couple of paragraphs. It could be a flashback scene, an early memory, holding one idea or insight or key phrase; that helps them reinterpret or outmaneuver.

It could also be a secret past traumatic event which actually holds deep meaning or even a power. *End scene:* the main character or an ally has died, the villain has triumphed. *Flashback cut scene:* that character was bitten by a dog when they were a kid, and are afraid of canines. But actually it was a werewolf. They've had the potential to wolf out all this time but never activated it until now... surviving an otherwise fatal accident. A secret immunity. If you revealed this too early or made it too obvious, it won't be a good twist; but it can also seem forced or shallow if the twist comes too quickly.

Instead of losing to *"Surprise, I'm a werewolf!"* to winning all in one scene, you can space it out. This where you'll have your deepest, most touching emotional scenes as well, when readers are paying the most attention and so are most vulnerable. When stakes are highest and anxious uncertainties reach a boiling point, hold that tension as long as possible.

Almost always, the point in most books is that *good* triumphs over evil just because. Friends and family and integrity have to win, or at least the *belief* in those things should be rewarded. In life this is not always true, but most people who read popular fiction will be expecting a victory. If it's an easy win, by a superior force, it's not a great story. If it's an unlikely win that proves justice and decency has a place in our universe, they'll be filled with warm butterflies for a few days.

EVERYBODY DIES

Find something you love and let it kill you.

What if you don't have a final battle scene? You will, but it may not be a manifestation of physical violence. There may not even be a clear antagonist. The point is that everything should feel life or death to main character, even if it isn't really: it's a death of their sheltered self, their pride, their ego... a shift from me to we. Death of self, and a rebirth, as something new, improved, changed. Every story. Otherwise, this story probably isn't worth telling.

Let's say you have a bunch of travelogues. They're all funny stories, but they probably won't make a strong book unless you figure out what you learned, how they changed you, and an overall theme or uniting purpose emerges. The *point* of your story, the reason it matters, is because of this learning, when your protagonist or narrator becomes changed through extraordinary, singular pressures unlike they've ever faced before. If you're writing a memoir, you may need to take a little creative license. Probably, in real life, there isn't *one scene* where all of this happens in a sudden epiphany. But you can create a meaningful transformation in hindsight.

For example, one of the ones I've used is the experience of going to a university job application and being laughed out of the room, because the staff had discovered an early self-published book I'd written. It was a pretty terrible day, and I felt frustrated and angry. It may not have been the day I vowed never to apply for a job again and be subjected to that level of disdain or condescension, but framing it that way is a more powerful story. That was the day my dreams of teaching at university were crushed, and I decided to make a living as a writer instead.

But I'll give you a few more examples: *Derry Girls* on Netflix is a fun teen drama about a bunch of Irish girls in the 90's. Mostly comedy, with episodes that establish the characters and drama. In the last episode of season one, a random sidequest exposes a deep secret about one of the group; the secret shatters how they see each other, and the group is divided and miserable. Then one of their groups gets laughed at during a talent show, and *all* the group comes together to support her, healing the wound, laughing and dancing together. At home, their parents are coming together for a different reason: the escalating political violence has resulted in a bombing.

Emma, Jane Austen's most satisfying novel, has very little outright violence or conflict; but the entire story displays Emma's social meddling and builds to a point where her interference causes enough harm for her to finally turn her eyes inward, do some soul-searching and come to a profound personal epiphany.

> Emma's eyes were instantly withdrawn; and she sat silently meditating, in a fixed attitude, for a few minutes. A few minutes were sufficient for making her acquainted with her own heart. A mind like hers, once opening to suspicion, made rapid progress; she touched, she admitted, she acknowledged the whole truth. Why was it so much worse that Harriet should be in love with Mr. Knightley than with Frank Churchill? Why was the evil so dreadfully increased by Harriet's having some hope of a return? It darted through her with the speed of an arrow that Mr. Knightley must marry no one but herself!

The critic, Michael Schmidt, comments: "Her repentance when it comes is abject and total. She is suddenly blinded like St. Paul on the road to Damascus. Religious imagery underlies this remarkable paragraph: St. Paul, meditation, heart, truth, evil, hope, and the thrilling image of the physical sensation that understanding brings with it, the dart/arrow suggesting Saint Sebastian."

Her inferior self has resisted change or self-scrutiny until the anxiety she feels at the harm and drama she's created is too large to be ignored, and then the self-doubt comes crashing down. It's only one moment of reflection, but it's everything... bound by choices and consequences until she cannot go on the way she was before, the only way to continue is through change, an unmaking, a reconfiguration.

As the I Ching (Chaos symbol) simplifies: "When the Way comes to an end, then change – having changed, you pass through."

Let's pretend, as an example, that your protagonist is a woman who got into the environmental movement early and has spent decades educating the public on the virtues of recycling, celebrating earth day, actively petitioning the city council to embrace modern recycling, a champion for ecological conservation. Then, suddenly, she discovers from a big news report that the *oil* industry was actually behind the vast recycling propaganda, that less than 10% of plastic bottles actually ever get recycled; that it was in fact all a big scam to allow businesses to continue selling millions of plastic bottles while allowing consumers to buy convenient parcels of fizzy drinks while assuaging their cognitive dissonance. She was never a champion of good, she was a tool of the vast corporations, her work helped them sell this massive deception and destroy the world's ecology. For *decades*. How might she be feeling? Her identity is stripped away. Everything she believed was a lie. What does she do now, where does she go from here?

In another example (also inspired by real events), an archaeologist discovers traces of tobacco on the fibers of an Egyptian mummy—which defies all accepted explanations. Her career is destroyed, as colleagues claim negligence or contaminated samples. She can either give up her research and fall in line, or combat the establishment and *prove* that Egyptians had already established a trade route with the Americas in 1213 BC. In the end, she takes samples from the intestinal tissue from deep inside the Egyptian Pharaoh Ramses the Great, rather than the external layers of skin and cloth, and discovers traces of cannabis, coca and tobacco, laid down in his body "like rings on a tree."

Once you know these formulas, you'll see them everywhere. Netflix is useful because the craft is so obvious; almost cheesy, but always well done. In *Rim of the World*, a band of misfits team up to save the world. When they finally reach their goal, delivering a vital key to a bastion of resistance, their contact is already dead. "It's over guys. Let's be honest, who do we think we are? A nerd, a criminal, an orphan… we've failed, it's over." They almost separate, disbanding the group because the objective is gone; but then come together again: the journey forged their friendship. The objective was the purpose, but now they stay together because they want to. They're resigned to die together, but then they accidentally make contact with an adult and tell them they have the key.

"What do we need to get it to work?"

"*Nothing*. There's nothing you can do. I'm sorry, it's over. There's nothing you kids can do against this thing. Now get out of there immediately."

The main character, the one with the most growth and progress, says simply, "No." He will no longer allow other people's limits to dictate what he's capable of.

"What did you say Son?"

"I said *no*. I made a promise and I won't let anything stop me. So I'm going to keep trying. We didn't come all this way to give up now. We're done being told what we can and can't do."

In order to reach the climax of your story's conflict, figure out what absolute forces, rules or societal expectations your protagonist needs to refuse or transgress. As Oscar Wilde writes, "Disobedience, in the eyes of anyone who has read history, is man's original virtue."

Queen's Gambit: Dead Queens

There are hundreds of TV shows or movies I could include as case studies in this book, but I've chosen something recent that illustrates a few major points. If you haven't seen *The Queen's Gambit* yet, starring Anya Taylor-Joy and released to Netflix in 2020, you might want to skip the spoilers in this section.

Beth Harmon is a young orphan who becomes a competitive chess player. She learns to play chess, and beats everyone, except the one best player in the world: a soviet grandmaster. She needs to represent freedom and democracy, against Communism. But along the way, she's used drugs and alcohol to visualize the board; she's ruined her relationships and ended up alone; she let the love of her life get away. The quest has cost her everything.

So, the ending, is not just about her *beating* her opponent. Of course she's going to do that. The secret key is what happens when she arrives at the tournament, unprepared, and the change that occurs in the middle of the "final battle." They play half a game and pause for a break.

She's given up the drugs and alcohol and is still winning, but she isn't sure she can beat the big boss without them. Her love interest arrives. He and all her ex-lovers and friends from home have been working together for hours to map out all the possible moves, to provide her with winning solutions.

She wins, of course, but the messages are clear: love and friendships matter more than crutches like drugs and alcohol. It doesn't just depend on her skills, it depends on the relationships (because stories are about people, who feel and are moved.) If it was just a girl playing chess, and she won because she was the better player, there would be no magic. The magic is, not in the supportive friends, but in the touching and surprising moments, when she realizes that she has supportive friends and they show up for her in a big way. But of course, *that's not all.*

Even though they fed her all the possible plays, her opponent still doesn't do what he's supposed to do, and throws her a last-minute curveball. She takes a deep breath and looks within. For most of the series, we've seen that she's a natural, intuitive player, and at first resisted learning any rules or playbooks or strategy (sound familiar?).

She's overcome that limitation by studying, and it takes her much further than she could have gone alone. She lost to this opponent the first time around, when she only had intuition. Now she's a master: she knows the craft, she knows all the plays and the rules; but it's her unique gift, her intuitive magic, that is needed at the very end, because it's the thing that makes her unique enough to win and change the game in a surprising way.

BATTLE SCENES

We talked earlier about fight scenes, but here are a few more pointers for your *final* battle scene. The hero might enter the arena with a flimsy plan. They might have gained a valuable piece of knowledge or information. They might have been given a new weapon or power, or learned the villain's weakness. (Or maybe not... they might find that just by going into battle on faith, whatever they need materializes in the critical moment).

I mentioned earlier that smart characters don't go to death willingly, so this isn't entirely fatalistic or tragic. Something that can work really well is, the protagonist only faces the antagonist to *buy time*—because his allies are already actively pursuing a plan of action and someone just has to keep the villain busy.

This is a great way to kill characters as well, incidentally: one character stays back to fight off the horde; you can make it more powerful by drawing straws, having one character get the losing role, but having another character shove them out of the way at the last minute and sacrifice themselves. I'd probably put a major side-character death earlier, going into the dark night of the soul, but that will depend on the story.

THE INNER & OUTER TRANSFORMATION

Another way to increase the conflict, is having an inner and outer battle at the same time. Probably not for a book one, but for a series finale, the stakes all need to be bigger. So while the hero is battling the villain, all the forces of each side are engaged in a full-scale war. All the characters you love are fighting an overwhelming force, bravely, to buy time for the hero to achieve one critical piece of the plan: to take down the shields, to steal the protagonist's power source, to free the mind-enslaved drones. While they're working on it, the villain discovers them, and fighting ensues.

So now, we can see cut scenes of the actual battle, the blood and gore, the fallen heroes... everyone *waiting* with faith and hope that the hero comes through.

Throw in some banter or dialogue to break things up, doubts or fears, threats or goading. Often the villain will criticize the hero's weakness or futility, and they'll respond by standing up for themselves—probably realizing that they have grown and won't be pushed around anymore; or that the fight is worth giving everything. There's probably a point where they realize they may not survive this encounter, and commit anyway, ready to face their own demise. By accepting this ultimately fatal conclusion, in a sudden twist, the protagonist reaches into themselves and finds the motivation to persevere.

With resolve and tenacity (and maybe some unlikely allyship or external help), the hero unlocks access to their secret weapon, resolve or insight, and overpowers the villain.

The final battle scene often includes a "death of the hero" scene, where the hero, or an ally/romantic interest, sacrifices themselves, and appears to die—with a long, heavy, tragic pause of trepidation—but then is brought back to life in joy and celebration.

This doesn't have to be a literal "battle." It's just the last, final straw, the most dramatic part of your story. It's what forces the protagonist to make a realization, change or grow. And it's the place where the protagonist finally has a clear victory.

CONFLICT MULTIPLIERS

While the fighting is important, the *drama* is more important, so don't forget about those difficult moral decisions, the taut relationships between allies or relatives, feelings of trust or duty or loyalty or betrayal. The things that hurt the most aren't going to be the pinpricks of a thousand faceless monsters, they will be the look of disappointment in a trusting ally when they realize their faith has been misplaced.

With that said, here are a few more potential ideas you can sneak into your final battle scene. The ruling premise is that *all* of the building conflicts or tensions, which have been sublimated, can creep out and wreak havoc in the third act. Use all your gunpowder. This is your last stand.

- A small fight that becomes a big fight. Little nuisances and sniping escalate into big fighting.
- Tempers build until people start saying how they really feel; the real truth slips out, or a cutting remark that can't be taken back.
- Anger leads to backstabbing; publicly revealing or sharing a devastating secret that blows up someone's life.
- This reveal sparks a slow-burn sideplot story that erupts. (oh, are we all sharing everything now? Well then...)

- Arguments escalate to a real emergency, accident or crisis. You've got to shut down the fight somehow, keeping tensions high without anyone backing down.

You also need to pair conflict with heart-wrenchingly sweet scenes. Imagine you've got five minutes to make a life-changing impact on your reader, what are you going to hit them with? The conflict will make them lean in and hold their breath. The protagonist is at their lowest, and most vulnerable, so the emotions are going to hit hard. Awareness of these meaningful incidents (that they weren't ready to appreciate or notice earlier) may be precisely what gives the protagonist that extra little push towards action.

- A cautionary tale reveal that makes the protagonist reconsider life choices and recognize fatal flaw.
- The slight win that shows what's possible; allowing a side character to get what they want.
- A meaningful memento of happy times, reflection on where they come from, what they're letting go, what they want.
- A reminder of what's important.
- An almost-action that fails. It's disappointing, and they learn they are still blocked by fear and resistance.
- Wise words of encouragement from an unexpected source.

In a contemporary novel or romance, without a clear villain, the antagonist will most likely be the block or limit that's holding them back, and the story is about building the momentum to *finally* leap into action, chase dreams, and smash through their limitations with a bold public declaration or a completely vulnerable share.

THE INDEFINITE DECLARATION

You'll see this most often in romantic comedies, but it's the hushed silence as the protagonist waits for an answer to their story question. They've finally snapped, allowed themselves to believe, hope or wish, risked everything publicly, and are now completely vulnerable. The universe, the love interest, the whole world waits with bated breath for a response.

Rather than a quick affirmation and celebration, you can draw out this moment—the critical moment of truth—that will decide the protagonist's fate. Is it a yes, or a no?

First, you can trick the audience with an indefinite declaration that appears to be negative.

> "I love you, please, give me another chance!"
> *long pause*
> "I'm sorry, I can't…"
> *flicker of disappointment, gasps from the crowd*
> "…I can't live without you."
> *swelling music, tears fall.*

Or, the love interest sacrifices themself, are assumed lost. Stunned shock and trauma, sad music… and then the hero's hand comes back over the edge of a cliff, triumphant resurrection. *Slap before kiss.*

YOUR THIRD ACT

The Third Act will mostly cover the protagonist dealing with their loss or failure, feeling overwhelmed, getting a pep talk or finding a meaningful reason to persevere, formulating a new plan of action, and/or being forced into a final confrontation with the antagonist. They'll succeed, but they'll have to give something up (or at least be willing to). In the process, they are forever changed, and when they return to the ordinary world, everything is the same, but they are different.

Think about your final battle scene again. Make it bigger, bolder. Make the setting distinctive and amazing. Picture the hero or heroine faltering, before coming back to triumph. What were they hoping for? What didn't they expect? What do they need to learn, discover or realize before their victory?

Final battle notes:

- Must be extremely challenging
- Villain has unexpected power or weapon
- Focus on the small detail
- Break up with banter, threats, gloating
- Triple the stakes after the hero has failed
- Real personal risk and external risk (selflessness)
- Death realization (and overcome)
- Epic Arena
- Flashback reveals crucial insight
- Inner and outer transformation

WHEN IS IT OVER?

How do you know when you've reached the end? When the main story goal or quest has been completed. What if you don't have one of those? Well... that could be a problem. You may have lots of interesting "vignettes" or episodes or scenes. Some of them may not even include your main character; the one who grows and changes the most.

Side stories or scenes are okay as long as they deepen the characters, provide contextual information to help see the forces of conflict, help show the stakes and risks (what's happening, why it matters) or create forward momentum (introduce the next necessary detour in the story). But there should always be a main drive or goal—even if it's just survival—that will be achieved once the main threats are eliminated or successfully avoided. It's also possible if the whole story has been avoidance, the final conclusion will allow the character to suffer what they've been avoiding, gain inner strength from the experience, and rise to triumph.

- Main story goal has been reached
- Conflict avoided or resolved
- Avoidance is no longer an option
- Change through confrontation.
- Worst fears realized
- Stop when enemy/threat is defeated
- Cliffhanger vs. epilogue resolution (afterglow)
- Return to the ordinary
- How do they feel? How are they treated?

RETURN TO ORDINARY

After the final battle scene, there may be another chapter, or epilogue, to wrap things up, which may include a return to the ordinary (look how far we've come), or a personal reflection (recognition of the change).

The hero returns, changed. They've won, though it's probably temporary (this villain was defeated, but he or someone new will return). The safety is short-lived and bittersweet. The hero once again faces the small challenges or bullies at the beginning of the story, but they seem so trivial now. The hero is no longer lacking; they've grown in confidence, and now have a group of new friends, and a new hope for the future.

The antagonist has been defeated, but the protagonist is forever changed. The shard of glass has been removed, but they have scars.

What have they lost? What have they gained? What object(s) symbolize those things? Think about how they feel the next day: what are they thinking? How are they treated by others?

Loose Ends

A loose end is a nagging logistics issue about what happened or how it happened. It can be filled in quickly, because it doesn't have an emotional impact, so you can tie up several loose ends quickly in a few paragraphs. Don't confuse these with twists or reveals, which should have a dramatic, emotional impact that changes the plot events. Reveals or twists should be shown in real-time, within a scene, so you can witness the reaction; loose ends can be given casually, but *only after* the main story conflict is resolved; otherwise you're needlessly reducing tension and intrigue.

But you do want to address or confront the main story quest or goals that have been the main motivation for action throughout the book: if you get to the end and you've introduced a whole bunch of cool stuff but never got back to the main conflict you introduced (the main story is always the *biggest* conflict or sense of urgent need, with the biggest footprint or effect on your world at large) then readers may feel disappointed or even cheated.

If this is the first book of a series, you don't need to worry about wrapping everything up, and you can even end a book on a cliffhanger (the hero defeats the villain; the book ends). It's nice to have a final epilogue with a bit of a temporary conclusion, a new state of being, a return to the ordinary world. But you don't need to wrap up *all* the loose ends or unanswered questions; or they won't feel the need to keep reading and continue with the second book.

INEXTRICABLY BOUND

I started this section with a few definitions of *casting*, but there's a big one I intentionally left out. Casting out demons, or a spiritual exorcism. Earlier I raised the idea that the Plot Dot was a kind of mouse-trap for our fears and insecurities. But in this section, the specific circumstances of the abracadabra both ensnare and banish.

Written as prescribed by Serenus Sammonicus, into a receding triangle, by removing a letter with each line until only the A remains, it's calling for supernatural aide but also binding it to a certain path or course, funneling it towards your purpose, channeling the celestial energies into an endless scream of torment until it becomes a quiet, stable hum of power. Again, I don't mean *literal* demons here: in my view, magic is a ritual-based practice that engenders creative confidence. Asking for help and believing that your request has been heard.

An archaic epic poem from the 7th century mentions the goddess Adrasteia, which means *inescapable* (she was later renamed to Nemesis, and then Fate). Her servant was a wizard called *Damnameneus*: which is also one of the six magical formulas referred to as the Ephesia Grammata.

His name is often used as a magical amulet in the same form as Serenus' remedy: an inverted triangle. The charm served to invoke or call the supernatural power by using its full name, and then slowly withdrawing letters until it is contained.

A hexameter on a charmed amulet reads, "Oh Subdoer (Damnameneus) brutally subdue the unwilling ones with constraints." The magical word starts at the beginning of a longer formula; the famous *grammata* might have served as incipits designed to help sorcerers recall the first verse of each section, to support memory. Basically a magical cheatsheet or cliff note. These powerful words were inscribed on oral incantations and amulets to protect people and places; or more specifically, to prevent or subdue harming influences. That's why it's a curse word, a word of power. (Every time you're quietly muttering *damn* under your breath, you may be unconsciously summoning a demon to subdue your enemies).

The act of the disappearing name results in the flight of the demon, using the same vocabulary in expulsion rituals, *then I flee, immediately I withdraw*. These days, *damn* can be both a curse, and also an expression of wondrous awe. Something remarkable or transformative.

In other words, abracadabra is *both* an opening up, and also a binding. We have called forth the wonderful and dangerously destructive forces in the universe; now we channel and constrain them until the transformative, ritual sacrifice is complete and the metamorphosis is done. The story is about the change: but first we need to let the genie out of the bottle, and then stuff him back in again.

The first "Jack in the box" toys featured a wind-up devil, that pops up on a coiled spring when the lid is opened. An anonymous poem called *The Bird in the Cage* uses the expression in 1570, referring to swindlers who exchanged purchased goods for empty boxes.

So you can think of the abracadabra as the shock and scare when "pop goes the weasel," or the surprise and awe when the tomb is revealed to be empty (the hero survives imminent death). The more you crank the gears, the more you bind the demon, the bigger the effect when it escapes its container.

The Egyptian *Book of the Dead* also references Osiris in conjunction with eggs, hares and resurrection. So as a final "trick"—imagine that abracadabra is pulling a rabbit out of an empty hat. Figuratively, this is the same as a resurrected Osiris. Mummies must be torn asunder and *bound* so that they can become *restored*.

Conversely, you can picture abracadabra as a kind of suspended paralysis. Your protagonist can't win by resisting his demons. The demon is inside him, it's his fear or limitation, his refusal to face his shard of glass. It's a *fatal* flaw for a reason: it needs to be cut out. The wound must be opened and purged, before it can be healed. Your hero must descend into the darkest depths, and face immense pressure; they must step into the void and be destroyed. But then they will come back, newly formed.

As Victoria Erickson writes in *Age of Wonder*, "Transformation isn't sweet and bright. It's dark and murky, painful pushing. An unraveling of the untruths you've carried in your body. A practice in facing your own created demons. A complete uprooting before becoming."

But there's a more fitting metaphor for the final act of your story. The spell at the start of this chapter also mentions "papers tied up with so many knots." Knotting is an old form of magic. At the end of the third act, just leading up to the final battle scene, our protagonist is bound, restrained, stuck, pinned, with the terrifying consequences of their own responsibility.

Earlier, I compared your story to creating a messy tangle: a knot so tight it can't be undone, which seems impossible to unravel, leading to the question, *how are they going to get out of this?* In old silent movies, the most obvious way to depict this scene was literal: a woman tied to a train track, and being saved (untied) at the last minute. An older version replaces the train with a dragon in need of slaying, to save a bound princess.

According to Mary Hoffman, a series of exciting events is not a plot. Imagine, then, that a good plot is like a well-tied knot. A good knot can be untangled, preserving the string unharmed. A *great* knot can only be cut.

This is the reason drama is the heart of our story, and why abracadabra represents the personal transformation of our protagonist. For a story to matter, it has to reach deep: but to truly reach the core depth of your character, they must be cut open or torn apart. This is usually rooted in a deep desire, or love, that they cannot live without, and are willing to sacrifice for. It's this vulnerability that leaves them open to real change. According to Martha Nussbaum in *Therapy of Desire*,

"Love itself is a dangerous hole in the self, through which it is almost impossible that the world will not strike a painful and debilitating blow." Or, as Rumi puts it, "a wound is the place where the Light enters you."

The Magic Words
The formula for powerful story

- ✓ Razzle Dazzle (distract with action) 25% - WHAT
- ✓ Hocus Pocus (engage with fun weirdness) 50% - WHO
- ✓ Shazam (charge with energy) 75% - WHY
- ✓ Abracadabra (reveal the unexpected) 100% - WOW

Attention, distraction, expectation, fulfillment.

MEMORANDUM

- Tie the knot until it can't be cut
- Bind the character with impossible choices
- Move past expectation of reward
- Stretch the critical moment before the big reveal
- Terror and horror (surface danger vs. personal unmaking)
- Deeper depths lead to a satisfying resolution

The alchemist has vanished, and you're alone in the dark library. The books are torn and scattered. It feels like you've been standing here for a hundred years. Reaching to put the book back on the shelf, you feel someone watching you and see an eye through a keyhole, just below the shelf. You slide the key in, and a hidden door swings open. You hear laughter and chase a spectral figure up a spiral staircase until you reach the top of a crumbling tower, and see the moon shining over the ocean far below.

A bundle of wood is waiting for you. You light the pile with your candle, and the fire roars to life. That's when you realize, you're surrounded by mirrors, and the light is blinding. Your beacon lit, you see an echo further up the coast, and then another, much farther down the coastline. Your triumph turns to trepidation as you realize how much further you still have to go, and that this tower did not hold the treasure you were seeking. You spin as someone whispers your name. A light rain falls on your neck, and a subtle gleam shows the blade of an ancient sword embedded in the rock.

You have earned...

★ The Talisman of Diligence ★

Mastery is the application of wisdom.

You've earned your third totem! If you've finished your rough draft, you will feel a thrill... for awhile. You are beginning to see the lengths you still need to travel in order to achieve your vision. You can see the whole shape of your story, but it's still just a rough sketch. This is your dark night of the soul. The imagination, the discovery, may lessen at this point. The fun stuff is behind you, now begins the arduous process of excavation and refinement.

> "It is worth mentioning, for future reference, that the creative power which bubbles so pleasantly in the beginning a new book quiets down after a time, and one goes on more steadily. Doubts creep in. Then one becomes resigned. Determination not to give in, and the hope of an impending shape keep one at it more than anything." – *Virginia Woolf*

You're now armed with knowledge and experience. Paradoxically, rather than increasing your confidence, your new-found awareness may generate feelings of dissatisfaction or overwhelm. This is the point that many authors give up, after the first draft is finished, but the necessary revisions seem endless. Take a moment to celebrate your journey, and recognize that you've taken a large step towards mastery. If you *don't* feel inadequate, at this point, or unhappy with your current abilities, it means this challenge hasn't been big enough to force your growth. Progression requires us to push past our limits. The first rough draft is a necessary, partial step to help you move closer to a book you'll ultimately be proud of, but we both know you can do better.

"Sword and mind must be united. Technique by itself is insufficient, and spirit alone is not enough."
– *Yamada Jirokichi*

Over the next few chapters, I'm going to lay out some revision strategies and also help you clarify each section of your book, while addressing and purging weak writing, to make sure your story shines.

Sanctify your space: Get yourself something sharp. It doesn't have to be literal sword or fancy dagger, but symbolically this token should represent something that *cuts through* hesitation, doubt and fear, something that *confidently persists*. It could also be a reminder to take action now. I suggest a desk cactus or plant, an action figure or victorious statue, or a decorative quill pen. If you're a bit more morbid, like me, you might want a *memento mori*, like a skull or an hourglass timer.

Perfect

CUT THE FLUFF, KEEP THE MAGIC

If the last chapter stretched your patience, thanks for indulging me. I could have simply added the tips and writing strategies of what to include or avoid in your last act, without all the literary trivia. And the truth is, it would have been enough. But I wanted to share some of my passion, and I wanted to make you feel a sense of exhilaration and discovery. Even, maybe, some fear and discomfort.

I could have simply referenced the story of Icarus, ignoring his father's warnings and flying too close to the sun. Rather than staying safely in the comfortable, prescribed middle—the medium distance that wouldn't put too much stress on the artificial constraints of his manufactured wings, Icarus reached for more: flying too high, before drowning in the depths of the sea. On its own, the story is a parable about the dangers of excess. But the *real* emotional core of the story, isn't Icarus at all, it's his father Daedalus, the skilled artist and craftsman, who had to stay behind to pick up the broken pieces of his fallen son.

In *The Icarus Deception*, Seth Godin writes,

> "We tend to forget that Icarus was also warned not to fly too low, because seawater would ruin the lift in his wings. Flying too low is even more dangerous than flying too high, because it feels deceptively safe."

I pushed you hard and deep, to go beyond the simple, structural level of your story, and reach for something more. More than you were capable of or comfortable with, perhaps. And while you can absolutely rely on the cheatsheets and checklists to help give your narrative wings structure, to lift your story higher, when the first draft is done—you'll probably be sifting through the failed wreckage. If Icarus is the hopeful fool who cared too much, Daedalus is the tinkering inventor who tries again and again to fix his mistakes.

In the first section of this book, we focused on writing books readers love: picking a direction so we wouldn't spin in circles. Then we committed to writing our rough draft. With luck, your creative attempts will have tempted the muse, and you'll have felt the wings of your writing soar with hidden magic. You may have breathlessly skipped over the waters of your imagination, daring the dark dangers below.

But just like our narrative drama, the stakes and challenges increase as we progress in skill and ability. We've now reached the Third Act of our Journey, the *final polish*. For thematic purposes, our task mirrors this book's tagline: cut the fluff, keep the magic.

If the previous section was fun and games, this part is painful transformation. The first pass may have felt organic and magical.

We allowed it to be messy and untamed, the wild Dionysian impulse towards reckless discovery. We were *foolish*, in that we were discovering fresh insights and stumbling through uncharted territory. It may have been more art than craft.

But now we need to turn to Apollo: the rational, organizing impulses of the logical brain. This work may not feel as good, which is why those "literary dilettantes" (who cultivate an area of interest, without real commitment or knowledge) may balk against the restrictive practices I'm about to suggest.

Some of this section might seem banal or pedantic. It's hard to make editing, revisions and grammar fun and sexy. But I warned you at the beginning that improving your craft wouldn't feel magical all the time. An amateur will love to watch the sparkles of inspiration brighten their page like fireflies; an expert might tear off their wings to see how they work. But a magician, one who has mastered the craft enough to summon his own deep magic, will capture them in a jar and allow their light to shine.

Some of this will feel like work. Be careful you don't run back to what's comfortable, or spiral out looking for simple or easy answers. Your addiction to *new* may prevent you from *mastery*.

> "Without ambition one starts nothing. Without work one finishes nothing. The prize will not be sent to you. You have to win it." – *Emerson, 1841*

A BEACHED WHALE

When I get migraines, my fingers barely hit the right keys and I end up with alphabet soup. Spellcheck sometimes guesses the closest accurate word somehow (amazing) but there are definitely sections of my writing that have stubborn typos and mistakes.

And although I'm usually a very careful editor, after you've been through your own manuscript a few dozen times, your brain can play tricks on you, assuming the letters on the page match what you have in your brain. I also send out emails when I'm sleep deprived—waiting until exhaustion lowers my inhibitions about contacting over 50,000 people at the same time —and my messages inevitably have a mistake or two.

My messiest, most inspired and thoughtful emails often get a powerful emotional response, because of the content. Here's some recent feedback:

> "I've subscribed to hundreds of newsletters over the years, only high quality stuff, but I've never enjoyed reading anything more than I enjoy reading what you write. Seriously, your artistry, generosity, outlook and style are beyond everything else I've seen. And I always learn something of practical value each time I read something from you!"

I'm not sharing this to brag, but to point out one important thing: you can get away with a lot, as long as you provide something of practical value. The writing and style and content can *enhance* the value, but they don't generate it.

Likewise, I would argue, a handful of typos don't destroy the value of a work, because the value isn't about the letters or the spelling. Most readers can overlook weaknesses in favor of strengths, as long as they are willing to be charmed and get what they needed from the content.

But there will always be a few people who can *only* see the errors, and use it as proof to discount or discredit everything else I say. And that's to be expected: people associate good spelling with good writing, even they really aren't the same at all. It's possible to be a great writer and a bad speller. Editing is important and we will focus on some strategies to make sure our manuscript is 100% clean: but it's not the *only* thing, and certainly not the most important thing.

In fact, when you've made it to the end of your first rough draft, you may feel elated and excited – you might start thinking about hiring an editor, getting a cover designed, and look into publishing. In my experience, however, a first rough draft is, at best, about half as good as it needs to be, and *editing* won't fix the real problems that lurk not so subtly beneath the surface. It might seem more like a bloated, beached whale, stubbornly impossible to move, flooding the beach with a foul stench and ruining the sandy experience for everyone.

If you follow the strategies, rules and guidelines we explored earlier, you will end up with a more powerful, more meaningful story, regardless of the words you use—which is why so far I've been very light about pragmatics like writing style or sentence structure. While other guides focus on the writing parts way too early, without touching on all the deep magic stuff, we've saved it to the end, because the feeling, the power of the story, must come first.

If you've made it this far, even if you feel like your story is incredible, it's still probably a messy, first rough draft. Your story might be brilliant. It might be genius. But remember, the magic happens in the reader. It pierced *your* heart, but will your words communicate and transfer that same emotional impact to your readers?

Editing, revising and proofreading are about making sure your story holds power even when you're not there to conduct the ceremony. It's the difference between a rite and a ritual: you aren't there to explain to readers what happens, or say, "this part is really powerful! Read it again and you'll get it!"

Readers must discover the scene or your ritual for themselves, the magic must be replicated, it's *their* process of discovery that matters. You'll never be able to experience your story the right way again, because you know what happens. So it's hard to see exactly how readers will respond to it.

It can be tempting here to give up and seek help, guidance or feedback. I'll talk about working with an editor later, but the truth is you're probably not ready for that yet. Often the first draft simply allows you to *see* the whole story; when you go through it again you may realize it's not actually all down on paper yet. But the task can seem gargantuan; there's so much that can be improved, what do you even start with?

It's easy to fix typos, punctuation or clunky sentences, but that won't help with the actual core issues. Not even an amazing developmental editor can fix all of this for you: they will point out the problems and suggest fixes, but you may need to do serious revisions before it's even ready for a final polish. Also, paying for editing will not make your book more commercial, if readers don't want to read it.

I've edited many dozens of books and novels, and consulted on nearly a hundred more. In my experience, most manuscripts need the *same* things tweaked, regardless of the genre, and there's an order and a process for what needs to happen first. So this final section will include a detailed breakdown of the editing process, in manageable chunks, in the order they occur. At the end, I'll give you some tips (and warnings) about working with a professional editor.

MY 4-STEP REVISION PROCESS

What follows is a guided revision process to help you move from rough draft to final polish. The main thing I'd like to stress here is that, we aren't just revising or polishing or proofing at this point. We'll still be doing significant revisions and rewriting. In my experience, while the "magic" might be present in the humming first draft, the "power" comes in revisions, when you cut and hone and channel; taking the magic that's there are supercharging it.

This part can feel brutal: if your manuscript is your baby, we'll be tearing it apart and moving things around. But this is surgery, meant to heal defects, so your creation can live its best life.

"When your story is ready for rewrite, cut it to the bone. Get rid of every ounce of excess fat. This is going to hurt; revising a story down to the bare essentials is always a little like murdering children, but it must be done." – *Stephen King*

We'll be focused on fixing specific issues, in an order that I think makes the most sense, from the happenings, to the motivations and descriptions, before finally moving on to the actual typos and mistakes.

In the first draft, we just try to put down *what* happens, in the most impactful way. In the second draft we focus on *why* it happens (character motivation). In the third draft we focus on *how* it happens (what it looks like, and stoking the emotional angst). All of that needs to happen before we even begin to worry about the actual words.

WHAT. After I finish a first rough draft, I'll go back and fill in any gaps or fix narrative problems, focusing on the events or incidents. Getting things in the right order so they make sense, so readers can read through the book without feeling confused or disoriented. The right stuff needs to happen, in the right order, or else more polishing is useless. I also want to make the "right stuff" interesting by adding as much conflict and tension as possible.

WHY. Once I'm pretty sure everything is in the right place, I'll pay attention to the motivations: why does this happen, why are characters doing these things? I'll need to create backstory, plant clues, establish facts. If they need a pair of scissors in the last chapter, I'll make sure to add one into the right scene earlier so it doesn't just appear. I'll make sure everything makes sense and is believable.

HOW. In the third stage, I'll look at how things actually look, and describe the setting, character movements, clothes and scenery. I want to make sure readers can picture it clearly. I want to avoid reference points ("small items") and change them to real descriptions ("a pot of tea, spools of thread and an orange crayon). I'll make sure I'm using expressions and postures, without overdoing or repeating any too often.

272

Through that process, I'm also fixing any typos or mistakes I find, but I'm not actively seeking them out and I won't worry too much about word choice or sentence structure. This is actually a 3-step *revision* process followed by a final, 4th step, which includes copy editing and proofreading. To keep our magical theme, I've structured the last four chapters like this:

- Phenomenon
- Provocation
- Elucidation
- Clarification

While the first sections were about learning incantations and casting spells, this one is about taking your magic public. We've prepared, we've practiced, but only in private. This final stage is about *performance*, not just writing secretly in the sheltered comfort of your own home, but getting up on stage, preparing to share your art with the world. And while the three inductive stages have been, *prepare, produce* and *perfect*, this isn't actually about making your manuscript flawless. We're merely trying to get it *done*, using the 11th century Latin perfectus: from "per" meaning to finish or complete, and "facere" meaning to make, or to do.

9

PHENOMENON

1st Revision: Happenings (What)

Most authors think the distance between a rough draft and a final proof is just a few rounds of editing or proofreading, but it's so much more. You've got your vision out on to the page, but revising it into something *really good* may be frustrating without a guide or roadmap. But even if the writing is beautiful and eloquent, and even if you fix all the typos and mistakes, it still doesn't mean your story is ready to publish or that readers will love it.

Often, once the rosy glow of accomplishments fades and you're in your tenth straight week of revisions, you can feel like you're drowning in mud. It is difficult to edit your own book, especially since so few guides offer a strategic plan for powerful revisions.

You might increasingly see the large gap between what you thought was nearly finished and the huge amount of work that still needs to be done before you publish.

At some point, it might be tempting to just hand it all over to an editor to fix it for you; but that's also something I wouldn't recommend. There's an absolute dearth of qualified editors who actually understand the highest level of craft, and even if you find someone efficient and competent to do a developmental critique of your manuscript, you'll be paying them to point out flaws and structural issues, not rewrite your book for you.

There's advice out there that cautions you to put your manuscript in a drawer for a month and forget about it, so you can come back to it with new eyes. That's not something I recommend, although I do suggest taking a break and celebrating your success before diving back in. Creative burnout is common at this stage for a few reasons. You might be telling everyone you *finished your book* and so now they're going to keep nagging you about when they can buy a copy.

Every time I finish my rough draft, I think I'm *almost done* and underestimate the time it's going to take to edit. A good ballpark would be, it'll take you as long to revise as it did to write the rough draft. In actuality, it sometimes takes me three times as long. That's because there are often several passes. It's rare that you can just go through and fix mistakes and typos and it'll be ready to publish.

The main thing I want to communicate here in this section, is that *nobody else* can do the brunt of the work for you, and also that the words on the page don't matter all that much.

I like to use the image of polishing a pane of glass: the scene, the story, outside the window, is the most important thing. Editing and proofing is important, because you need to be able to see through it. Small smudges will distract and cause readers to focus on the glass, not the picture behind it.

But just because the glass is *clean*, doesn't mean the view is interesting enough to hold the attention. It might not be, in which case I'll ignore that clean pane of glass and stare at the walls instead.

At my parents' home in Oregon, we watch the fat squirrels hang like secret agents from the bird feeder to steal their seeds; we toss peanuts and if they're too slow or clueless, the bluejays swoop down to steal their treats, often cramming two or three in their beaks before feathering off again. Sometimes one of the neighbor's cats swings by to check out the action, and hides predatorily in the tall grass by the birdfeeder. If there is something exciting to watch, we don't see the smudges on the glass. If there is nothing exciting to watch, we don't look out the window.

THE EDITING PROCESS

Some people loathe revision, but while it can be frustrating, it's also where the magic happens. I tend to do as many as seven passes of revision, and the *really good* stuff only happens late, after my story is already pretty much done, when it's fine, when it's good, then you can make it better.

While it's true, like we discussed earlier, that some of the your genius "aha" moments might have come in the flurry of creative abandonment, picture those like priceless jewels strewn into the mud. They can enhance an already engaging story, but alone they will be lost or devalued. If I wanted to extend this jewelry metaphor, it would look something like this:

First, we select the most precious stones.
Second, we cut the angles so they refract the best light.

Third, we set them in a gold or silver setting.

Fourth, we polish the ring and put it in a display box.

The *craft* of cutting and setting allow the best viewing of the beautiful gemstone. The *art* of creating a pretty setting increases the value by allowing it to be held, used and adored. The *magic* of the final piece is transformed through all the hard work it took to get there.

Sometimes, however, the things you love the most don't actually fit in your story, and it would be a mistake to leave them in. Flaws or blemishes, for example, that make the stone unique and give it character, may also reduce its value. They can even be a distraction, which is why we have the common writing advice *Kill Your Darlings*.

This is one of the reasons revisions can be so traumatic. You have all this great material, scenes and world-building, excellent characters and it's all *good* but not all of it *matters*. It can be difficult to see the forest for the trees, which is why we're going to focus on the forest first.

SURVEY THE LANDSCAPE

You've successfully made it out of the woods and through again, but it was probably a messy process. You probably took a lot of wrong turns, got half-eaten by mosquitoes (annoying doubts and insecurities), were stalked by wolves (gripping fears of obscurity), and spent a few hard nights on the ground crying yourself to sleep. The journey was worth it, to you, but will readers suffer that much discomfort for the journey?

Your job this time through is to map the clearest and easiest way through the forest, noting the important bits, so that readers won't get stuck, scared or bored. This time, you're a guide, not an explorer.

Imagine you're standing on a hill looking out over a wide valley full of sweeping pine trees. You know that once you go in, you'll lose your sense of direction in the mists. You won't be able to see the sun or the mountains to get your bearings. It won't be an unpleasant journey, as long as you know where you're going and feel confident that you'll get there. But when night falls, if doubt creeps in, you might start getting anxious.

So the first step is to look out for the landmarks: the places you'll stop to make camp, the phenomenon you can actually observe, *the happenings*. The causes or explanations don't matter yet; you can fill your guests in about those around a campfire, as long as everyone is comfortable and enjoying the trip.

FIRST PASS REVISIONS (What)

The easiest way to start, is to take a break from your manuscript and try to map out your story in a journal, or on a whiteboard. I'll often keep a section in the manucript I'm working on called notes or scenes. Whenever I get stuck, I'll make a simple bullet-point list of *what happens*. The trick is, to see how each incident or event triggers the next. We'll be troubleshooting your story, to make sure it flows and makes sense; while removing obvious plot holes or logical inconsistencies.

Instead of a casual walk through the forest, let's say you're building an emergency escape route. Let's say the ground is on fire, the air is full of blinding smoke and sparks and flame.

You need to create a system of rope bridges and wires, hundreds of feet in the air, that cuts through the whole forest and stretches from tree to tree. Which trees are necessary? Which ones don't get connected? Keep in mind, while traversing this new pathway, you can still *see* other trees; and on a clear day the view might be worth the trip, but it's the active, old-growth trees holding it all together that make the journey possible.

Sometimes I'll have to make a checklist for each section, each act, or even each chapter, if I'm really stuck. I often get flummoxed by the specific order of the events or reveals.

Where does this need to go so that it will create the most drama and conflict? Who knew this information, when did they find out, why haven't they acted on it yet? In other words, we'll be engaging in the Old English practice of *werifesteria*: to wander lovingly through the forest in search of mystery.

In my first revision, after getting to the end and taking a few days off, I'll search for anything that isn't explained or doesn't make sense. I'll fix any typos or small issues I see – often my first draft is riddled with spelling or punctuation issues – but mostly, I'm trying to experience the story as an inexperienced reader would. I'll write paragraph-long notes in the side of my document, even full scenes, which I'll need to go back through later and add into the main material. I'll comment on anything that something doesn't belong, that it needs to be moved, or that it's already been said elsewhere. I'll raise questions about missing information, flag lack of conflict or tension, brainstorm additional content.

If we're still using the rope-bridge metaphor, I might be cautiously testing my wires to make sure the trees can hold my weight without breaking. I might be measuring the distances to make sure they're uniform.

My chapters tend to be around 4,000 words, with a scene break in the middle. There are no hard and fast rules for chapter length, but remember, a scene break or chapter break marks when *something has happened.* Long chapters can be an indication of a slow plot, or failure to announce key events. Thrillers will often have shorter chapters or simple vignettes of a few pages, because, of course, *less is more* and tension comes from a lack of information, not the abundance of it.

What's happening?
- Is it interesting?
- Is it plausible?
- Does it make sense?
- Is it necessary?

You can fix a boring scene with the scene checklist I shared earlier, and you can avoid some of the biggest mistakes if you read through my list of 25 signs of amateur writing. If you don't want to cut a scene, then you need to find a way to add conflict and drama. *Any scene* is okay as long as something changes or happens at the end, so find a way to get there. A nice, pleasant, otherwise boring scene can be brilliant if it ends with a shocking twist or a callous remark. Nice, sweet feelings will make the insult cut deeper because it's unexpected.

STORY QUESTIONS

In the first pass of revisions, you'll be mapping the terrain, which means you may discover new plot holes for the first time. That's fine, and we'll discuss those in more detail in the next chapter. It's enough here to flag them and keep them in mind.

The story questions are what will build suspense and intrigue. The character's progress through the story will depend on a pressing need to know what is happening and reacting to events while searching for answers. This will keep the momentum and pacing tight, so it's not *just* about what is happening, it's also about knowledge gaps that must be filled in later on, at the best moment.

The protagonist, and your readers, don't know exactly why all these things are happening yet. It's probable there's a bunch of motivation and backstory that needs to be added, but that can't be done until we recognize that they're missing. So think of this as more of a land survey. You'll probably need to write some new scenes or content to develop the story you already have. There will also be a lot of resource management: shuffling or relocating crucial passages where they're needed most, and then building up urgency by having characters feel anxious or uncertain.

They should speculate on the fears and dangers occasionally, to make sure readers follow their most pressing concerns. How will I do this, what if this happens, what's the worst that could happen (and it should be bad). So while it's mostly about the *phenomenon* of what's actually happening, it's also about the emotional responses triggered by those events. The nagging lack of knowledge, and the quest for answers, should drive a significant portion of your story.

Drama is the unfolding of unresolved conflict; the events in themselves are critical, but they should be unexpected and resist easy attempts at explanation. If they figure out one thing, it raises more questions; pursuit of resolution raises more conflict or challenges. Thwart every attempt, but in a surprising way.

There should be a sense of wonder and mystery, to fuel doubt and insecurity. Even if there is no faceless antagonist with an agenda out to stop them from uncovering his dastardly plans, a vague feeling of *something is amiss* should prevail.

In my landscaping example, imagine the forest is covered by a thin mist that obscures the view. Hikers can see the details, but not the horizon. At the top of the hill, once they've completed the journey, they can look back and be amazed at the scope of the realm, and appreciate the scenery—noticing the major landmarks that they passed along the way.

Don't have characters ask leading questions or guess the surprise you're going to reveal much later. It won't be a twist or reveal unless the answer is *different* from the easy and predictable; not something the character has already wondered about. Be careful to scrub hints, mentions or explanations that come too early.

While these happenings should be events or incidents, that doesn't mean it's all fight scenes and bad guys. The slow, moody chapters where your characters reveal vulnerabilities matter also. They can't be the whole thing – something real must change in every chapter that allows the plot to move forward – but adding in different kinds of conflict to every scene will make your book much more satisfying and keep readers hooked.

The main point here is to focus on showing the conflict unfold in a real scene, something tangible readers can watch play out, that triggers the next sequence of events. The tenuous rope bridge that stretches the misty gap just enough to arrive at the next wooden platform.

SHOW DON'T TELL

It's easy in the first draft to slip into a narration or plot summary rather than active scene; I'm sure you've heard the ubiquitous advice to *show not tell* but you'll rarely be given exact support to help you identify your telling or strategies on how to show it instead, so let's address that here.

Why does it matter? It's the difference between witnessing a car crash and having someone tell you they saw one. It's reportive narration instead of engaging experience. It matters, because if someone is describing or telling you how it all went down, you know the action is concluded and the stakes aren't real. If they're a very good story-teller, they might dramatize the event, and you'll be begging to know *what happened next*, but it's less impactful to be told, rather than held spellbound, in rapturous captivation.

Enthrallment takes active participation: some people say you can't put someone under hypnosis who isn't already open to it. The most egregious examples of telling, are revealing critical story details or twists in a casual offhand remark. That's a book-to-wall-flinging offense. But it's often used by amateur writers to explain what's happening so readers can appreciate the scene or story, in the form of a ten-page history dump before we get into the action. In the most harmless usage, which we'll talk about later, it's telling readers information that they can't *see* in their mind's eye.

> She laughed nervously.
> *I know that she's nervous, but I can't see it.*
> She laughed but the humor didn't reach her eyes, and she scratched the back of her hand nervously.

Adverbs are fine (more on that later) but they are a quick fix that communicates information, not scene description. Too much and it's a blank screen without any visuals.

Another common problem is, accidentally revealing the action before it happens. Before you let readers see the scene, you explain to them who the characters are, why they feel this way, what happened between them six years ago, and why they have this or that object with them.

But then you're saying the same thing twice; you've already told readers the details, and now the scene is just playing out what you've already explained. Repetition is one of my pet peeves, in all forms, so I will check carefully to make sure I'm not sharing information that readers already know.

> She was so nervous, she didn't hear him come in.
> "I'm home!" he shouted.
> "Oh, sorry," she said, scratching the back of her hand. "I didn't hear you come in."

This is telling *and* showing. Every scene needs something new, surprising, and you take all the power out of the scene by telling them what happens first.

Maybe it's because you know that the scene is weak or unclear: it doesn't make sense without the added information. And that's *fine*, for now. First, you go back and "fix" it by cramming the information in right before it's needed. But that comes across as heavy-handed or clunky. You really need to go back several chapters or pages earlier, and find a more suitable place to drop that information, where it's not immediately obvious why or how it will matter. If it appears when it is not relevant, it can show up when it's needed, without seeming like a clumsy bandaid.

The more tense or conflicted a scene, the less characters will suddenly remember small details or anecdotes or memories about stuff; nor will they spontaneously appreciate their surroundings or experiences, unless it has a surprising novelty factor. If the character wouldn't think it, then the author is feeding readers information directly, even if it doesn't make sense in context. Heavy-handed just means, you're being too obvious with your craft and readers can see you, pulling the strings behind the curtain.

That said, of course the writing style will depend on the genre. Some books are nearly all narration, and the strong narrative voice adds commentary throughout the story events. Shakespeare famously repeated himself, saying the same thing in several different ways, to make sure his mixed audience would get all of his innuendos or crafty metaphors. I wouldn't recommend that these days, unless you're making up your own words, which I also wouldn't advise. But if your narrative voice hasn't introduced themselves formerly to the reader as a literary device or integral character, or explained how they are involved in this particular story, be wary about chiming in to steer the reader's experience.

CAPTIVATING PERFORMANCE

It's the difference between a dress rehearsal and a final performance: in practice, the actors have a script and run through lines, the director narrates out loud or refers to staging cues based on where the sets will be positioned, when they're finished.

But with a live audience, the entire show must be performed without scripts. Actors have memorized their lines, are in costume, interacting with the props, moving with intention and dramatic purpose.

Show Don't Tell is an easy shorthand for one of the biggest writing mistakes an author can make: getting so involved in the story, that the narration interrupts the action. It's hard to teach this clearly without showing exactly how to do it with writing examples, but I actually came up with three tricks recently to identify and remove "telling" from your writing.

#1: Who is saying this? With the words on the page, identify the passages where the *author* is speaking directly to readers; the narrator is the one talking. In the description, for example, there may be some extra adjectives thrown in:

Then she grabbed her cool, pretty coat.

Who thinks it's pretty, the character? Or the narrator? Especially if it's an action scene, be careful about interrupting the story, to "break the fourth wall" and talk directly to readers. You need to erase yourself from the scene and let the story do the work. This applies to your actors or characters as well. It should feel like readers are invisible voyeurs. If actors break character and present supplementary material (crucial to the story but irrelevant to the current scene action), it reveals that they are aware of an audience and spoils the effect.

New information, changes, and reveals, need to happen within the context of the action, within the scene, so that your characters can react and respond organically. The more tense the scene, the more annoying it will be if you step in to explain things. It's like watching a movie with someone who constantly interrupts or says, "this is the good part" or "did you notice how he stashed the murder weapon behind the clock, that's important later."

#2: What are your characters doing? Anytime you have information – context, backstory, a quick aside or postscript – find a way to remove direct telling and put it into the actual scene through dialogue or action. Otherwise, the narrator is having a discussion with readers directly and the characters are frozen in time, waiting for the narrator to catch up. Details that appear alongside the experience of the phenomena, the dramatic unfolding of the scene, exist outside of time. When they appear, it means your characters are just standing there, waiting until the story is ready for them to move again... which means *nothing is happening*. Sometimes you can fix it by including a bit of action, especially character movement, a physical task that keeps them occupied and allows readers to picture something, while their minds are otherwise engaged. If you *need* them to have a flashback or memory or think through the story questions, do it in a slow scene with a monotonous task, like keeping guard or doing the dishes. But rarely are a character's stationary, internal musings the significant material in a given scene.

Telling happens outside the story. You've bypassed the characters and whispered something to the audience, so it can't impact the story or plot directly. It only affects the readers' experience or understanding of the plot.

Sometimes this can create suspense: readers know it first, which creates anxiety (assuming the information will cause conflict or drama). They're waiting for the shoe to drop, waiting for characters to discover it, and for the ensuing fallout. Make sure this scene happens and is satisfying (don't sweep it under the rug later or make it a non-issue by de-escalating conflict).

However, giving too much information can also remove the surprise or conflict altogether. It might feel flat. Readers and characters should usually discover the same thing at the same time. When the character responds separately later, to something we already knew, it can feel forced, melodramatic or anti-climactic.

Dramatic story is the unfolding, unresolved conflict that happens to your characters: the emotional experience of unexplained phenomena. Remember, the most important things come last; and the most impactful information needs to be earned, not learned.

Small details, that are merely information to stop readers from asking critical questions—like *wait* where did she get shoes from, she lost hers after the dance three chapters ago—those can be told. You can sneak in trivial details quickly, in a sentence when needed. But any *dramatic* details, that have an emotional impact and will affect the characters' actions, should be gift-wrapped and delivered with solemn reverence.

#3: What does this look like? If this was on TV, with a camera and a screen, what would you be watching? A character standing there thinking about his past, motionless, frozen in time while a narrator sets the scene? At least give them something to do, to keep their hands busy.

Also, before you have a character's mind spontaneously churn up a random cerebral fixation, give them a *trigger* — a reason to recall that specific childhood memory or whatever. We tend to keep our traumas hidden, except in times of great stress. So even if a trigger prods repressed anxiety, the more important the happening, the more your character will resist it, especially in the beginning. Show the resistance, before the reveal.

Avoid starting your story, or including scenes, where your character just sits down and reflects over all the important things that happened in their life, breaking down in tears over what they lost during The Event years ago.

Avoid narrating extra context that's not in that scene, not on the camera, not in the room. "Little did little Tommy know, that in just a few short years, he'd be leading the rebel alien army..."

Why would I care at *all* about watching little Tommy's childhood saga, if I know there are aliens coming? You can't ask readers to "see" two scenes happening at once, and we will always want to watch the more interesting one. You're basically saying, I know this childhood stuff is boring but don't worry, it'll make sense later when we get to the good stuff. In a good short preface, ending with that sentence could be a strong hook, but once you've mentioned aliens, every scene without aliens will feel dull. The solution is to start closer to the real story sooner, and make all the childhood backstory reveals come out later, near the height of dramatic conflict.

Be careful of showing *and* telling, because this is redundant. When the narrator tells or explains something new to readers, and characters are then surprised by it, reacting to the thing, it weakens intrigue; and characters don't usually chronicle their lives out loud.

If you have to do this, show what happens first, then tell if you have to fill something in with details. But don't tell first and then show, otherwise the characters are just repeating what readers already know.

Picture it like a gunshot. The gun goes off, bang. A sharp, singular event. When you have to add more, start with the action, then fit in descriptive details or backstory, if it's relevant; but keep in mind it will slow down an action scene, so limit it to a few sentences, not a full flashback or time jump.

> He pulled the trigger. The bullet ripped like an explosion through the wood, sending up a shower of splinters.

> "Oh no!" she shouted as the gun fired, diving under cover and covering her ears.

> "He's got a gun!" someone shouted across the room. The shooter, had, in fact, stolen the gun from his father's locked cabinet after dosing him with a strong sedative. It wasn't hard to guess the password, it was his mother's birthday. Today. Six months after she'd passed.

If it all went *before* the event or phenomena, we won't be surprised to watch the event unfold, because there would be no intrigue: we saw it coming, we know what happened and why; it doesn't raise any new questions or suspense about what's coming next.

Be careful to avoid common phrases that can seem stale or empty. *What does it look like,* to dance like nobody is watching? Show what you can see, not what you can't see. It's the difference between reaching into your analytical mind's drawer of idioms and expressions, and using your imagination to visualize something fresh and new.

Be especially careful every time you comment on a character's thoughts, feelings, mood or state of being. If someone notices that someone else is distracted, *what do they see* that leads them to that conclusion? If it's all internal, readers can't picture the scene, and picturing the scene is everything.

I DON'T REALLY CARE, DO YOU?

Technically, *show don't tell* should come later when we talk about scene description. But this first pass is really just about taking the story you have and moving things around; getting rid of the information dumps or filling in plot holes. It's possible you have *all the right* information and *none of the* dramatic story-telling. It's also possible you've written a plot summary, an overview or description, without actually writing any scenes at all.

The biggest danger here is that narration creates distance between your readers and your characters. Everything is 2nd hand reporting. None of it has the immediacy, the conflicts, the stakes. Pretty words are fine for a poem, but you can't *ask* readers for their extended attention if they don't care about what's happening. Remember, the secret of magic is the unknown. If they can see your cards, they'll raise or fold, with no risk or uncertainty, which takes all the pleasure out of the game: it's just a mechanical, boring transaction.

Your first draft might only be the *outline* of a novel: you've told yourself what happens, but it isn't actually written yet. Later we'll talk about description and scene building, but at this point it's important to learn how to recognize the difference between telling and showing so that on your first readthrough, you can mark sections that need to be removed, rewritten, or integrated into the story.

The main thing to keep in mind here is that a series of scenes or information is emotionally unsatisfying. It has no power, because there's no resistance. Energy is caused by escalating conflict and unresolved tension. String the bow and draw it taut.

- Force your characters into impossible situations, wrought with conflict
- Have them dig themselves deeper, refusing to give up or change their ideals or desires. Their resistance creates tension.
- Force them to finally have to sacrifice it all anyway, and in *that* revelation, the bow is released with a satisfying resonance, the arrow pierces the target.

KILL YOUR DARLINGS

My uncle is an eco-friendly logger. Rather than bringing in heavy machines to clear a forest, he's called in with his horse and sled to cut down *one* tree at a time without damaging the surrounding forest. He does this to keep the other trees happy and healthy.

When you were telling yourself the story, you might have relied on backstory infodumps, and that's fine. But now, you're telling the story to readers. You need to learn how to cut down and remove trees, without damaging the integrity of the ecosystem. Sometimes several pages of work can be reduced to one, clear, powerful sentence. Save everything you cut to another section or document as a backup, in case it becomes useful or you find a better place for it. But focus on your bare-bones outline.

Make sure that *what happens* is the focal point of every scene; that each scene is building towards an event or reveal or change; that it triggers the next stage in the chain of events that will ultimately lead to the peak drama experience that devastates your character. A lot of things can seem trivial or accidental at first. Ending a scene or chapter with a shift in mood or a rhetorical question can work well.

This first revision will probably include some heavy cutting or rearranging. Get rid of too much information or save it until you can work it into a scene later. Get rid of infodumps and backstory flashbacks, especially in the first few chapters.

It will also probably include a great deal of *new* writing: if your scene wasn't fully fleshed out, if you've gone through and added comments and questions, you'll need to do another pass and add in that new material before smoothing it over. You may have *telling* that can be revised into *showing*.

But don't get too caught up in minor details; we're tearing up the terrain and stacking piles of debris. Use the scene checklist to make sure each scene has conflict and tension. Focus on showing what happens: the unexplained weirdness that demands (and defies) a rational explanation, forcing your protagonist to engage.

Bring your ax. Keep it sharp. Hack through the landscape until you can move through it without getting lost or stuck. Then you'll be ready for the next stage of development.

> "Editing might be a bloody trade, but knives aren't the exclusive property of butchers. Surgeons use them too."
> – *Blake Morrison*

MEMORANDUM

- Map the whole journey
- *What* happens? (phenomenon)
- Remove trees to clear a straight path
- Don't pause and explain (allow the mystery)
- Unfolding action, without commentary
- What's actually there, how does this look?

10

PROVOCATION
2nd Pass: Motivations (Why)

One time in California, my grandmother bought me some sugar cereal. My parents didn't allow it, so I tucked in ravenously when we got home. But there were weird little black spots in it, which I took out and placed on a napkin while I kept eating. It wasn't until they began to move around that I realized they were tiny bugs.

Grandma was outraged; we went straight back to the store where she yelled at someone over the counter. To add insult to injury, he implied something like *our store is clean, maybe you got them from home.*

In the first pass of revisions, we sculpted the landscape. We cut and moved trees. We cleared valleys. We exorcised narrative infodumps or backstory and found a way to fit them into scenes. We focused on information management; how and when to reveal the crucial pieces of information, hopefully at the end of scenes or chapters. It's rough, but we're pretty sure we've got all the right pieces in all the right places, and we're getting close to a clean rough draft. It's probably not *good* yet, but it's all there.

Now that we can see the lay of the land clearly and how it all fits together, the second round of revisions is when we focus on the *why it matters*. You might have the actions mapped out, the physical manifestations of story that we can see; but the *why* is the emotional core that we can *feel*. On a more basic level, it's also why do your characters do the things they do. It can't feel too random or you're a cruel or clumsy puppetmaster, forcing your protagonist to make bad choices to further the plot.

In this section, we'll focus on motivation, depth, relevancy and fixing plot holes (anything that distracts readers from the big picture and causes them to slow down; anything confusing, that doesn't make sense, that doesn't fit). It's a bump in the road, not just a "hole" or lack of information, but an inconsistency or a glitch in the matrix. A bug in your cereal. You may not even notice a few of them; the sugar masks the taste and you crunch through it. But once you see enough of them, and recognize what they are, they're *all* you can see and it'll spoil your appetite.

PROVOKE DESIRE, NOT IRE

A provocation is the deliberate arousal of anger, but it can also be of desire or interest. We want to prod and poke our character until she's forced to react. At the same time, we'll be hooking our readers' attentions. The key here, is that it has to be deliberate: the intentional removal of key information, so it can arouse skepticism before being delivered in a satisfying way. You lead readers to ask questions, and then satiate their desire. However, if you *accidentally* lead readers to ask *other* questions, that you don't resolve, they'll feel let down and frustrated. We want to stoke their desire, without provoking ire.

Typos are annoying but endurable. A plot hole is a more serious sin of omission. It makes readers distrust the author. They'll have to wonder if you're simply negligent, or actively malicious. It's only a mystery if there is an answer, otherwise it's an annoyance.

You can use my scene checklist from earlier to make each scene count, focusing especially on the three types of conflict to keep tension high, until the thing happens, but why does it *need* to happen? Why does it matter to your protagonist deeply enough that they are forced to act? Why does it hurt?

These two questions will help you find your plot holes:

1. Why are the characters doing this?
2. Why does any of it matter?

The first question is pretty basic. You need signposts or open discussion as characters walk through (or dismiss) their decisions. Show your work, but don't be heavy-handed by repeating everything. But also, don't have characters go from one place to another without letting readers know exactly what they're doing, why they're there, what they're hoping to achieve.

The easiest way to do this is with a short story recap between action scenes. Discuss what happened, make new plans, and remind readers of the stakes and obstacles (these are two different things: stakes are bad things that may happen; obstacles are things that will stop you from preventing those bad things.)

Authors sometimes see behind the text and understand that the motivations are implicit, because you brought it up two hundred pages ago, or you thought it was obvious. But that makes machines out of your characters. Remember, every *decision* is a point of potential strife and conflict. The decisions should get worse and worse, until each choice delivers terrible consequences. The decisions should be difficult enough that they sometimes wrestle with direction, but any choice is fine as long as there's a plausible explanation for it.

Luckily this stuff is easy to fix, but you have to *find* the hole first, which is tricky, before you pave it in. These are mostly information gaps, so you can correct them with a simple sentence or two. Asking the two questions above will help you see the *absence* of information, so you can start brainstorming solutions.

INEVITABLE NECESSITY

Hopefully, you've already figured out *what happens*, but it might feel a bit flat. You need to figure out the main *spokes* that support your narrative, and they should be pulling in opposite directions (conflict), while keeping your narrative moving forward (momentum, discovery, revelations). They're probably already there, but you may need to add a couple more for balance – and then you just need to pluck them a bit. Make them thicker, make them capable of supporting all the weight.

We may have all the right material, but it's not obvious, it's at the wrong time, it's not experienced. If you're using my outlines, you may have covered the pivotal turning points; like ancient pillars buried in sand. We'll need to dig them out again, until we can see clearly from one marker to the next. Wrap your narrative around these spokes until it's strong and tight. Lift the main threads of your story to the surface, bringing everything together.

First, basic needs (what is happening). The risks must be high, and they need emotional reasons (something they care about) to do things even if they're dangerous or uncomfortable. Then psychological needs (why does it matter), leading to an identity-forming crisis that transforms them. The more they struggle, the tighter the web binds around them until the confrontation is inescapable. But the story only works if they *keep moving forward,* into increasingly uncomfortable situations. It's your job to *provoke* a proportionate response, with whatever inspiration, intimidation, rewards or punishments necessary.

SPECTACLE & MYSTERY

A short story or poem is a spectacle, even if a mysterious one. It can all be scene at once, or poignant fragments. Its simple façade invites deep contemplation. Gladiators are a spectacle. The fighting and the conflict, bright swords glowing under the hot sun, the lions and dust. But the results, while unexpected in every instance, while dizzying and electrifying, are not mysterious. Some will live, some will die. Spectators don't ask questions, they're too attached to the outcome. You can keep a story going on spectacle and readers may love it; or they'll get bored of the repetition and say it's flat or without depth. If you find your readers, the action might be a benefit—as long as you can keep supplying them with equally effective doses of adrenaline and endorphins.

In my opinion, the stories that hit hardest, that leave an impact, rely on a fair bit of mystery. They may not be as punchy or exciting, but they cut deep, they enthrall, wrapping tentacles of curiosity around your brain until your eyes are glued to every flaming letter.

Your readers will be asking questions as the story progresses, which will put an uncomfortable pressure on them. It's *your* job to relieve this pressure. As Michael Schmidt writes in the biography of the novel:

> "There is pleasure in the anxiety the reader feels, a teased desire for clarity, the teasing exquisite, the urgency of the desire overridden by the pleasure of it… a deliciously agonizing and protracted fictional foreplay, creating, sustaining and augmenting anxiety, until the release in a daylight of explanation that lets the reader gratefully down…"

Your goal as an author, should be to so impact your readers that they can't stop thinking about your story, until they wear it out like a threadbare sweater, poking fingers in the holes. In other words, the better your story, the more susceptible you may become to critical readers who go through it a second or third time asking *why*.

What is this magic? They will ask. Why is it affecting me so? How has the author achieved this? If you've anticipated their questions, you'll be able to plant little clues, that will be discovered gratefully by diligent readers. If you haven't, their dissatisfaction will fester.

DEUS EX MACGUFFIN

Until you've finished the first pass of revisions, you may not even know what happens yet, much less why. But in your second pass of revisions, to make your story satisfying, you need to create compelling reasons for *why* things happened or characters acted the way they did.

A story question is a deliberate omission of information that is satisfactorily resolved. A plot hole is a gaping logistical issue that is not raised nor explained, or a weak character motivation that feels flat or forced.

The deeper the spell cast, the more readers will yearn for a satisfactory resolution, which can lead to a bigger let down if their doubts aren't mollified. If the premise of the story doesn't hold water, they will still be dazed and enamored, but they may feel cheated—their hopes and faith soured as they realize they've been sold snake oil.

Stephen King's *It* has brilliant suspense and gripping visual horror, but in the end it's all just a giant alien spider. It doesn't exactly mar the entire story—the climactic spider fight isn't really the main point. Something had to be there, something plausible, and it works well enough to justify everything that came before it.

I could argue that King's shape-shifting, ancient alien creature is a form of *Deus Ex Machina*; a divine force appearing suddenly at the end of the narrative to wrap things up nicely. It works, but it's kind of cheating. But the holes *must* be filled, or you'll leave readers dissatisfied.

It's a bit like a *macguffin*: an object or event that furthers the plot and character motivation, necessary to get the story going, but insignificant in itself.

A macguffin is incidentally integral to the story. There's nothing specifically wrong with this—filling a plot hole with dung is better than not filling it at all. Use whatever you can to get the story where you need it to go. But I would suggest that you put greater thought into the driving forces of your antagonist (the creature in *It* was motivated by a primitive yet powerful goal: survival, by any means necessary.)

One of the most egregious *macguffins* is from an influential book you've probably never heard of: the *Castle of Otranto* by Horace Walpole, first published on Christmas Eve in 1764. It's been hailed as both the first romance, and the first gothic novel.

In the first scene, a random giant helmet kills the protagonist's son. We don't know where it came from or why it exists or where it went after. It's a striking visual image (we'll talk more about that later) but it doesn't make a lot of sense. It didn't have to, at the time.

The idea came to Horace in a dream, he wrote his novel in a week, and it became a huge bestseller. He penned it in his castle, and even though he had his own printing press, he paid to self-publish anyway under a pseudonym, pretending it was an old manuscript he'd just discovered. The author writes,

> "I have given rein to my imagination till I became
> on fire with the visions and feelings which it excited.
> I have composed it in defiance of rules, of critics, of
> philosophers."

At the *time* there was nothing else like it and almost no competition. But *now* it read like really bad fanfic. It's powerful, captivating, and has probably inspired every famous novel in the last two centuries, but there's no craft or style.

It's doubtful that something similar would succeed today. Readers and agents are inundated with options and have learned how to reject books *quickly*. They could be watching Netflix or playing video games. We've also, as a society, become much better at expecting scrupulous, well-told stories, and are less likely to be transported by a manipulative manuscript (Gothic literature presents imposing visions to deliberately induce anxiety).

You can still crank out a ridiculously high-drama, emotionally captivating novel in a few weeks that *wreck* your readers. And it can even be kind of a mess. But it has to basically make sense and be a positive reading experience. (We'll talk more about the difference between quality and cleanliness later, it's a whole thing.)

As long as you can keep the razzle dazzle going, readers may not stumble over plot holes, as long as you keep them breathless and distracted. But that's exhausting, like being stuck with a guy who does all the talking without giving you a chance to respond. Energy vampires have to constantly scale up their gestures, expressions and vocal machinations to keep your attention as long as possible (probably so you won't notice the deficiencies in his character or personality; but the intentional distraction only serves to highlight flaws).

They start a story and once you're listening politely, they stretch it out. You can't take your eyes off them, because the story never wraps up, it expands, it mutates, it jumps, and you forget what the point was or how it started, but now you can't wait to get away from it.

You want suspense and intrigue, but you don't want readers to be confused or impatient. They will *wait* for answers, as long as they *trust* that they're coming. You need to have the characters raise or ask the questions early, so that readers know this is obviously weird or unusual; that the author is *aware* of the problem and will probably do something about it eventually. That this omission was intentional, not accidental. If nobody acknowledges the weirdness, or the characters take it in stride, readers may doubt it will be resolved.

WHY DON'T THEY JUST...

Imagine your character is walking down a long hallway with open doors. One of them is on fire, and they go through it anyway. For this to make any sense at all, we'd need to see all the options. All the other doors need to be locked, or filled with something worse. This door needs to be important and necessary.

If readers can imagine an easier, simpler way to get what they want, your characters should be able to as well. Why don't they just stay home? Why do anything at all? Especially as stakes rise, so must their motivations. This doesn't mean you need to dump your backstory motivations earlier. But when faced with a very difficult choice, leave space for deliberation. The bigger the decision, the longer they should need to think about it or brainstorm. Don't have the answers come easily. First, show the problems; all the closed doors and terrible consequences. Then, have someone offer a possible solution. The answer to plot holes is *closing* doors to limit options, or increasing the motivations to justify an otherwise impractical decision.

RAISE AND DISMISS

Often plot holes can be fixed by allowing characters to raise or ask critical questions, and then be given simplistic answers. They may not fill the entire hole, but they're good enough for now to keep things moving.

Have your characters point out or explain their fears, goals, and options, and have them get shut down by logistics. We *need* to go do this, but we don't have a car right now. So let's do this instead.

One common criticism in young adult literature is that a bunch of teens get in trouble but refuse to ask parents, teachers or adults for help. You could fix this by having them *think* about asking for help or *almost* asking for help, but the conversation derails into conflict, or dad needs to stay over at the office or take an emergency trip, or grandma gets sick and the protagonist doesn't want to bother her.

You can also have someone who simply makes a unilateral decision, and the others go along with it reluctantly. Disney's *Mandalorian*, for example, shuts down debate and discussion by having a character say *this is the way* which forces compliance. One of my childhood friends, if he didn't get his way, he'd storm off in a huff, ruining the game.

Show the decision as a process. Raise the problem or story goal, and suggest possible answers (without guessing the right one). If you have them make a good plan based on reliable information that actually works out, you'll have reduced a lot of the conflict or suspense, so it doesn't have to be perfect. Their motivations or assumptions might be flawed. You just need enough direction for limited, short-term action with plausible enough rationale to put them where you want them to be for the next thing to happen.

It doesn't have to be perfect, but it has to be there. Maybe the hallway is still full of unlocked doors, but each one has a *do not enter* sign on it. You're corralling characters towards the ending that they need to experience. Without signposts, the infinity of possibilities will make their ending unrealistic. Why didn't they at least try all those other doors before they stepped into the burning room?

If their motivations are strong enough (their pet raccoon is on fire!) then of course they'll ignore all the other doors, and that's fine too.

LIMITED WINDOW

The easiest way to add urgency is to set any kind of arbitrary deadline or window of opportunity. This can be a great impetus to get the story rolling quickly, or add drama in the form of a hanging guillotine. Something bad is going to happen soon, and we must *do the thing* before that happens! An ultimatum that threatens to destroy their status quo (and also shows how they're stuck). Either *do this* or *take that*.

The more urgent or pressing the obstacle or impending threat, the less you need to justify a character's rational response. They may not even think about it at all; they might just run out into danger. They also may not over-analyze something that appears to be a trivial, irrelevant goal. Before they begin their mission, they need to pick up the dry-cleaning, but stop for a cup of coffee, which then spills accidentally all over their fresh clothes: they duck instinctively, just in time for a bullet to shatter the glass behind them. In this example, you don't need to explain why they were thirsty. You *do* need to explain why the bullet missed them at the crucial moment. And if they'd stopped to pick up their coffee or dry-cleaning *after* the bullet incident, it wouldn't make any sense, because now their only concern should be self-preservation. (You could explain that also, if they needed a cup of coffee to calm their nerves; but they wouldn't stand in line at Starbucks for it if someone is trying to kill them).

EMOTIONAL CONSISTENCY

If plot events are triggered by a character's emotional state, make sure you justify their outburst. Why are they so angry, happy, flirty, and what internal thought processes are responsible for their external display of emotion?

If they must make a bad decision, give them a reason to be irrational, and do something out of character. In romance, just as the two love interests are very nearly together, an ex shows up, which causes the protagonist to get drunk and depressed and nearly kiss another guy, which creates even more conflict between them. At some point, when the stakes are high enough, you can get a side-character to ask them *why*: why are you willing to risk everything for this? Why can't you just let it go? That's a great place for a full-disclosure backstory or reveal, or a deep introspection.

Most of the time, however, your protagonists shouldn't have *time* to worry about fulfilling their needs, or wondering about who they are, at least until after the midpoint. Your protagonist is probably not seeking personal fulfillment, but will react based on *who they are* and *what makes immediate sense;* what seems like the best option at the time.

At the beginning, they may just be stumbling around in a clueless fog, but the more they come to recognize and understand what's happening, the more it begins to matter to them, the more deliberation and personal motivation they will need to keep going.

RELEVANCE

People sometimes talk about the unpredictable, yet *inevitable* ending; when all the pieces finally line up in a surprising way. It's difficult to pull off, but immensely satisfying in retrospect.

An easy way to get a little bit closer, is just to keep track of the relevancy of each scene: how is *this* related to the *real* story conflict. Your characters may be willing to go on side quests if it's relevant to their main story quest; but if they get completely derailed and seem to forget entirely about their Big Picture Mission for too long, readers will get antsy and ask "what happened to all that big exciting stuff before? Was it all a lie? Did it even matter? Why should I care about this little boring stuff when we haven't found out what happened with all that big stuff?"

Often you can save scenes that don't seem to fit by allowing your characters to reflect on, think about or draw conclusions. Not too often (or they'll just be anxiously worrying about the same problems without taking action), but every once in a while, they can refresh or sum up what they're doing and why it matters. Alternatively, they can explain why they *aren't* freaking out or anxious about those big events, with any number of excuses: maybe "someone's got to hold it together" or "I have to concentrate on something small I can control, or I'll fall apart."

You can also give them an insurmountable block until you're ready for them to progress. They can briefly worry about the unresolved story questions and ominous dangers out there, and lament helplessly that there's nothing they can do about it right now because they're stumped on a critical clue.

This, incidentally, holds for most of the early *Harry Potter* books: someone is trying to kill him, and it's *essential* he do something like study or prepare so he can pass his test or challenge successfully and unlock the next piece (or at least survive)... but Harry is too distracted with girls and butterbeer.

Like most heroes, he's a luckless (but kind) buffoon, who gets saved by his loyal friends despite having few abilities or charms of his own. His flaws are more excusable when he's a young child, and get him into necessary conflicts that speed his growth and maturity. It *works* because the world is so rich and interesting, and the trivial accidents that take place along the way find a crucial role later on.

The scenes, dialogue, action and everything else will be fine as long as the story spokes support your main characters' decisions and actions. Once everything is finished, they'll fade a bit or be covered up by all the little details, but they need to be there, or all the little details will be easily blown away by a few big story questions or plot holes.

Going back to our forest example; we've removed the trees and cleared a route, but now we're cutting through brush and creating a path—so readers have a sense of depth and can see a little further down the road and appreciate what's happening on a deeper level. In many cases, a small plot hole can be filled with any random excuse. She left the gun at home because she thought it might rain and didn't want to get the gunpowder wet.

"That's not how guns work!"

"I didn't know that!"

The point is not to trivialize or make light of a dire situation by allowing for dumb mistakes.

"Where's the gun?"

"I forgot it in the truck!"

"How could you be so stupid!"

Even that though, is better than saying nothing, getting into a shootout, and getting injured without ever mentioning what happened to the gun she had earlier or why isn't she shooting back. Sometimes fixing plot holes is simply a matter of keeping track of all the objects they have with them. Just be careful not to give them a Mary Poppins magical bag filled with a solution to every problem; remember we want to *create* problems, not dissolve them. We need a key for *this specific door*, not all the doors in the hallway.

If you've previously used a solution for a similar problem, you'll need to explain why they don't use the same solution again. In *Prisoner of Azkaban*, Hermione uses a time-turner which drives the whole plot of that book; but it would be too easy a solution for the larger issues later on in the series. They are destroyed in an episode in the *Order of the Phoenix*, which is confirmed in *Half-Blood Prince* when Hagrid considers using them again: "We couldn't have done," said Hermione. "We smashed the entire stock of Ministry Time-Turners when we were there in the summer."

1. Why are the characters doing this?
2. Why does any of it matter?

The first question can be resolved with misdirection and sleight of hand. Many of these small questions are nagging details; they don't really matter to the main story but are essential to get readers to their destination. All you're trying to do is keep them rolling smoothly forward. We just need to check-in with readers periodically and remind them of what's happening, and why. You might think it's obvious, but each time a character rushes off into a new scene to do something, they need to consider the risks and rewards. Is this something they *really* need to do right now?

The further you progress along the story, the greater the stakes are going to be. While they may have helped out a minor character with an early favor, they'll be more selfish with their time and energy as the main story becomes all-consuming. Their motivations (practical or emotional) will need to outweigh the escalating dangers, or be imperative to the fulfillment of the main story quest.

In my experience as a casual gamer, who plays most games on easy mode so I can hack through them, I'm there mainly for the story and scenery. Sometimes developers will *force* me to complete all their banal sidequests; to track down 3 keys to unlock a treasure chest; to grind for leather and iron ore to improve my armor or weapons before I can enter a new realm.

At best, this makes players experience more depth and appreciate the world worth saving, which will show off hidden corners of the world and ultimately increase enjoyment. At worst, however, I get lost and forget what I'm even supposed to be doing. I'm a highly trained assassin helping a drunk husband get home safely. But it's kind of like firefighters rescuing kittens out of trees. It's not what they're for; but it's why we love them.

CHARACTER MOTIVATIONS

In 1943, Abraham Maslow published a paper in the Psychological Review outlining the five tiers of human motivation. They are commonly called the *Hierarchy of Needs*.

1. *Actualization* – purpose, realization, confidence
2. *Esteem* – status, achievement, respect
3. *Love & Belonging* – friendship, family, sex
4. *Safety* – security, employment, health
5. *Physiological* – breathing, food, water

People's motivations will change depending on which level of fulfillment they currently enjoy. In most cases, characters will be motivated by 3~1... *until* 4 and 5 get challenged. The most pressing need will always block out the less critical need.

Robinson Crusoe is interesting because of the inane detail about precisely how his mechanical inventions afforded him food, water and shelter. He's only thinking about survival, but that conflict makes the small details relevant. J. M. Coetzee writes:

> "For page after page—for the first time in the history of fiction—we see a minute, ordered description of how things are done."

These details only matter because the protagonist's physiological needs are threatened. Likewise in *Castaway*, Tom Hanks figures out how to eat and drink before he creates Wilson, his exotic volleyball companion. If your book doesn't have life-threatening challenges, your characters might begin seeking love and belonging, and finally move up towards actualization.

One Stop for Writers has a detailed list of character motivations, along with examples. Positive motivations include protecting a loved one, finding something lost, finding a friendship or companion, avoiding financial ruin, proving someone wrong, pursuing knowledge, realizing a dream, repaying a debt, escaping confinement or doing the right thing.

But there's also a list of "dark" motivations: evading responsibility, pursuing a toxic desire, becoming the sole power or authority, achieving dominion over another, getting revenge, keeping what one has, correcting a perceived mistake, taking what one is owed, obtaining glory at any cost, profiteering, promoting chaos, or ruining someone's life.

Both the regular and "dark" motivations can be traced back to Maslow's driving forces: basic needs, psychological needs, self-fulfillment needs. When people pursue these needs and are *not* allowed to get them, they become bitter, self-righteous, defensive, angry, and sometimes manipulative. The system let them down: they were optimistic, happy at one point, until it was all taken from them unfairly.

Notice how close some of them are. Getting out of debt could be a hero's motivation; years later, they could have an addiction to profiteering or hoarding so that they'll never know hunger again. Maybe they had a little sister they couldn't save and now they want to bring down the rich and wealthy.

The *Count of Monte Cristo* is mostly a revenge quest plot, where one man goes through extraordinary lengths to reclaim the life that's been stolen from him. While it's presented as righteous justice, it could also be seen as a fanatical need to get even.

The difference between a hero and a villain is *often* that the villain is coming from a place of power. Their basic needs are probably already met; they aren't in immediate danger; they aren't faced with bewildering circumstances and a lack of information—they may be incapable of change or growth, which is why they aren't the heroes. The hero meanwhile, starts from a position of relative weakness and goes through a positive fulfillment arc. They may not get what they think they wanted, but they do get what they need.

The hero can be subjective depending on who is telling the story, but it's generally the sympathetic character who is most changed through the narrative. Both heroes and villains tend to operate outside of the law or societal expectations. The difference between a revolutionary champion and a dangerous insurgent is mostly whether or not they succeed, come to power and rewrite the history books.

YOUR ANTAGONIST

I haven't really talked about how to create your antagonist yet, and it's kind of a big deal, so let's address it here.

Your antagonist is the driving force of challenges that oppose your protagonist's story quest, either active or passive. It's the *thing that must be stopped* or *he who won't be named*.

We don't have to understand the antagonist's motivations until near the end, when it's all revealed. They are important to figure out, because without them the entire novel can be reduced to unfortunate circumstances of chance.

They might have to do with the backstory about how this crisis ever came together; the villain's personal motivations; the brewing cataclysm that scientists predicted but everyone ignored.

The key thing is, while the protagonist has the power to change or evolve, the villain does not: the protagonist removes his fatal flaw and is healed. The villain considers it, but refuses.

Otherwise, the entire spectacle could have been avoided or reduced with a simple conversation or a few rounds of therapy. The villain is obstinate and refuses to change their opinions, no matter how much damage they cause.

This is typically why characters such as Captain Ahab are seen as villainous characters, with an egomaniacal pursuit that leads to inevitable destruction. But even Ahab has his reasons. The whale stole his leg and made him a cripple. He believes in science, not superstition. He refuses to accept a miraculous, demonic whale, and is constantly at odds with his more credulous crew. It's not *just* a revenge quest plot: he's trying to prove to himself and his men that the universe is fundamentally indifferent, which means anything is possible, nothing is preordained, his missing leg is an unfortunate accident. The opposing view, that he's being *punished for his hubris* and should learn to accept his limitations, is an identity-shattering crucible; he can't accept that without giving up who he is. He's sympathetic, but villainous because he can't change without destroying himself. But *if he had won*, he would have been gloriously heroic.

A hero is basically the same thing, only they triumph in the end, and their victory is usually predicated on a deep personal shift or transformation. They *deserve* the victory because they've *paid for it*, through what the narrative has cost them. They don't always choose to change willingly, or deliberately; they are forced to change.

These obstinate, opposing forces with autonomy and purpose cannot both succeed in getting what they want without clashing heads. Their beliefs and motivations are the coals that fuel the fire of their passions.

But the villain should be the stubborn one, and the hero should be the kind one (they are forced to act to reduce the potential damage to things they love or care about). And even then—at the very end of the fight scene, the hero often shows mercy by refusing to kill the bad guy. The bad guy regroups and attacks while his back is turned, and the hero is forced to act in self-defense; or the bad guy gets taken out by a supporting character, keeping the hero blameless. Alternatively, the hero *becomes* villainous in his single-minded pursuit of noble ideals, but that's literally a different story.

My main point here is that a story can quickly unravel if the underlying conflict behind it is unjustified or easily resolved; or if the timing and logic don't hold up. These motivations might just be a few quick paragraphs towards the end, but they're the critical anchors that make the resolution feel inescapable.

Your antagonist's motivations are probably the engine that keeps your story running. At some point, readers will want to look under the hood and see what's there. In horror you can get away with *because they're evil*; and not every villain needs a sympathetic, redemptive story arc, but they should still have a rational purpose behind their actions, or the entire premise may feel like a farce.

Likewise, protagonists shouldn't be motivated purely by abstract concepts like *truth* or *justice*. If it isn't personal, it doesn't hurt. Why should they stand up to this bad guy? Why is this fight their responsibility?

The villain and hero are probably motivated by the same deep thing, based on their character, but expressing it or pursuing it in different ways. The hero ultimately gives up what he wants for others; the villain refuses to change. The protagonist is moved by the story and flexible enough to adapt; the villain is inflexible to his own destruction.

There's a Mayan story I like about two types of trees that are usually found growing together. One is poisonous (Chechen), the other is the antidote (Chaca). They produce the same fruit, so their seeds are eaten and spread by the same birds, even though their effects are diametrical. The Mayan lore recounts the tale of two ancient lords, the brothers Kinch and Tizic, that loved the same woman, Nicte-Ha. They fought, fueled by jealousy, and died in each other's arms. Their final request was to see Nicte-Ha again, so they were reincarnated as the trees that share one flower.

WEAK AND DUMB CHARACTERS

Throughout this book I've been referring to "smart characters" — what I really mean is, characters who don't do dumb things for no reason. I've had authors push back against editorial comments about character motivation; offering examples of books with irrational, inscrutable protagonists who don't deign to explain themselves or act with intent. The books are murky and obscure, which can be a type of power.

But even Kafka wasn't *Kafkaesque* on purpose; his style is less of a deliberate choice than a limit of craft. He was never a professional writer, and when once presented a bound set of his stories, he said:

> "My scribbling ... is nothing more than my own materialisation of horror. It shouldn't be printed at all. It should be burnt."

Kafka succeeded because he captured the essence of the age; but also because his best friend edited and published the unfinished manuscripts that Kafka never meant to see the light of day.

Of course there can be some irrational characters. Some of your side figures may need to be capable of deceit and treachery, even for base motivations like jealousy or petty rivalness; and your antagonist should probably be capable of malice or cruelty.

But these are often unlikeable roles, created to add stubborn opposition. If your protagonist does have negative qualities, she's probably not aware of them at first, and learns to overcome them through the story. Your protagonist will probably also make mistakes, and this is fine! What they won't do is act randomly, with no purpose or agenda, no hope or expectation, like a drifting, inhuman specter.

Your characters should very rarely make *stupid* mistakes, which means – every difficult choice or action they make must be explained or supported. A reason, even if it's a bad one. At first, they will shy away from causing pain or unnecessary villainy. Later they might choose morally unscrupulous behaviors or actions, but only in service of a greater good. Or they can be forced into treachery (risky situations that don't agree with their own internal compass) by giving them a firm ultimatum (do this and get everything you've ever dreamed; or get out forever).

If you *have* to get them to do something awful, make sure you've exhausted every other possibility, and give them the decency to feel wretched about it. I'm not saying don't have your characters do dumb things. You *should* be having your characters make all kinds of terrible decisions; forced to do things they loathe, so that they hate themselves and the situation that has brought out the worst in them.

It's also *fine* to bring out these issues, when they're tired, or hungry, or drunk, their worst tendencies might leak out. Even good characters might slip up or make mistakes that increase the tension and conflict. But it can't be trivial or trite. It can't be "oops, but oh well." That way leads down a dangerous path to ethical relativism, and once your heroes have lost the moral upper ground, even in small decisions, readers may not trust them with larger ones.

This ties in with the decision-making I talked about in the last chapter. Showing the challenges and plot events is what happens, but you also need to show the characters wrestling with difficult decisions that reveal character. Without it, you've only got a set of meaningless incidents.

"To uncover the plot of your story, don't ask what should happen, but what should go wrong. To uncover your story, don't ask what the theme is, but rather, what is discovered.

Characters making choices to resolve tension—that's your plot. If your protagonist has no goal, makes no choices, has no struggle to overcome, you have no plot." – *Steven James*, *Story Trumps Structure*

Your protagonist needs to have a strong, consistent internal compass, and it needs to be revealed through incidents that establish their character. This is *who they are.* Without it this reliable core identity, we won't be able to tell a story that forces them to change.

- ✓ Plot holes are unfixable story questions that tear readers out of their suspended disbelief, and make them question and doubt the entire enterprise. If they're big enough, they'll throw the book across the room in frustration.
- ✓ Plot holes can be skipped over by entertaining plausible motivations or justifications for the characters' actions, and showing your work: what do they need to do next, what's their plan, what do they hope to achieve?
- ✓ Making decisions are what creates our unique identities; stories are about character. Show the struggle to decide; that's who your character is, and what your story is about.
- ✓ Nobody is perfect, but their actions will be determined by their experiences, by who they are and what they've been through. They can be an irrational *mess*; but they will be consistent. Eventually you need to show how they got that way, and if it's your protagonist, find a way to improve.
- ✓ Conflict and stress can create turmoil that allows careful consideration to devolve into irrational, reckless behavior. *Provoke* them into making mistakes.

MEMORANDUM

- *Why* do things happen?
- Prod and poke
- Raise and dismiss
- Sticks and carrots
- The antagonist can't change; the protagonist does
- Spectacle and mystery
- Internal consistency
- Explanations of occurrences or appearances

11

ELUCIDATION
3rd Pass: Descriptions (How)

When I was a teenager, I took a bus through Argentina with a bunch of international exchange students. It included dozens of hours of barren tundra. It was hot and dusty and boring. But while the experience was monotonous, the countless hours aren't what I remember. I only remember the songs or games or conversations I had with my friends; the stunning pink glitter beaches made of crushed abalone shells, the icy chill of Ushuaia, the Southern-most city in the world. Most readers won't remember the words on the page. They will remember the images you put in their brains, and the way those pictures made them feel.

What feels like ages ago, I mentioned that the individual words of your story are like the leaves on a tree. Assuming you have a strong structure and a story that matters, now, finally, we can begin to talk about the actual vocabulary and sentence structure. But keep in mind, we're still not editing, not really.

We're *presenting*. We're not polishing the glass; we're making sure the images behind it are worth viewing. Without the details, your story has been unfolding in dark, featureless corridors. Now we're turning on the lights.

Description is not about pretty *words*: a dazzling vocabulary might actually be a hindrance. It's about the artful arrangement of scene specificity; the props and background sets representing the world through which your characters move.

We've left it until now, because there's no point in dressing up or elaborating on a poignant scene until we're sure we've got all the right pieces in all the right places. Description should be used in service of a story worth telling. Otherwise, rather than a tree, it's like one of those exotic flowers that bloom for one night only, every three years, before fading into the darkness.

HOW DOES THIS LOOK?

In this third stage of revisions, we'll be going through and fixing the details, focusing on the main question, *how does this look* or *how, specifically, did this happen?* We need to embellish our wireframe scenes, and incorporate (give body to) elements to help readers picture what's happening. This may also be where we begin enhancing important passages, like our intros and outros (first and last paragraphs of a scene), our transitions, our worldbuilding, settings, costumes and body language.

In this chapter, I'll share some tips on how to recognize weak writing or blasé descriptions, and change them to powerful, creative world-building that sets your book apart and burns a deep, lasting impression on your readers.

I leave the scene description and setting until the last round of edits before the final polish, because they are adornments, like a garnish of parsley. They won't actually make the main meal taste better, or be more satisfying, but they will enhance the subtle perception and enjoyment.

SPOTLIGHTING

The trick with description is to highlight a few key objects that cast the right mood for your current scene, without devolving into a pedantic inventory. Remember, the magic happens in the spaces between. You want to leave room for readers to fill in the gaps, to help them *actively create* and step into your fictional space with their own imaginations. But you need to steer them in the right direction, or they'll wind up in a featureless void and can't picture anything.

Imagine you're on a dark stage that's semi-furnished with props. Everything is there, hovering in darkness, waiting for you to give it purpose. Whatever you choose to light up with the spotlight of your narrative prose, readers will assume must be important or relevant.

If you show a gun, it should be used later. If you spend a paragraph describing an old woman in the market, she needs to be critical. The more something *matters*, the more detail you should give it: a character's careful analysis of a particular object or setting hints at their *interest*. Therefore, it's a mistake to give careful descriptive detail to *everything*. Characters shouldn't notice random weird things or characters if they don't matter to the story.

According to American novelist Walter Lippman, we imagine most things before we experience them. "We do not first see, and then define, we define first and then see."

"The only feeling that anyone can have about an event he does not experience is the feeling aroused by his mental image of that event: a representation of the environment which is in lesser or greater degree made by man himself. In untrained observation we pick recognizable signs out of the environment. The signs stand for ideas, and these ideas we fill out with our stock of images."

The more something matters, the more you need to describe it in detail so readers remember it later. Readers come to the text with their own preconceived notions, so you don't need to fill in every specific detail: focus on what's unique or different about familiar scenes, settings, objects or characters.

If you're trying to set up a surprise twist by dropping a clue, without an early reveal, you can use description to:

1. plant *red herrings*, things that seem like they might matter but ultimately don't or
2. lightly touch on things so they're established, but don't dwell on them so readers are surprised.

Show the thing, but discount it at first. It's probably nothing. Change the subject. If your characters wonder and fret about it and it keeps coming up, it's heavy-handed, clumsy foreshadowing.

DESCRIPTION IN ACTION

The biggest mistake I see is a dump of description in a stand-alone paragraph, with no action. For this to play well, description should fit into the flow and cadence of the actions in the scene.

Elements should be introduced when they are being *noticed* or *used* by your characters.

Description always belongs at the first instance – the first time your protagonist arrives at a new setting or meets a new character, they will be more likely to notice the distinctions of the anomaly. The unfamiliar always catches our intrigue. Unless it's absolutely unremarkable, in which case, the protagonist needs to be given a reason to notice it.

> There was a telephone on the wall and a chair in the corner.

> Kaidance's eyes were drawn to the bright red, rotary telephone that seemed out of place with the earth-toned living room. The mustard yellow easy chair in the corner beckoned; she'd been standing up for hours.

Be careful not to add a more detailed description later, for something that's already familiar, unless your protagonist's needs, interests or moods have changed enough for it to now be more relevant.

In a tense action scene, however, the character won't be looking around and observing, unless she has a purpose (her eyes cast around the room desperately for some kind of weapon, but the nursery was filled with stuffed toys and piles of soiled clothing).

In a slow, thoughtful scene, characters may *zoom out* and casually take in the main elements. In a dramatic, violent scene, characters will be flooded with adrenaline, causing them to *zoom in* and focus on tiny details. If they're running from the bad guys, they won't stop to admire and comment on the scenery: they'll only notice the obstacles in their path of escape.

If the first encounter with a new setting was rushed, and the character didn't have time to slow down and observe their surroundings, then the second time when things are calm they may notice more details. Add description in the place it makes the most sense depending on the protagonist's mood and goals.

Don't focus on the banal or trivial stuff—the teapot boiling—unless it's about to become a weapon to ward off a home intruder. Or, the shrill scream of the teakettle adds a note of tension to the conflict bubbling beneath the surface of an otherwise calm scene.

Try to break up description into short sentences that support the action without feeling like they're crammed in at the wrong time. Introduce a new setting in a paragraph or two, but after you've already hooked with action or speech.

The main point, is that description is at the service of the mood of the scene; it can be used to enhance the pictures readers see, how clearly they are able to envision what's happening, which will make the conflict more vivid and resonant.

GET THE BASICS EARLY

Introducing the main characters or settings can be tricky at first, when you're trying to establish details without slowing down the pacing or action. But try not to let a few chapters go by without telling readers what a scene or character looks like. You want to establish who the characters are and what they want or don't want in the first chapter or two. You can add depth or nuance later.

But you don't want to introduce new core characters or setting description in later chapters, after they've already filled in the blank spaces with their own imaginations: it makes readers feel like they can't trust the text. They've spent chapters getting to know a character and suddenly it's not at all what they were picturing. Some surprises can be good if it's critical to the plot. A character might notice a smaller mark, tattoo, unique eye color once they're paying close attention. At first, however, they'll only get a vague impression.

When describing your protagonist, try to avoid showing them casually looking at their own reflection in the mirror and commenting about their appearance. It can make them seem vain, unnaturally self-conscious, and overly concerned with their appearance. Find a way for their appearance to be a reflection of their personality, and demonstrated through motion or action related to their current story goals.

When danger is imminent, characters will be focused on the here and now. In slower scenes, they will be more reflective and thoughtful, looking *back* or *ahead*; so commonplace items might trigger a flight of fancy—an old memory or a sudden epiphany around a central problem they've been facing.

Show the *object* when it first appears to establish that your protagonist is aware of its existence; show the *detail* when it becomes relevant or interesting to their pressing need or current mood. Also, the more they're focused on one thing, the less they'll focus on all the other things.

You can also use description intentionally to slow down a tense scene that comes before a great climactic choice or decision. Choosing to go forward despite the risks; stepping into the abyss, pregnant with possibility and unknowing, drawn forward irresistibly like a magnet. Acute awareness of the importance of the moment through detailed scene description: the details, the sweat, her heartbeat, gulping in fear, chest tight with anxiety.

In this third pass of revisions, it's a good idea to go through your manuscript and look for *first instances*: when they meet new people, arrive at an unfamiliar location, first mention some mysterious object or figure. The first time they hear something new is a good chance to explain, describe, or even ask questions about it that another character can supply answers to. It can even be very useful to have a *novice* type character, whether or not it's your protagonist, so that you can have someone as unfamiliar with things as your readers: so unfamiliar terms can be taught without needing a glossary.

LOCATION DETAILS

Google street view is great for virtually "walking around" foreign or local areas and getting a feel for the scene. Be wary of *how much* historical or geographical accuracy you put into a book. While the details can be interesting, it's easy to bog down a manuscript with research that doesn't actually support or improve the story. You can also use Pinterest to search for images and make a "mood board" for a particular scene or setting. But try to make your scene *more than* the normal stuff you can find online. Make it particular and interesting. Show it used, lived in, with a sense of deep history or pathos; this is a place that has already, or will, develop your characters.

In particular, think about your touching moments, where the deep reveals, vulnerable conversations or backstory discoveries happen. Where do you want these conversations to take place? These will be pivotal scenes, even if they're happening in transit, with your most memorable words. Set them in a nice setting. It's like putting fine wine in a decanter, to give them extra space that improves the depth of the experience.

It may also be important to figure out distances and placements. Where is everything in the room; how far are locations set across the city? Make sure your characters are moving in consistent directions. Again, write what's best for your story, not necessarily for accuracy: figure out how they'll get around, where the furniture is placed, where the car is parked, where they left their keys. If you want them to pass through somewhere to pick something up for a critical mission, make sure it's on the way; or if it's necessary to complete the mission, make it *out* of the way to increase difficulty (the more motivation, the less easy it can be; the less motivation, the more easy it should be).

MOOD OF SCENE

A scene should have one main mood; you can strengthen the mood with foreboding or foreshadowing – but use the scene description to establish the ambiance. Add things and colors that make readers and the main character feel a certain way. You can increase dread or sadness if you want to, before something bad happens and have readers anxious and on high alert; or a light happy scene just before something bad happens, so it's unexpected and has more shock value.

Don't show the mood of the scene by making your characters irrationally moody; if the scene pulls the emotional direction, the characters should actively resist it.

I felt a chill run down my spine, but I shook my head and pulled myself together. It's just an old warehouse... the ghost legends are just stories. It's not *really* haunted. Still, the macabre decorations and broken, abandoned toys made me uneasy.

Resistance is the secret sauce of most scenes, especially those weak in actual conflict. If the characters feel buoyed by happiness and fulfillment, something in the scene reminds them of a painful past or challenging obstacles yet to face. If they're already depressed and anxious, mirthful laughter or bright colors might seem like a deliberate mockery. The disagreement between a character's inner mood and outer surroundings creates palpable tension *while* describing each, without either feeling unimportant or boring.

COLOR THERAPY

Colors have a psychological impact on our subconscious. You can use this to your advantage by thinking of each scene like a mini painting or still-life. If you took the feeling, emotion, action, surprise or reveal that happens in a scene and wanted to capture it in a photograph, how would you organize it? The deeper the color, the deeper the mood or feeling.

According to American psychologist Dr. Robert Plutchik, there are eight primary emotions that serve as the foundation for all others: joy, sadness, acceptance, disgust, fear, anger, surprise, and anticipation. There are different versions of color wheels, some that are much more in-depth, but here's a simple basis to get you started.

- **Yellow:** *serenity, joy, ecstasy*
- **Light Green:** *acceptance, trust, admiration*
- **Dark Green:** *apprehension, fear, terror*
- **Light Blue:** *distraction, surprise, amazement*
- **Dark Blue:** *pensiveness, sadness, grief*
- **Purple:** *boredom, disgust, loathing*
- **Red:** *annoyance, anger, rage*
- **Orange:** *interest, anticipating, vigilance*

This isn't a comprehensive list: turquoise can symbolize communication or compassion; black can mean sophistication or power; pink can mean sensitivity or romance. My point here is only that you should consider a general color-scheme, at least for your big, major scenes. This will also help you keep track of the general mood you want readers to feel in that section.

One of the things I recommend in *The Plot Dot*, and I do in my own books, is try to incorporate a "flash of color" which could be a totem or object with emotional resonance that draws the eye of the imagination and grounds the scene—this will probably be the opposite of the general mood color. It's the focal point of the still life you're creating, and creates vivid contrast. Drops of blood in the snow; a bright blue cape against the gray of a castle wall; the orange flames of a fire burning against the navy blue of the night sky (if the object glows, it can even cast a halo effect on everything else in the scene.)

Even a simple object can communicate a lot about character: a protagonist's pink unicorn pen that she's far too old for but won't give up because it's the last thing her father gave her before he disappeared; she's both embarrassed by it and protective of it.

ANCHORING

A totem can even drive plot events, and "anchor" major backstory or character reveals. It would look something like this: use, lose, find, relinquish. First, the character is shown possessively clutching or admiring a sacred object. They might even have a good luck ritual before important events. Then, it goes missing; throwing them off their game, giving them an excuse for poor behavior, causing a major slip up or accident. You can add drama by having them accuse another character of stealing or hiding it.

Next, they find it again and *now* they finally reveal the backstory of what it means to them; it probably represents their fatal flaw or a critical trauma that shaped their fears and core identity. The story is revealed after it's shown to be important, and after she feels comfortable enough with the new friends to share personal truths. Finally, they pass it on, let it go, in a gesture that represents their personal growth.

You can also create an anchor that represents unresolved plot events or story questions; a token or keepsake they picked up during a crucial scene that reminds them of the central conflict, the stakes, the dangers. The more important it is, especially if it represents unanswered questions, the more a character might study or deconstruct it. It may even reveal a crucial clue or step forward when they finally noticed some deeper component or hidden mechanism.

While I'll mostly focus on clothes—what are they wearing, where did the change in outfits come from, why was the costume change necessary—at this point you may also want to introduce some extrasensory details like smell, taste or touch as well. Scents can be powerful emotional anchors, while also revealing history or character. You can use them like color, to reinforce the mood of the scene, or trigger memories.

> The stench grabbed me by the throat and made me double over, covering my nose. The deceptive sweetness of air freshener, like minty pine, and whiskey, felt like the year my foster father brought a hooker to our family Thanksgiving.

CLICHÉ & CUTOUT

A cliché or a cardboard cutout is usually a kind of shorthand. Rather than describing what something looks like, you're referring to external, shared knowledge. He cut the bread like Chuck Norris chopping ninjas. He laughed like a hyena on meth. Some of these might be interesting, and fun for readers who get your meaning.

But beware reaching into your readers' experiences for a picture, rather than giving them something fresh; it can't help but be derivative.

If you say, "she's very beautiful, like Madonna meets Jessica Rabbit," you still haven't told me what she actually looks like.

It's not real description, it's symbolic for something else that needs to be retrieved. A placeholder, like *insert typical blonde newscaster lady here.* Cultural references could enhance the story, especially if they're relevant to your characters, but there's a chance your readers may not be familiar with the references.

Clichés could also be common phrases to describe a mood state, like *he was a blubbering mess.* What does this mean, what does it look like? They stood *slack-jawed in dumbfounded awe* – this is a caricature of actual surprise.

The higher the drama, stakes or conflict in the scene, the more careful you need to be to avoid clichés or shorthand references, because they feel flat or cartoonish. They don't feel *real*, they feel like a summary. They trivialize and minimalize the real emotion in the scene.

Also, if I haven't mentioned it earlier, if your characters are breaking down in tears or hysterics or maniacal laughter every chapter, then they're too volatile and the plot events are impacting them too harshly. Save the tears for the powerful scenes that hurt the most.

It's *fine* to begin with clichés or shorthand—barely fleshed out, invisible characters, with no personality or form. The faceless, ridiculous *goons* or *henchmen*. But try to focus on a few unique distinctions that bring your settings and characters to life in a new and refreshing way. Describe what actually is, not a screen or filter or reference.

THE RIGHT WORDS CUT DEEP

You don't make something hurt by using more words. You use the *right* words. Sometimes, authors attempt to explain why and how much something hurts with a lot of description.

The character is thinking about how much this hurts; it's almost worse than that other time... (jump into backstory or deep existential reflection). Stay in the scene, focus on the details and feelings, not the thoughts.

Thoughts come later, after the shock wears off. Real pain is almost all feeling. As a good rule of thumb, characters are either in the world or in their head; they're either *thinking* and ignoring their circumstances, or they're *experiencing* and noticing every detail.

Wordiness in general, especially when it's fancy or purple prose, may appear like good writing, but can actually be useless drivel. Worse, it can be deliberately harmful to your story. Pretty writing stands out and draws attention. It can support a story, but it can also be distracting. It makes readers pay attention to the writing, the words, rather than the story. The more proud you are of your clever sentences and word choice, the more likely it's a passage you'll need to cut. Excessive description that interrupts the flow and seems out of place can be trimmed down to interesting essentials.

Don't use words readers will have to look up. Don't speak in foreign languages to show off your knowledge. Don't spend three pages on the history of civilization (unless it's essential to story, and even then, cut it down to a few paragraphs). Use the least amount of words you can to describe what happens.

> "In many cases when a reader puts a story aside because it 'got boring,' the boredom arose because the writer grew enchanted with his powers of description and lost sight of his priority, which is to keep the ball rolling." – *Stephen King*, *On Writing*

ADJECTIVES/ADVERBS

You've probably heard people say to avoid adverbs; I would scan your manuscript for adjectives as well. They're fine for the unimportant stuff. They can be useful to show transition, mood, or expression. But they are no substitute for actual description, and can easily become hyperbolic or melodramatic.

He stepped quickly.
She said loudly.
He shouted hysterically.
She danced excitedly.

Adverbs are not descriptions, they are symbols for shared experience. The first two instances above are probably fine. The latter two, are reducing complex scenes to grammatical shorthand.

He shouted hysterically is telling. You can still use it, instead of describing exactly what shouting hysterically actually looks like, but if you're using too many adverbs, then you aren't actually describing what is happening in your story, you're just planting speech cues to help readers fill in the blanks.

Generally, there's a better way to say things than with an adverb, which is why it can be useful to look out for them and replace as many as you can with actual description. Adjectives may point to similar problems: narrative summary rather than actual scene-building.

How does he shout excitedly? What does this look like?
How does she dance excitedly? What does this look like?

This might be a good place to ruminate on the crutch of *very*, when you're trying to stress something important. If something is "very good" there are dozens of better words you can use instead. Similarly, if something is "extremely shocking" you're trying to force implied conflict that isn't actually present in the scene. Telling readers they should be shocked won't work; you have to actually shock them with your content.

Adjectives and adverbs are fine in moderation, especially for unimportant scenes that you *don't* want to dramatize. But they can quickly spread like weeds: if you have to use two adverbs in a sentence or three adjectives in a row, there's almost certainly a way to be more precise with your language.

HOLD YOUR ASSES

Sometimes authors will cram several actions together into a compound verb: she begged, cried, and stuttered. These are basically three different actions, so you're reducing it to a "set" rather than one specific action. You're asking readers to picture doing three things at the same time, which reduces the action to absurdum.

In addition to trying to show action through compound verbs, be wary of showing separate actions happening at the same time, with connecting modifiers like *as* or *while*.

Use one action per sentence unless they truly happen at the exact same time. Otherwise, start with the action (what) and follow with the descriptive modifier (how)

For example,

> I followed him into the scary chamber as my heart pounded.
> My heart pounds in my chest as I follow him into the scary chamber.
> Following him into the scary chamber, my heart pounds.

Before this works, it needs to be preceded by a detailed description so we understand why it looks scary; what scary

338

means to the protagonist. Action, then a description of the action.

> I nearly bumped my head on the hand-carved, low-hung doorframe that had been engraved with archaic symbols.

> On the hand-carved, low-hung doorframe that had been engraved with archaic symbols, I nearly bumped my head.

> As I studied the hand-carved, low-hung doorframe that had been engraved with archaic symbols, I nearly bumped my head as I entered.

> While Jack poured us both a thimble of whiskey, I paused to study the hand-carved, low-hung doorframe engraved with archaic symbols, nearly bumping my head as I entered.

In moderation, extended sentences like this can work. But even then, *as* or *while* can slow down a tense scene. Especially when *as* involves something needlessly confusing; it can imply extra words that aren't necessary.

> He was barely coherent as to what was happening
> He was barely coherent.

Check your asses and whiles. They imply two things happening at just the same time; usually one thing is actually happening first, and the other thing is a response or reaction that happens next. If two things are happening at once, the biggest, most interesting action should come first. It can be confusing to have *as-as-as* and a couple of *whiles* which shows stagnation, not momentum or progress, especially if it's a bad habit and it happens often. So during revisions, this is a simple thing to look out for and rewrite.

Melodic, languishing sentences have their place in description, when you have the time and space for them. But during fast, high tense, anxious scenes, with beating hearts and emotions high, try to avoid needlessly long conjunctions.

Finally, if it's a surprise or a twist (a new experience important enough to qualify as an *event*), show the detail after the reveal. A profound shock will be momentarily blinding. Characters won't be studying the details or looking around, rationally investigating the apparition's qualities. They will turn their eyes inward, calculating and processing the new information and what it *means*. You want to break quickly once the thing is revealed, the insight is realized or recognized. Later we can delve into a deeper flashback of how it went down, or a careful description of attributes.

HOW TO LIE TO READERS

I mentioned earlier that dreams can represent false stakes where there is no real conflict, so I'd avoid them, at least in the beginning. But they *can* be used to plant fake pictures in your reader's mind even when they aren't true in your story. Planting imaginary (untrue) images in your books can be used to characterize the setting and mood of a chapter.

This is usually done via metaphor, simile or analogy. You can sneak them in to add gravity and vivid imagery to your chapters. For example...

She said, swaying like a serpent before it eats its prey.

This would work in a chapter that's dangerous or scary or violent. But it wouldn't fit in a normal, non-threatening chapter. While useful in description, comparisons can actually be distracting, especially in a tense scene. Just when you've got readers gripped with the immediacy of *this scene*, you're asking them to picture something completely different. If you have several detailed metaphors in the same scene, it will become a smorgasbord of visual imagery. Readers have trouble holding several different scenes in their heads at once, especially if they're contradictory. Make sure, at least, that the new image reflects the *mood* you want them to feel, otherwise don't use it at all.

Ask yourself, will getting readers to picture this thing help them understand what's happening, and feel the right feelings, or distract and reduce drama from the real scene that's actually taking place? Metaphors can feel creative and satisfying, when you use mental gymnastics to search for and find a fitting comparison, you'll be tempted to think it's stronger than it really is. Use them sparingly, and only when they can enhance, rather than lessen. Also, if possible, find a way of presenting them as the imaginative lens of the narrator or protagonist, rather than the author's additional commentary.

For example, I have a scene where my protagonist goes to a Halloween party. She has a mask, but is wearing plain, boring clothes (because it doesn't make sense for her to have a fancy dress). *But* I want readers to see her a certain way, even though I can't actually put her in a ball gown, so I do this:

> My dark hair is tied up with this bird's nest of a bun that
> holds the mask onto the top of my head, with tangles
> and spikes and long feathers jutting out to the sides. I
> wished I had an amazing black cocktail dress like I've
> seen in fashion magazines, with sequins that glittered in
> the moonlight. I imagined the long tails floating silently
> behind me, hovering just above the cold November dirt, as
> I drifted, like death, among the gravestones.

That's a half-accurate depiction. Many parts of the setting, and her clothing, aren't actually in that scene, but I can serve them up anyway and put them in reader's minds. They will see her in that dress that she's not even wearing. They will see fog and moonlight even though there isn't any. But that's good: I want them to feel that chilly gothic atmosphere.

Long extended fables, anecdotes or dream sequences, on the other hand, should mostly be cut, unless they very clearly help the protagonist figure out what to do next, or represent the surface fear and anxiety. Maybe a teacher or ally tells them a myth or legend to motivate them. While the conflict is completed (no real stakes) the images presented can generate deeper emotion. So images that conjure a heightened or changed state of emotions can work well to demonstrate the way your protagonist is perceiving their environment, based on internal state of mind. This, in turn, can justify their actions:

"The way in which the world is imagined determines at any particular moment what men will do. It does not determine what they will achieve. It determines their effort, their feelings, their hopes, not their accomplishments and results." – *Walter Lippman*

In one of my LitRPG novels, I have my character fight a dragon in a video game. Even though it's mostly a contemporary science fiction, readers also get to experience some extended, fantastical scenes. I love my virtual reality dragon-fighting scene. It's probably one of the things readers will remember about that book. But the stakes aren't real, so while it's visually cool, it also doesn't matter. It's kind of okay because she leaves it with a confidence boost that helps her take action, and deal with the real-life challenges she's been avoiding. Something *changed,* and it's necessary to the plot, so I can get away with it. As St. Paul writes, "Everything is permissible, but not everything is beneficial."

BUT OBVIOUSLY

Beware of little markers like *it's clear* or *it's obvious* or *obviously* … often times this is the author trying to convince readers of a thing without doing the work of establishing it through description. Strong-arming us to accept without proof that things truly are the way the author wishes them to be.

She was clearly frantic.
He was obviously just trying to get attention.

This is like using *very* for emphasis instead of choosing a stronger word. But it also means it's clear *to the character*, which can seem judgmental or dismissive or impatient: which is fine if that's what you mean to portray. It can make them seem hasty or unreliable, and doesn't increase the visual imagery. *Is* it clear or obvious? Or is the character's prejudice showing through? What signs or indications give the impression of this observation? How are the characters or readers meant to understand this, without actually seeing it?

Whenever you're commenting on visual appearance that implies personal opinion, be careful to consider ask yourself,

- **According to whom?**

Who is noticing the attractiveness of the attractive barista behind the bar; is she even seen by the main characters? Is her appearance or the libidinous appraisal and approval relevant to the story? Story needs to happen through a character's eyes; it matters or is emotionally relevant because of what we know and feel about the main character.

It was clear... clear to whom? Who is reflecting on these descriptive details? What is guiding them to remark or comment on particular attributes? How are they forming their assessments, especially of *other character's* internal states or emotions?

Sometimes authors try to impress upon readers how amazing their world is by giving their characters almost comical overreactions. Only use facial expressions if the emotion and meaning aren't clear from the text. If they aren't necessary, cut them – they come across as exaggerated, and they distract from the words. Especially if they have several, radically different expressions in the same handful of paragraphs. If what the character is saying is very important, make the words powerful by making them good, not by showing the character's reaction.

You *can* show characters react to an impressive scene; you can even frame a new scene deliberately and have them take a moment to appreciate the majesty of the setting. You just want to avoid using your characters to contrive artificial praise, *instead* of supplying accurate description.

Similarly, be careful to avoid an impassioned, rehearsed speech that makes a case or an argument, which is then reaffirmed positively.

"What a great way to look at it!" or "You're absolutely right!" or "Yeah, wow, I agree, I never thought of it like that, you've changed my mind!" These can sometimes be not so subtle, self-congratulatory pats on the back; and most likely represent the author's imposed viewpoint.

Plus, it's not good story, because there's no conflict. Instead, the speech needs to be interrupted, silenced, refused or challenged. That's where the conflict lies, in repressing the truth, not giving it a podium.

"Creating art is never about judging. It's always about letting different views on life collide. That's the conflict you are looking for, because these are the themes that cut deepest." – *Ben Shapiro*

DIALOGUE

I'm not sure that dialogue belongs here in the description section, but it is true that the best place for description will be in dialogue tags or to show movement that breaks up conversations. Facial expressions and body language can be included to replace adjectives or adverbs.

You don't need to describe the *way* they say every sentence – especially if the tone or emotion changes every time they open their mouths. But you can add description or active presence as sentence tags; so that instead of a dump of passive details, followed by a visually empty, stagnant exchange of words, the scene and dialogue become interactive. Usually, almost always, stick with "said" and show nuance through descriptive details. Said can also be omitted as long as the speaker is obvious.

> "Yes, that's exactly right." He moved over towards the book shelf, removing a volume and handing it to me with an awkward smile.

> "Yes, that's exactly right," he said, removing a volume from the bookshelf and handing it to me with an awkward smile.

An adverb often *hints* towards what could be a more detailed metaphor. You can also use italics to stress certain words, and change the meaning or sentiment expressed.

> "Yes, that's exactly right," he said predatorily.

> "Yes, that's exactly right," he said, prowling closer like a caged lion stalking his next meal.

346

"Yes," he said, his eyes glowing with a manic ferocity. "That's *exactly* right."

When possible, remove empty, inciting words like *moved, went, started, began.* Don't show the beginning of starting to get ready to prepare to do the thing. Just do the thing. Also, you can use description to convey tension or conflict that isn't apparent within the words or dialogue. Adverbs may help speed things along, and be better than a row of extended, confusing metaphors, but the most important thing will be the conflicted, emotional responses that make the conversation meaningful.

"I know, can you believe it?" Susan gushed.
"It's been so long since we've seen him," Amy mused, her eyes filling with misty tears.
"Well, I bumped into him a few weeks ago," Susan admitted sadly, glancing down and running her pink nails against the wood table, obviously ashamed.
"You beast!" Amy screamed angrily, as she threw her glass of wine against the wall. The bright red stain crept down the bricks, sputtering as the ruby drops fell into the warmth of the glowing fire.
"It wasn't on purpose," Susan said, a tight smile on her lips. "He just showed up at my work unannounced."
"And you didn't think to tell me?" Amy whispered, narrowing her eyes while picking up a piece of broken glass and curling it into her fist, nursing a quiet rage.

The problem here is the rapid emotional changes come too quickly and make the characters seem volatile. Emotions should be shown in dialogue or body language and facial expressions, rather than "told" in narration with adjectives or adverbs.

You generally want more scene, dialogue or action than description; otherwise they can slow down the drama of the action and feel like padding. However, longer descriptive portions can be used intentionally, to give space for brooding pauses that allow feelings to ferment and fester. They are great to *interrupt* heated conflict, allowing characters to be impacted by new events or reveals, as their emotional reaction builds towards an outburst.

Simple Dialogue Rules

- Use contractions. People almost never speak without them, unless they are being especially careful to enunciate, like during a tense conversation.
- Don't say each other's names. After being introduced, unless it's necessary to direct their question towards one person, characters probably won't be constantly using each other's names.
- Almost always, you can get away with *he said, she said*, but that only refers back to the last character mentioned. If there are more than a couple characters, be careful here.
- Try to avoid a descriptive title: if a character hasn't been named yet so you're just calling him the *young boy* or *green-hat guy* or whatever, it can get old fast.
- Skip banal small talk. Don't let people talk about unimportant things. Everything should have tension or conflict, so if they are being nice on the surface, there should be deeper emotional undercurrents like distrust or anxiety.

- Don't allow a character to launch into an extended soliloquy or argument to illustrate their backgrounds or beliefs. If someone knows them, they've probably heard it before: so they'll just say *okay grandpa* and tune them out. If it's a stranger, why would a stranger sit and listen to this announcement unless it was absolutely relevant?
- Give them something to do, so they're not just sitting around talking; the task should be related to their next most pressing story goal.

TORTURE PORN

During especially violent or harrowing action scenes, we should zoom in on the close details; the beads of sweat and blood. But some authors write stories that glorify the sex or violence: the stories are actually thinly framed narrative filled with explicit sex or brutal torture scenes.

There's nothing wrong with writing smut or sadism, unless it completely eclipses the story or surprises your readers. You need to focus on who your audience is, what genre you're writing and what they expect. Both erotica and crime thrillers may have visceral scenes (images that affect your nervous system, that you can feel in your internal organs), but the descriptive details need to enhance the conflict, tension and suspense already at play. If not, you're banking solely on shock value, or the macabre (things that remind one of death). Even so, save your *most* impactful, gross, physically sublime or rapturous scenes for later in the story, so you can build towards them. If they happen too early, they'll cheapen the effect later.

349

Also, stay present within the main character's point of view or reaction. If it's a grisly murder, do they cringe and close their eyes or stare in rapt fascination? If they walk in on a partner cheating, do they notice they're using her favorite blue sheets or do they cry and run out immediately? The details they *notice* will depend on their *response*.

If the vivid, quivering scenes that are the best described and filled with life and realism are the brutal rapes and murders, this says more about the author's morbid curiosity than a character's realistic experience of it. I'm not shaming the use of graphic detail, but if your novel has a lot of gratuitous violence and sex, the big picture, *why is all this happening stuff* will probably need tweaking. Ask yourself, why is *this scene* so much more vivid and detailed than anything else?

INSTALOVE

Earlier I talked about ways to make readers fall in love with your characters, and each other, but this seems like a good place to expand that into showing *romantic* interest.

"Instalove" is a common reader complaint, a designation for characters who fall for each other because they're both very pretty, but without unique character attributions, which can make the ensuing romance seem shallow—especially if they're willing to risk everything for someone they barely know.

Instead, whether in romance novels, or any other genre with potential romantic interest, you should start with resistance and hesitation: give them reasons to ignore or fight against their budding attraction. Physical appearances can be noticed but discounted, even spun into a negative.

> Sure, I mean I guess he's hot in that dangerous, I haven't
> showered in a week, I smell like bike-grease and Mexican
> take-out sort of way. But I *hate* guys like that, especially
> when they think their good looks let them get away with
> being jerks.

This confusing friction between appreciating the form but resisting the attraction, can make a protagonist actively avoid personal encounters, which is why you need to force them into physical proximity, despite reservations. I mentioned earlier how to use the Kabe-Don and the smirk, for example, to showcase an attraction that's vaguely threatening or unwanted.

She'll start noticing tiny details about how he does things or how long his eyelashes are, or the yellow fleck of gold in his left eye, when they have the opportunity to spend time together, and after revealing incidents have shown that there's more depth to him than meets the eye. Remember, details show *interest*. Once she's started to admire his character, she may observe his features more carefully.

But even then, she resists, she scoffs and reminds herself that this *could never happen*. Taboo and forbidden fruit are tempting for a reason, because of the risk, the "we shouldn't" or "we can't" or "what if they find out." There must be risk and consequences, there must be resistance and avoidance, so that through the story events, the characters grow to a point where their attraction overwhelms all the very practical barriers between them, and they come together anyway... *"but we must."*

If a satisfying story resolution involves making the core challenge more difficult and challenging, so it has a profound meaning and forces a change, likewise in a romance novel, you can make the relationship more profound, and their desires more overwhelming, by creating more barriers and obstacles.

What if my novel doesn't have any romance?

In my opinion, it probably should. First, it's about having a bit of sex appeal or eye candy. Second, it's about the complex relationships and conflict that a potential romance provides: feelings, wants and desires are put at cross-purposes against the greater scheme of resolving the plot. Simply put, it's an extra layer of tension and intrigue.

Romance is about vulnerability: it's giving the heroes a weakness or complication that can be used against them. If they don't have anything they *care* about, it will be harder to motivate them into doing dangerous things. Nobody cares about the whole world; your hero shouldn't risk his life to save everybody else's. Unless it's his duty as a space marine, but even then he's just following orders. It's not as heroic to just do what you're told, nor as meaningful. Breaking orders and protocol, risking everything for your family, your crew, your friend, or your true love – those are endearing qualities readers can root for.

It also doesn't have to ever bloom into *physical* romance. It can be two characters who are attracted to each other, and always challenge each other to be better, without revealing their feelings. It can create drama if the feelings aren't reciprocated, or tension if two main characters already have history but couldn't make it work.

You can have one guy kiss the girl early, which adds complexity when she starts to fall for his brother or best friend. You can begin with a "fake" kiss—where the characters are playing a role or it's just pretend—which makes them doubt or blow off more serious feelings later. Story is about transformation, so you don't want to start with a simple, breezy relationship: start with fights and bullying, make them enemies so they'll have more ground to cover before they can become friends, and then lovers. You can also force them to be on opposing sides, each led by their individual principles, so their feelings for each other cloud their resolve. One might even betray the other, or falsely assume that they've been betrayed.

INCLUSION

You may also want to consider the importance of inclusion and representation. Ideally, it shouldn't come this late in your story, or be patched into during revisions to make your novel more politically correct. I admit, when I'm writing I tend to write from my experience, and don't consciously figure out the race or sexuality of my characters. There's even a danger in trying to appropriate or speak for identities that you don't represent. But this can lead to the illusion of a standard, normative experience that leaves no space for some readers to find themselves in.

A few years ago I was at a writing conference and loudly interrupted a conversation about love triangles. Although they're often seen as a problematic trope, I enthused my support: it's an easy tool to increase drama and conflict, and can work really well. I'm against avoiding useful tropes just to try and be different. But someone explained to me how they present a picture of sexual heterogeneity that can be uncomfortable for readers who don't fit mainstream depictions of love and romance. By writing them, I'm communicating that *this is normal*.

Most of my readers like my books. The majority, like me, probably don't think that much about side characters. But I have at least one fan who messages or tweets me regularly to ask whether this or that character is gay or bisexual or whether they'll get into a relationship with so-and-so. And I've always been like, "I don't know, I haven't really thought about it yet." In other words, their sexual identities don't matter that much to me; that's not what the story is about. They're in the world but they're along for the ride; I don't feel a duty to give them a satisfying conclusion, autonomy or self-direction.

I've even made the mistake of making side characters gay and killing them off for drama, not realizing this is an all-too-common trope (not allowing marginalized, minority roles to be main characters or have a happy story arc of their own).

Some readers can easily find their desires represented in the majority of popular fiction. They expect to, so they don't care that much about the smaller details. But for *poc* (people of color), bi, gay, queer or trans identities, they do not see themselves often in main character roles. They see people like them being sidelined into supporting positions. They root for people like them to *matter* in stories because they don't seem to matter in real life, and they're constantly reminded of that fact, in both reality and fiction.

When I get messages like that, questioning the sexual identities of my characters, it's because readers are latching on to the slim roles that might mirror their experience; hoping that they have been included, as a token representative character who participates in the story. But being *recognized as existing*, isn't really enough. These characters matter, not because they are the concern of the majority of readers, but precisely because they aren't. I'm not saying write with an agenda, but do be respectful of your audience, and consider including a realistic diversity of strong characters.

TRIM & SCULPT

Details are like accent marks. They cause readers to slow down and pay attention. If it doesn't *matter* to the story, doesn't spark a reveal or backstory; doesn't evoke a certain mood or emotion; or there's no reason for the character to suddenly notice and fixate on some random trifle, then cut it. When you develop a scene, you're giving life to it. Develop what's important.

The *most* impactful scenes, probably the major turning points, will leave the biggest impression, so they should be *lit up* brightly, with more description, and the details should be unique and interesting, while also maintaining the mood of the scene. Don't say a chair, say an antique stool with a broken peg; a stern chair of polished oak, engraved with pictures of dancing elephants; a fuzzy pink sofa with pink hearts and a coffee stain in the shape of an octopus.

Remember, in the third stage of revisions, the *elucidation*, we're asking "how does this look?" or "how, specifically, did this happen?"

The 5 big rules of description

1. Readers will remember the pictures you put in their heads, not the words on the page.

2. Description should serve and be bound to the story, not distract from it.

3. It should be squeezed into and around the scene action, when the protagonist is using or exploring.

4. Show what's *different*, not what's the same.

5. Leave space for readers to fill in the gaps, but get them started in the right direction so they aren't surprised later.

MEMORANDUM

- *How* does this look?
- How do the pieces fit?
- How does it make sense (details)
- Transportation/movement/location
- Object permanence
- Flash of color/totem
- Break up dialogue with movement
- What's she/he wearing?
- Mood and ambiance
- Spotlight what's important
- Highlight pivotal scenes

12

CLARIFICATION

4th Pass Revisions: Erratum

If you've successfully wrestled your manuscript into shape, and gone through the *what, why, how* stages of revision I've suggested over the last few chapters, you'll have already made significant improvements to your story. But it may have been a messy process, and there's a good chance that quite a bit of it is still rough or full of mistakes.

And that's fine: we've left the little problems towards the end on purpose. But now that we have a strong story, a view worth seeing, it's time to polish the window. I've named this section *erratum*, which is commonly used to refer to a list of corrections or errors in a book, but stems from the Latin verb meaning, wandered, erred or strayed.

We have explored the forest, moved the trees, cleared the path and enhanced the experience of the journey. Now we need to clear the debris so readers don't stumble. This requires more than just the pedantic corrections of spelling or grammar. It's also about adding the highlights that bring out the depth of the story through contrast.

If this was an oil painting, first you'd figure out the idea and arrangement, sketch the scene, block in the main color shapes and dark shadows. The fine detail work would come on top; the final bright white reflective spot in the eyes that give it life, or the subtle gleam on metal surfaces.

As I mentioned earlier, absolute perfection can never be reached. At some point, it just has to be *done*: also these tiny details probably won't be noticed or appreciated. But the value of the art is in the presentation. Not only the absence of obvious flaws or defects; but also the final layers of varnish to preserve the colors, the frame you choose and even the materials you pack your art into, the empty white space that gives it gravity, the discrete tag on the wall. All of it gives a sense of value and purpose.

At this point, the final stage, we're probably done with our heavy edits and revisions, and we'll be cleaning it up and making it presentable by removing mistakes or problems, focusing mainly on little details like word choice, punctuation, sentence structure, grammar and spelling. There are two things we need to do in this final stage of preparation: clarify the writing and remove distractions, so that the *erratum* (miscellaneous imperfections) don't interrupt our reader's experience or cause their attention to wander.

CLEAN IS NOT THE SAME AS GOOD

Specifically, if the previous chapters have been a deep, developmental edit, now we'll move on to secondary levels of editing. A "line edit" would focus mainly on improving the style, word choice or sentence structure; the overall quality of the presented material, the efficacy of the individual phrases. A "copy edit" would focus on more general mechanics, like spelling, grammar or punctuation. A final proofread, would ideally catch typos or errors after the book has been formatted.

These definitions can be fluid, and many editors offer a one-pass service that fixes as much as possible at the same time, but we'll divide this chapter into these broad distinctions.

- Repetition, consistency, details
- First paragraphs, ending hooks, conclusion
- typos, spelling errors, punctuation

Editing your book can be a struggle, which I hope we've significantly reduced through tackling the major issues in the last few chapters, so before we begin, I'll offer some examples to frame the discussion, before attempting more practical suggestions.

THE CREATIVE WAR

The 2016 movie "Genius" is a biographical drama about Thomas Wolfe and the editor who got him into print. Starring Colin Firth, Jude Law and Nicole Kidman, it plays with the romantic ideation of art and the dichotomy between two men who want to publish a great book together. At the beginning, the title *genius* seems to refer to the pure, uncivilized, manic, raw, passionate energy that produces the work. The book belongs to the author, says the editor (Max Perkins). "My only job is to get good books into the hands of readers who love them."

However, to make the book marketable, the editor softly recommends trimming a few chapters and choosing a more commercial title. These suggestions turn into a flaming feud between the author and the editor, which ruins the friendship. But the roles are still clear. The editor's job is to take the *art* and turn it into a *product*. The author creates only for himself, the editor makes the work accessible to other people.

At the celebration dinner, after selling 15,000 copies, one of Thomas Wolfe's supporters, feeling rebuked that the editor is getting all the praise, offers this subtle barb, which subverts the meaning of the movie's title:

> "We should give Mr. Perkins all of the credit. After all, he's the genius who made all of your dreams come true. He's the one who shaped that massive collection into a marketable bestseller. Putting it into the eager hands of readers everywhere."

In fact, Mr. Perkins takes his editorial role far beyond simple proofreading and copyediting: when Fitzgerald comes in looking for handouts, because *Gatsby* was a flop that didn't sell, Max gives him a pep-talk and some cash to see him through.

As depicted in the movie, artists are the tortured geniuses who know nothing about rules, society, expectations, holding a job, paying the bills. So editors and patrons—who do know about those things—need to hold their hands and sometimes, believe in them when they don't believe in themselves, and pick up the check so they can do their great work.

This contribution is worthwhile, because artists are the source of *beauty*. But this creative energy needs limits and boundaries. Thomas Wolfe's description of a man seeing a girl and falling in love is masterful and powerful. Perkins reads it out loud.

> "You don't like it."
> "You know I do. That's not the point."

The point is, it's overwritten and stylized, and detracts from the main message and flow of the story. It's beautiful, but *unnecessary*. An editor's job is to cut out decoration, the unnecessary embellishment, and focus on the story. So they trim all that wild beauty into a manageable, digestible, enjoyable shape for the masses.

The process is both a negotiation and a mentorship; the editor acts as a father-figure and writing coach. "What was it like when you were falling in love for the first time?"

> "It was a lightning bolt."
> "Then that's what it should be. A lightning bolt. Save all the thunder."

That's a great line, but it's harsh. It cuts out half of the experience. It discards the hour of growing rumbles in the dark, the sudden flash that puts all of that noise into context and illuminates everything, the quietening and static electricity that lingers afterward. A lot of contemporary writers focus on action and plot and have very little downtime, and very little beautiful writing, because they've learned to do things this way.

In the end they cut out "her eyes were blue, blue beyond blue like the ocean, a blue he could swim into forever" and left "her eyes were blue."

Max and Thomas slave over the book every day for two years, arguing about what to cut and what to leave in. Both men sacrifice their personal relationships and family for the book.

Wolfe compares his writing to Jazz. It's an art. It pours out of him. "To Hell with standard forms! Be Original! Blaze new trails!"

At this point, it *seems* like Thomas is teaching Max how to let go and loosen up. And that this is a positive thing. But a minute later, while Tom stays out and parties, Max goes home and gets to work.

Tom's messy, theatrical lifestyle erupts in a frantic consort's suicide attempt, which Tom blows off coldly. Max goes home to his wife, newly appreciative of his nice big house, his loyal and faithful wife and his family.

While Tom has the creative passion and energy, left to his own self-destructive devices, there would never be a book – Max has to come in and sternly tell him to *stop* writing. He pulls the pen out of his hand and sets it down.

In a final gesture, Thomas writes a dedication to Max, but Max says "I wish you wouldn't. Editors should be anonymous." Max says editors lose sleep over how much influence they have over authors. "Are we really making books better? Or just making them different?"

The movie reaffirms the romantic view that art is unstable and necessarily tragic, and that to create art you need to let go of the rational mind and lean into your boundless, irrational passion. That's the advice you'll get from most big creativity gurus; the advice most authors cling to defiantly.

It's wrong however, and dangerous, because that's not the way publishing works anymore. Editors aren't going to fight with you to make your book better. If your book isn't already good, already clean, they probably won't offer you a deal; and if they do, they'll expect you to make whatever changes they see fit. Not to mention, if you don't format and style your submission according to the strict rules of the publishing house, they'll move you directly to the reject pile. And that's just in traditional publishing.

In self-publishing, you hire your own editor and pay them for their time. They'll do their best to improve your book, but you are free to accept or ignore their recommendations. And although they may hope your book will be successful, they aren't incentivized to work extra hard to make it a success. Perkins could afford to spend two years on a project and still make a windfall on its success, because he's earning a share of its profits.

Freelance editors will put in as much time and effort as they've been paid for. After that you're on your own. Authors often expect editors to "get" or "appreciate" their book, but this isn't necessary to do a good job, and often hints that the author is reluctant to make suggested changes that will make the book more commercially viable.

CREATIVE VS. RATIONAL

Metaphorically, we could say Mr. Perkins and Thomas Wolfe represent our logical and illogical mind, our Apollo versus our Dionysus. Creativity versus logic; magic versus craft.

Modern authors must internalize these roles, and watch them bicker over every line we write. This can lead to frustration or creative indolence—avoidance of the work that seems too hard to complete.

> *How does writing work?*
> Well, you type & you delete. You rethink. Then you do 187 minutes of research and correct it. You reread & wonder if you have a grasp of English. Then you revise.
> *Then you're done with the book?*
> Then you move to the next sentence.

But the truth is, that's an ugly generalization: there is more than one way of writing. Not all writers are pantsers, servants to the unrestrained flow of inspiration. Some writers are slow and methodical. One type of writing is no better than another type. Surely a book written irrationally is not necessarily a more creative book, nor a more enjoyable book, than one written deliberately.

I can't help jumping in here to share the concept of Nábrók, or *corpsebritches*—the making of a pair of pants from the skin of the dead—believed in Icelandic witchcraft to produce an endless supply of money. Just because you put on your "magic pants" (the ardent belief that discovery writing or pantsing necessarily increases the value) doesn't mean the book will sell.

As the movie points out, the editor is the one focused on the market, on sales, on readership. The editor knows what people want. The editor sets rules and guidelines that enable the writer to continue writing. The editor is the stable, solid, wealthy, happy individual doing a job they're great at and getting paid well for it.

The writer or artist, meanwhile, as depicted in modern media (and often in real life) is selfishly committed to the whims of their own inspiration, an emotional mess, always poor, always struggling, never thinking about other people yet covetous of the success of his peers.

You do not have to choose between them.
You can be both an editor, and a writer. But you do have to decide who is in charge, and recognize that both provide integral value to produce a work of value. You can let the writer plumb the depths of their boundless passion, write whatever they feel inspired to write, and then exhaust yourself trying to self-edit that hot mess into a saleable book; or you can decide to let the editor set some boundaries.

They'll consider the market, they'll help plot the story—at least a bare-bones structure—and have the final word about what to cut and polish. Letting the editor in *early* rather than after the book is written, is the easiest way to slash your writing time and enhance your book's final quality. You can still be creative and inspired when you're writing the scenes, the dialogue. Your characters can still do surprising things that change the story. But the editor's fundamental pursuit will be figuring out what really matters, and cutting everything that doesn't.

SYBARITES (FANCY WORDS)

I've mentioned fancy words a few times earlier, but haven't pressed into the details of what this means specifically. Things can get tricky at this point because we'll be doing two things at once: both improving word choice to avoid repetition, and also removing unnecessarily elaborate or ornate prose. But how can you tell which is which?

A *sybarite* is a person who is self-indulgent in their fondness for sensuous luxury, so the key here is whether you're writing for your readers' benefit, or your own. As Dr. Seuss cautions,

> "The writers who breeds more words than he needs,
> is making a chore for the reader who reads."

Someone posted something online that resonated with me. They said the main difference between *literary* and commercial fiction was the commas... I responded with this little quote:

> "Commas are pauses, in which to savor, the harmonic
> discord of each, individual, lulling, syllable. A comma says,
> appreciate, this word, that I've chosen, for you."

In other words, while this is a bit simplistic, literary fiction is about the author's choice of words, and the simple feeling of pleasure at well-wrought syntax. Commercial fiction is usually more about story and reader enjoyment.

In literary fiction, the words are enough. Sometimes it works! Sometimes literary fiction also has a great, powerful story, but sometimes it's an imposition, self-aware of its grand claims. It may still sell a lot of copies, even if most people can't actually stomach it.

What I hope to impress upon you here, is that literary fiction is a *style* of writing, not necessarily a genre, and that what I call fancy writing (often referred to as "purple prose") does not indicate a better quality book. It can actually be a sign of weak or amateur writing; a form of overcompensating, self-indulgence.

Literary fiction is often *harder* to read, which can make it less enjoyable (or, only enjoyable to a very small audience). This is actually the main value or benefit: the challenge of reading a difficult book provides feelings of erudite accomplishment. It's why I spent a year editing an out-of-print 18th century treatise on solitude, in which the writing was so beautiful it was almost unintelligible.

And that's *why* (some) people take pleasure in it: they put in the work, because they've been told it's good. Part of the satisfaction and appreciation comes from the challenge it offers. But the more opaque it is, the heavier social influence you'll need to convince people it's worth their time.

As I told a friend over cocktails in Lisbon once, "you're trying on purpose to write for a very small, very picky audience. You're choosing to work harder, for less pay, in the hopes that a small group of high-brow critics deem you worthy, deem you good enough." And that's fine, as long as you accept what it is: as long as you care about those accolades, even if you need to get a real job to support yourself (because even most famous, traditionally published authors don't make a full-time living with their books).

> "Art that has long lasting value cannot be appreciated by the majorities. Only the same, small percent will value art's patience as they always have." – *Kurt Cobain*

If you resonate with this general idea, that real art has lasting value only when it isn't appreciated by the public, ask yourself the follow-up question: where does its value come from? Future nameless citizens who will enjoy it enough to pay for it, even though people today don't want it?

These ideas may be a kind of coping mechanism, that allows you to write what you want while ignoring the market's general disdain for your work. It can even be marginally delusional: in the belief that *great writing* is enough, even when it is used in service of a mediocre story. The other problem I often encounter, is that people who love the sound of their words and believe they are writing literary fiction are *actually* writing in commercial genres.

They see *Shades of Gray* or *Twilight* and think, I will write a better book than those, and because those genres are so popular, readers will value and appreciate my enhanced writing, and my books will sell as well. But this assumption fails to account for the fact that the majority of people *like* popular books for a reason; they love them just the way they are.

You personally may feel like most popular books are "bad writing" – but they were good enough to build empires and make a universe-sized dent in modern culture. They were perfect for their audience, and that's why they succeeded.

Writing in a particular style or genre doesn't necessarily make your writing better or worse, and, professionally speaking, won't increase the value of your book, which is market-driven. Spending much more time writing a book that fewer people read and enjoy, doesn't make a lot of sense, unless it's more about *you* than it is the *reader.*

The impulse would be to suggest higher quality books will be stronger sellers over a long period of time, and therefore worth the investment and labor costs. This is rarely true. In fact, the publishing industry has been notoriously bad at selecting winners, and most classic books are only famous today because they unexpectedly did well on the market in their time.

The fastest way to lasting literary success is to ignore the critics and gatekeepers and capture the imagination of the *largest stratum of the reading public*. No matter how you write, or what you write, the value of the book will be calculated by the number of people who enjoy reading it.

I'm not saying you should write in popular genres, if you don't want to. But it's a fundamental, career-ending mistake to assume that if you avoid all cliché, all rules, all order or structure, or banal considerations like "who will enjoy this" and just write "great books" that they will in fact, actually be considered good, by anybody.

> "High and fine literature is wine, and mine is only water; but everybody likes water." – *Mark Twain*

My main point here, is that beautiful words aren't all that important, and it doesn't matter where you put the commas. Even if you do choose the prettiest words, it won't hold up without a good story: you're just the man behind the curtain, all smoke and mirrors, all razzle-dazzle and illusions of grandeur. The story comes first, the structure, the purpose, the point. The magic isn't in the showmanship; it's the work's ability to affect a particular audience.

I'm not saying don't choose the most beautiful words. I love pretty words. But the words can become a distraction. It's like the author interrupting the story and saying, "Yeah the plot is good but aren't I clever for presenting it with this stunningly creative vocabularly?"

A while ago someone sent me this email:

> My favorite advice from you is still, "No one cares about your beautiful words." Well, that's how some of us get caught like fish in a basket: so focused on crafting phrases, we're unable to turn around and swim into the open waters.

I really like this metaphor. Many authors are sitting in their boats on dry land, painting protective sigils on the bow before sealing the hull and making sure it *floats*. Beautiful words, for poetry, are all that matters. But for a book, beautiful words can be irrelevant or showy. At best, they are pointless and empty embellishments, without tangible meaning behind them. At worst, they are holes that will sink your craft.

Ancillary details support the edifice; they are extra pieces that matter. Redundancies are superfluous and distracting; they mar or spoil the effect through excess. It can take a sharp, impartial eye to recognize the difference.

FINAL TOUCHES

If it sounds like I'm pontificating a bit, I hope it's edifying rather than demoralizing. Many authors have told me my *laissez faire* attitude towards writing has given them confidence to hit publish and get their book out there, rather than being paralyzed by doubt that their writing isn't "good enough."

What I've been trying to communicate, is that the precise cadence or style of your writing doesn't matter all that much, so don't worry about it. It is what it is. It's unique to you. It almost certainly isn't the *main value* of your book, nor is it the *main problem*. As Alexander Hamilton said to Thomas Jefferson,

> "There are approximately 1,010,300 words in the English language, but I could never string enough words together to properly express how much I want to hit you with a chair."

This is basically the same as "a picture is worth a thousand words." Whatever words you use, are only rudimentary symbols meant to evoke emotional images. But at this point, now that we have a strong story with plenty of dramatic conflict, you do want to go through and trim, smoothen, enhance and correct, to clarify and elucidate. And in my experience, the *really* good writing comes in the late revision stages, when you replace the common, basic words with the clever and creative ones.

What follows is a list of the *biggest* issues I'll be focusing on in this last, critical round of revisions, before moving on to a final proofread. Some of these I may have mentioned earlier; many of these match the issues and problems I lay out in the list of 25 first chapter mistakes you'll find in the *Grimoire*.

Repetition and word choice. Skim through your manuscript looking for patterns or crutches; things you've said multiple times; the same word repeated several times in close proximity; specific phrases or expressions that show up too often. You should also be on the lookout for any passages that make you stumble or slow down. You may need to read sentences out loud for clarity, so you can rewrite or revise them. Try to break patterns or repetition, or sentences with the same structure. This is where I'll be Googling synonyms every few minutes looking for a better word choice.

Fancy words are kind of like descriptive details: they will stand out and call attention. Use them for the *powerful* scenes, the important bits. If you use them *everywhere*, however, they'll actually lose power and make everything seem ostentatiously ornate, and without purpose.

Intros and outros. When presented with a list of items, people tend to remember the first and last thing. Pay attention especially to your first and last few pages; but also the first and last sentence of each scene or chapter, and make these as strong as possible. See if you can tweak them to increase momentum, by ending on a question or unresolved conflict.

Italics and bold for emphasis. Use as little as possible. Don't use punctuation to show emotion, loudness, or import. When you stress or call attention to everything, it all loses meaning. I probably removed half of the italicized passages in this book, and there are still too many. You can use italics to mark when a character is putting stress on a word, otherwise it's the author marking important things to make sure readers notice them. As Jane Welsh said in 1821, when her betrothed Thomas Carlyle started underlining words in the books he lent her, "I can detect the sense and provide the emphases myself."

Never resort to ALL CAPS or *?!* to show elevated emotion, surprise or shouting. That's punctuation, not story. It's like saying, I'm not good enough at writing to show an accurate emotional display within the context of the scene, so I'll just punctuate it. You're writing a book, not a screenplay. You don't get to say, "he exits stage left, obviously angry." If you need anything more than a single exclamation point or question mark, you need to revise the scene to actually make it exciting and make the conflict and tension real.

Consistent punctuation. Consider how you use words, phrases and proper nouns, which can be tricky. It's not a big deal as long as they're consistent and uniform, and you follow your manuscript's internal rules. But you have to notice, make decisions, choose the best option and then use the search feature or find/replace to fix them all. Also, it's always one space after a period.

Repetitive gestures. You need to break up dialogue with gestures, but be careful about getting into habits. Search for how many times your character smirks, crosses their arms, leans against a wall, rubs their chin or raises their eyebrows. *The Emotion Thesaurus* is a great resource.

Anything other than "said." Be careful of any speech indicator others than he *said, she said.* Use them sparingly, they get distracting. Focus on the words spoken, and real description, not fancy adjectives or adverbs. Thoughts are hard to get right, I usually just put them in italics, without the "he thought" designation.

PROOFREADING

The above sections addressed some basic style considerations; now we might be ready to move on to a final proofread, focusing on grammar mistakes and typos. Most likely, you've already been through your manuscript a few times, and caught a bunch of errors already. The ones that remain—and they're there—are stubborn and recalcitrant. They can be difficult to spot on your own.

> "The greatest of all faults is to be conscious of none."
> – *Thomas Carlyle*

Luckily, you can probably get away with an editing or correction software like Grammarly or ProWritingAid at this point. I've tested both extensively and found that the former catches more actual mistakes and issues; while the latter offers some advanced guidance for identifying weak writing and improving style.

I would take their suggestions with a heavy grain of salt, and ignore most of their rules about comma usage, but they will help you find most of your mistakes, if you don't give the robots too free a rein. As one author commented,

> "The horrors I have seen coming out of such monstrosities… authors will be blissfully unaware of the atrocious treatment your work had received."

If the meaning is clear and it's not a clear spelling error or typo, don't stress. If it's actually a mistake that means something else, fix it. Fix everything you can, but don't change things just to be technically right if it doesn't feel natural to you.

WORKING WITH EDITORS

A lot of authors are so excited to have finished their book, they send it off to an editor right away, but that's probably a mistake. As I mentioned earlier, a developmental edit *might* catch some of the major, big picture issues most authors get wrong. But the thing is, these are common and predictable, which means they can be learned and avoided.

Plus, it's really hard to find a developmental editor who is actually qualified to not only point out plot holes, weak writing, missing character motivations, lack of conflict, or poor pacing, but *also* to suggest precise solutions. They're out there, of course, but they aren't cheap, and even if they dramatically improve your book's flaws and help get it up to par (passably good), that doesn't necessarily mean it will be more commercial or sell better: they can't rewrite or fix the actual content. Not all books will earn, even if they are well-written, so splurging for an editor is not always a sound investment. (This is where *some* people will feel shock and outrage, and insist that *every book* needs an editor; but that would mean only those writers with a disposable income deserve to publish, a proposal I absolutely reject).

A line edit will improve the *style*, and make it smoother and more readable, but it won't fix the critical issues or improve the story. Like I mentioned earlier, the writing is important, but it's not the main thing. Which leaves copy editing or proofreading: but at this point, you're mostly paying for someone to find and fix typos, spelling and grammar issues, and while *most* professional editors should perform better than a spellcheck software, in my experience that's not always the case.

Even if you're a strong speller, typos are easy to overlook when you're in the flow, especially little ones like *it's/its their/ they're/there* and *to/too*. These are also hard to catch with automated software, but I wouldn't spend a lot on a proofreader to catch basic mistakes like this.

Before you pay for editing: read this book again. Seriously. Or at the very least, use the scene checklists and handy cheat-sheet materials in the *Grimoire*. Pay special attention to the list of first chapter red flags. You may not be able to catch and fix everything yourself, but the more you do, the less time your editor will waste fixing simple mistakes or basic punctuation, so they can focus their attention on the big stuff that really matters. Also be careful to remain open to their suggestions and feedback, rather than staunchly defend the uninformed choices that led to the development of the final manuscript, which may have significant structural problems that you are reluctant to acknowledge.

I'm not recommending you publish with typos or errors; of course you shouldn't if you can avoid it. Give them something substantial to complain about or they'll tear you apart for little mistakes. Unfortunately, while I do the best I can, I rewrite and overpolish so much I'm usually writing new words even in the very late stages, which makes it hard to catch any typos on release. I am usually very quick to have a clean, revised edition up after launch, but those negative reviews complaining about typos don't go away. This book launched with at least 10 errors (just .0001% of the total wordcount) and early reviewers made sure to mention it. Do the best you can; but keep in mind even most traditionally published books that have gone through multiple rounds of editing often have a few typos. A friend of mine spelled his own name wrong on the first edition of his book. While this is glib, if you aren't making mistakes, you aren't trying hard enough.

FORMATTING

When editing, I fix typos, punctuation and grammar mistakes, sentence length and structure to improve flow, while also commenting on big picture stuff like character motivation, pacing, dramatic tension and story holes. Then I'll run it through a few careful rounds of software to see if I missed anything. Finally, at this point, I'll also go through and do light formatting, and make sure to remove all the notes and comments in the margins; I'll add headers and footers, a title and copyright page, about the author and call to action section, and prepare the documents for uploading. Formatting is easy to learn and infuriating, even for those who have mastered it. I've made templates and tutorials to help you get a handle on it, but my soul dies a little every time I need to do it myself.

PURIFICATION

To return to our magical theme, if the last section involved scrying through a crystal ball to see how things look, this section would be like smudging our tools with sage. Research has shown that cleansing a space by burning sage can kill 94% of airborne bacteria: an ancient practice, thought to be a superstitious ritual, that actually works better than many modern disinfectants. 94%

accuracy is also about what to expect from either human editors or automatic software, which means, out of every 100 typos you catch, there are 6 more waiting to surprise you. Do try to get your book as clean as possible before you publish, but try not to obsess or overreact if your book goes to print with a handful of mistakes.

Instead, cultivate an aura of thankful gratitude for what you have created: you have done momentous work, and learned a great deal about the craft of writing. You have achieved clarity, skillful mastery, and deep reverence and respect for the words you've summoned; binding them to your will with intent and purpose, in order to express your captivating narrative.

MEMORANDUM

In the early stages of this book, I relied more heavily on my tree example, applying the structure we explored in the first section.

- The *what* are the roots which ground the story (happenings)
- The *why* are the branches which poke and prod (motivations)
- The *how* are the color and shape of the leaves (description)

During the second section, which introduced the four magical words, we focused on the main story questions for each quarter of your story, the *what, how, why* which revealed the *wow*.

It was less easy to come up with the final piece for this endmost section on editing, but if I had to choose one, it would be:

- The *now* are the final touches that demonstrate completion (fulfillment)

Instead of the drama or fruit being pierced to reveal deeply protected secrets (wow); we could view it as peeling, slicing and presenting in order for the fruit to be consumed (now).

Magic rituals or spells often end with a sense of urgency, with phrases like *in this very hour, immediately immediately, quickly quickly, before sunrise,* or *now for me fulfill this matter.* Modern variants might include "it is finished" or "so mote it be." Mote is a variant of *must,* so the meaning can imply "as it is required." The more common conclusion to an earnest prayer is *amen,* which means "so be it" but also conveys faithful confirmation or witness; *belief* that the request has been heard, and the action is already in motion.

If the writing of a book can be seen as a very long, difficult magical ritual or earnest prayer—the attempt to use words to convey meaning, to change or inspire or beguile (in the sense of "to help the time pass pleasantly")—then this final stage represents the conclusion of the work, and the readiness to let go and trust that it will be well received.

1. **What:** what actually happens (happenings, *story*)
2. **Why:** why does it matter? (provocation, *motivations*)
3. **How:** how does it look? (elucidation, *description*)
4. **Now:** is it ready? (clarification, *erratum*)

- Repetition, consistency, details
- First paragraphs, ending hooks, conclusion
- Typos, spelling errors, punctuation
- Preparing the book for consumption
- Meeting the requirements
- Surrendering the work to fulfill its purpose

You pull the sword from the stone. A clap of thunder is the only warning you get, before the tower is struck by lightning and splinters apart. You're thrown into the dark, rushing waters below. The weight of your cloak pulls you down into the reeds, and skeletal branches of coral scrape your ankles.

You succumb to darkness, but are carried by the tides and eventually drift to shore on a wide beach. You choke up water and gasp for air. Large timber of an abandoned shipwreck form an open hallway, like ribs of an ancient beast. You see footprints in the sand just ahead, and stumble forward between the massive boulders. You duck through a narrow passageway, into a secret grotto. Leaves tumble in slow motion through the air, and your vision focuses on a gnarled tree that fills the cave, a shaft of light illuminating it from above. At its roots, a crystal clear pool of pale blue water beckons. You cup your hands and sip the cold, rejuvenating liquid. It washes away your wounds and fills you with health and abundance.

You have earned…
★ The Talisman of Clarity ★
Excellence requires judicious appreciation.

You've earned your fourth totem! Ancient mystery cults or secret societies operated on the basis of strict social silence. Our word for *mystery*, most likely comes from the Greek *initiation*. For the uninitiated, the sacred experience is a deep, ineffable, personal insight. It has meaning *to those who have experienced it*, but this meaning can't be communicated into words. To the uninitiated, it may even seem ridiculous.

New initiates had to follow strict rules and codes of conduct, to prepare them to fully experience the transformative event: so that the wisdom and insight could take root in fertile ground. First you'd be told the myths, the stories, you'd practice the rites, but only on a surface level. You wouldn't be shown the deeper meanings until much later, once you were prepared, once you'd proven yourself worthy and capable.

Magic is about mystery, about withholding, about limiting knowledge before revealing it suddenly in a flood of light, overwhelming the senses, a sudden spontaneous bolt of realization. An insight that strikes like an arrow to the heart. The literal definition of "epiphany" is *to be shown*; but this misses the mark. You need to be in a state of actively desiring, of *wanting* to see, of being acutely aware of your lack, desperately searching for the answer to a specific problem, before you will *recognize* the solution when it is presented to you.

Magic only comes to those who are prepared and willing. Those who have seen the fatal lack, the missing vitality, and who will recognize and accept the value of what they're being shown. The "trick" has the effect of a wondrous feat, only if the initiate has been exposed to the impossibility of its accomplishment. *After* the initiation, once they'd gone through the experience themselves, the rules and prohibitions were no longer necessary.

If nothing else, I hope this book has allowed you to see things more clearly; to respect the challenges while appreciating the process; to agitate the desire for answers and solutions. The imperfect scaffolding and strategies I've provided are meant to lead you deeper into the wilderness of your own imagination, to confront the limitations in your own sacred practice, and they will take you far if you trust them. But eventually, at some point, you'll be able to leave all of these suggestions behind, and deftly manipulate into the abyss of your choosing, with whispering wings of fire and beauty.

> "Rules such as 'write what you know,' and 'show, don't
> tell' while doubtlessly grounded in good sense, can be
> ignored with impunity by any novelist nimble enough to
> get away with it. There is, in fact, only one rule in writing
> fiction: Whatever works, works." – *Tom Robbins*

I've done my best to structure this book in a way that allows for genuine, personal insight, and deep flashes of inspiration. But *you* are the magician. I'm simply holding up the mirror, to show you the reflection of the person you already are, the person you could become, and the magnificent things that you've yet to produce.

The power has taken root within you.
Feel it burning.
Feed the fire.

Sanctify your space. Find something the represents the depth of your vision. It *can* be a crystal—I have a big chunk of green fluorite on my desk that's supposed to be good for creativity. But it could also be a bit of jewelry; a bracelet or a pendant, either natural crystal or just for fun. I would even get something gaudy and showy; it's not for public viewing; it's for the privacy of your writing space and practice, something you wear that reminds you of your magic. (As a reward for this book, I'm getting myself a garish ring in the shape of Zeus). It could also be, however, a sacred receptacle for your potent energizing elixir (a coffee cup). The important thing is, how it makes you *feel*, and that you only use it when writing or working your book.

Conclusion

When I was writing this book, a friend of mine asked an important question that I wasn't fully prepared for. What do you want this book to do for you? What do you hope it will achieve? In other words, what's the point?

My first reaction was defensive, even though the question is beyond reasonable. Why spend hundreds of hours, wrestling with the text, trying to put all my thoughts and ideas into words? There are far better, easier ways to make money. Very few books make a living, even those from established authors. Why do we do this, if not for the money. For the praise and adoration? Unlikely. I propose we do it for the intoxicating challenge of attempting something difficult, something beyond us, that forces us to grow and improve, because only an arduous quest grants us that feeling of accomplishment and purpose. As someone wrote to me not long ago, they wanted to leave something behind to show that they were here. But is a book just an epitaph for a well-lived life, or something more?

For my part, dissatisfied by the available resources and overwhelmed by the hordes of struggling writers who had no shortage of enthusiasm but were suffering from craft problems, I wanted to find a way to share the tips I've learned. I've walked these darkened halls a hundred times, and although each author's journey will be unique, I hope I've been able to provide you with some useful tools and resources to help you explore a little less blindly, and arrive at a satisfactory conclusion to your book that fills you with pride.

If, as a side effect, I've also helped you to feel a little more confident and a little less alone, or if my stories brought a side dish of entertainment or inspiration, I'll count this book a success. But the real merit of this book will be *your* story, not mine. If this book helps create a thousand more, each a small improvement, and raises the bar for writing and publishing in general, I'll have achieved a great feat, with your help.

Magic requires an investment of time and intention; it doesn't happen quickly. The best magic shows up when you're ready for it, when you're prepared enough to handle and contain it. In reading this book, I hope we've begun an alchemical process that attracts greatness to you, in subtle ways you may not fully perceive at first. Continue the work, preparing the field, so that these energies may be allowed to blossom. Knowledge has power when you use it: but you must *earn* it, not *learn* it.

Not everything I've mentioned will work for you. I've tried to simplify an impossible subject, but the path forward may not be easy. Only the lion-hearted will accomplish the task.

An artist is never satisfied with the details, afraid to hear or listen to public reaction, and hones in on the quiet voice of their unique gift, to the exclusion of everything else. A craftman *makes it work*, is prepared to fail 40% of the time, never gives up, and keeps getting better.

You can be a fool *and* a magician, excel at the art *and* the craft. Never lose the wonder. With each new level you unlock, you'll witness unexpected miracles that seem to defy your creative abilities, rising from the abyss of your imagination like magic.

Throughout this book, you've unlocked secrets and earned talismans that represent the integral idea that creativity is a gift to be shared, and the four stages of *ambition, knowledge, diligence* and *clarity*. As you build your own tower, you may feel like you're going around in circles, but each loop gets shorter as you climb to the top.

You are now initiates, but your own adventure is just beginning. Choose joy, aim for value, practice your craft. I've shown you the path and prepared you for the journey. But it's only a guide. The real magic happens when you put pen to paper and create magic of your own.

You've reached the end of your journey.
What do you want to happen next?

You see, I want a lot.
Perhaps I want everything
the darkness that comes with every infinite fall
and the shivering blaze of every step up.
You have not grown old, and it is not too late
To dive into your increasing depths
where life calmly gives out its own secret.
– *Rainer Maria Rilke*

PS. Don't forget to skip back to the *Grimoire* for some bonus resources and content. If you liked this book, and want to help a friend deepen their writing practice, please spread the word!

ONE PAGE SUMMARY

Prepare: INCANTATIONS

1. **Basics:** *Filling Your Cauldron*
2. **Impossible Quest:** *Story Seeds*
3. **Plotting:** *Map the Journey*
4. **Raising Stakes:** *Keeping Secrets*

Produce: CASTING SPELLS

5. **Razzle Dazzle:** *Distract with Action*
6. **Hocus Pocus:** *Engage with Fun Weirdness*
7. **Shazam:** *Charge with Energy*
8. **Abracadabra:** *Reveal the Unexpected*

Perfect: CUT THE FLUFF

9. Phenomenon: *Happenings* (what)
10. Provocation: *Motivations* (why)
11. Elucidation: *Descriptions* (how)
12. Clarification: *Erratum* (now)

AUTHOR'S NOTE

I could have made this book half as long, by only focusing on the specific strategies, without all the extra stories and insights. I made a deliberate choice to take a bigger risk; knowing that the magical theme might alienate some authors. Some people have told me it's "not like my other books" and that's absolutely true; but this is the first one I've dared to share more of myself. I've opened my heart and made a sacrifice.

Unfortunately, by sharing more of my passions, I've also made the book overwhelming and defiant – it doesn't cater to quick skimming or simple insights. There are hundreds of unique writing strategies in this book, but presenting them as a bullet point list wouldn't really get them to sink in, or leave a lasting, emotional impression. The first reviews of this book were *terrible*. According to them, this book is worthless, without any redeeming merits or qualities, and unnecessarily confusing and overwrought. It's garbage, not even worth *trying* to read.

In truth, while these reviews were disappointing, they weren't unexpected. I could have written a simple book, with less heart and soul, and it might have fared better with a general audience. But my intuition (as well as many years of research) steers me towards the following conclusion: that a *good* book will be viewed as "fine" by most people. But a *great* book, people will either love or hate.

It's very possible I've missed the mark, and made it needlessly confusing and lengthy, allowing fewer people access to the content, which was not my intent. But it's also possible, that those of you who actually did put in the effort to read the whole thing, found value in it. I've done my best, and while it's not for everyone, time (and you) will be the judge of whether or not it proves to be a valuable resource.

Earlier in this book I mentioned the Myers Briggs Type Indicator (MBTI) – an introspective self-report questionnaire indicating differing psychological preferences in how people perceive the world and make decisions. Although I'm much more familiar with astrology, I appreciate what the Myers Briggs system reports about my personality type, which is the *Logician* (INTP).

> Through observation and intuition, the keen-eyed INTP
> easily spots inconsistencies and solves problems. They
> thrive on exploring and explaining how things work.
> Creative thinkers, they uncover new information and
> explore unconventional methods. INTP's are often able
> to spot ways to improve on an already brilliant solutions.
> Drawn to theories and insights, INTPS seek to find
> understand and then to explain, in often charming and
> witty ways.

My great strength has always been to zero in on flaws and problems nobody else can see, striving for understanding and efficiency, and finding a way to express, simplify and organize difficult abstract concepts. It's possible, with this book, I've allowed my "charm and wit" too much free rein, but it serves a purpose: to draw a line in the sand, and establish a personal voice that can't be easily erased or ignored. It's my sincere hope that this book leaves a lasting impact, and that you have been enriched through the reading of it.

THE BEST IS YET TO COME

The *Grimoire* section at the back of this book is much more than just notes or a summary: it's an extensive collection of significant and useful supplementary material that didn't fit inside the core structure of this book. You can keep reading to discover new insights, or access the bonus video series and optional Study Guide on *writethemagic.com*.

Grimoire

(appendices)

An *appendix* is a vestigial evolutionary trait that no longer has any obvious purpose. In rabbits, hares, and some other herbivores, it is involved in the digestion of cellulose; but in humans it serves no function and can sometimes be harmful.

For this book, I've developed a lot of *extra* material that could help you digest the main contents, but would be distracting if encountered too early. So I've decided to include many of them here, in a special section I've called the *Grimoire*—basically a textbook of magic or a list of spells, but focused more on specific strategies and practical application than basic pedagogy.

The term probably originates from the Old French *grammaire*, which was used to refer to all books written in Latin, and came to indicate something that was hard to understand. They were "magic" in the sense that they held inscrutable, illegible wisdom that was purely symbolic: a code without a key. I've also added these materials online for your convenience.

writethemagic.com/grimoire

Need more help? If some of this content resonates with you, but you want to see more examples of how to actually put it in practice, I have a bundle of writing courses available that explores some of these strategies in greater detail. As a thank you bonus for purchasing this book, I'm including a discount link that will let you sign up for 81% off, but only for a limited time. If you're ready for more advanced editorial feedback, there's also the option of getting a personal critique of your first 5,000 words; I'll tell you exactly what you need to improve in order to give your book broad commercial appeal.

writethemagic.com/videos

If you're ready to think about publishing or book marketing, I have several free books for you, but I recommend you start with *Guerrilla Publishing*, because it comes with a useful video course, and you'll be introduced to a new book or resource each day.

writethemagic.com/freebooks

25 SIGNS OF AMATEUR WRITING
(first chapter red flags to avoid)

What follows are some insights I've collected, after providing feedback on hundreds of first drafts. I've tried to only share general examples that I notice frequently in the majority of inexperienced manuscripts. There is nothing implicitly or inherently wrong with any of these: they are simple, common mistakes, made by authors who haven't learned through experience or education that there's a better way to present or communicate relevant information.

These are the things that will make an agent, or a reader, put your book down and give up on your story. It might be best to save this section for the editing stages, but I'm sharing them so that as you're working on your first rough draft, you notice them when they appear and can flag them for later revisions.

1. Purple prose, big words. I talked earlier about the difference between literary and commercial fiction; purple prose or fancy writing often indicates a vocabulary in search of a story (or hiding the lack of one).

2. Incidental notes to readers to fill in backstory. She opened the door and screamed (story). Her neighbor, Bill Voss, who once saw her skinny dipping over the fence and was fired from his job three weeks ago (distracting infodump) dropped his microwaved dinner of peas and meatloaf and ran over to help (story.)

Bill noticed the broken window and the bloody footprints on the floor and immediately called the police. Dan Andrews, the police chief, showed up 5 minutes later in his cruiser with flashing lights (story). Bill and Dan had been friends since playing on the high school football team together, and although they went to different colleges, both had moved back to the small town and met up frequently for poker games and BBQ's (distracting infodump).

Craig Smith stopped downstairs for a ham and cheese croissant at the local coffee shop, tossing a $5 bill into the tip jar, like he did every morning (story). The owner, Cynthia Megden, had saved his ass once when the family dog died. He was at a work conference and his wife Doris was at Pilates, which left their two daughters alone with a dead Chihuahua. Cynthia heard the screams, brought them downstairs for hot chocolate, and even buried the animal in the backyard (distracting infodump). A $12 cup of coffee seemed like the least he could do. He grabbed the steaming cup of caffeinated elixir, the Styrofoam cup warming his leather gloves, and walked out into the rain (story).

Done well, this can be a nice quick way to introduce relationships or characters (although it's still telling, not showing). However if it happens almost every paragraph, then your story is like a broken projector that keeps blacking out – you can't relax and get into the drama of the scene because you keep getting pulled away.

This leads to scene fatigue or overwhelm; where you're being presented with a collection of mental pictures. Ask yourself, are you developing one, great picture slowly and adding in emotion? Or are you showing them a slide deck and expecting them to cram like they're studying for a test tomorrow?

3. Too much description. She's walking slowly over the mountain peaks, her teal dress fluttering behind her in the wind, sparks of ember and ash hissing through the air like falling stars, the glowing emblems on her wrists sparkling against the snowy landscape.

Description is really important, but it has to support, not distract. And you can describe the whole scene really quickly, like I've done above in one sentence. But in the beginning, people want to know what is happening and why it matters. They don't care what color her dress or hair is. Ideally, description should be used when the character is noticing things; and they will only notice things the first time they see them (not familiar items or locations), and only when they are relaxed (not seeking immediate survival).

You want to describe the things your characters notice and pay attention to; but they won't notice anything that doesn't interest them. The easy way to introduce a romantic interest is to suddenly be obsessed with each little detail; but romantic interests, in the beginning, are usually dismissed at first: "sure he was handsome, in a conventional sense, but that didn't excuse his behavior." Later, when the protagonist begins to actually think about him in a romantic way or you're building romantic tension, that's when she'll notice how long his eyelashes are or the spots of yellow in his crystal blue eyes, like gold flakes in a mountain stream.

4. Confusing timeline. Something happened last week, a month ago, ten years ago. Does it matter right now? Do you need to mention that thing? Readers are struggling to connect with your *now*, with what's happening to your characters in this present scene. If the character is sitting around thinking of something that happened earlier, or notices something that is different from earlier – it has a good chance of throwing readers out of your story because they have to stop and ask, *wait is this happening now?*

5. The first chapter is like an earthquake. Readers are looking for solid ground so they can read comfortably. Everything that makes them lose track, get confused, have to read backwards or skip forwards, anything that takes them out of the story or forces them to stumble is a red flag, and it's dangerous. Three strikes and in many cases you're already out. Nobody will read the rest of your book, because you made the barrier to entry too high. (This is not because readers are lazy, it's because – like agents – they've learned to recognize signs of weak writing quickly so they don't waste time reading more when there are better books out there).

6. Multiple Adjectives. 1 or 2, tops. 3 or 4 and you're showing off. Her luscious, mermaid green, flowing hair cascaded over her bare, supple shoulders, as she reached out her sparkling, pink, glossy fingernails towards her fizzling drink. Side note: adjectives are not real descriptions.

7. Navel-gazing characters. Janice looked out at the backyard, noticing the overgrown grass, remembering the day they'd had a picnic on the fresh-cut grass, before her husband died, and he was still around to mow the lawn. (Actually, this isn't terrible writing, or a bad start or character introduction.) The problem is, in the first chapter, we don't know who Janice is or care enough about her to feel sympathy. We are waiting to see what happens. What's going on now. Why the author is telling this story.

Imagine it's a coworker telling you a story on a ten-minute lunch break. You'd want them to skip the details and get to the point. The first chapter should have very little history and a lot of action. Have things happen. Don't start with sitting on a couch, eating breakfast, waking up. Start just before their life implodes. Yes, you need to create sympathy and introduce the characters first, and your historical vignettes may reveal personal information, but they need to happen much later.

Show the character through reaction with plot events; you'll want them to be likable, so on the surface they probably seem cool – someone you'd want to be friends with, based on one meeting. They probably seem confident and aloof, but also kind and honest and just. They have principles that they stand up for, which makes them stand out. (Your heroes can start with a heroic temperament; or, even if they aren't yet strong enough to take action, you can show them wishing they were strong enough to stand up to bullies. Noticing the bad actions of others can be a type of heroism, or at least a symptom of heroic tendencies.

However, someone's wishes or thoughts or reflections aren't what makes someone heroic, it's their actions: don't assume readers will like your characters just because of what they've been through, or what they're thinking. Start with action, good behavior, and introductory episodes that force your protagonist into something that reveals their hidden strengths and moral compass.

Save the personal reveals for when characters are feeling vulnerable, when it makes sense to the story. After readers already like them and care about what happens (pity and fear), then you can make them fall in love with your characters through a deeper historical episode or backstory. Otherwise, you're trying to make readers fall in love with complete strangers in chapter one: that's too big an ask. Treat it like a first date, keep it light and feature their best qualities.

8. Needlessly clever metaphors, that make you think about and picture something that's completely irrelevant to the scene (side tip: metaphors are useful to put pictures in people's heads and make them feel things even when you don't actually have those things in your book).

9. Too many people (and each one with a full-on description about her appearance and backstory). Don't introduce your reader to a dozen people at once, what they're wearing, and how they all know each other, and expect readers to remember or care about any of it.

Tim sat next to Bob, who was larger and heavyset. Tim noticed the way the sweat pooled in the skin-flabs around his nipples and waist, staining his white T-shirt. His dark hair was well past a trim, but he didn't believe in living up to society's ideals of masculine grooming.

This is OK description, for one character, but what if there were several? Does it matter that Bob doesn't believe in living up to society's ideals? Will it affect or impact the plot? Is it revealing that Tim knows this about Bob – or is he guessing? How does Tim's revulsion to Bob change the mood of this scene?

Generally, description is described to show interest. When someone is attracted or repulsed, they start noticing things. Having a character suddenly get very interested in very small descriptive details – the way the outer rim of his green eyes were fiery yellow, like veins of gold – is a great way to show romantic interest way later in the book. But it can also be used to show whatever is important. And if too many things are important (described in great detail), then nothing is important, and readers will begin tuning you out or skipping over your descriptive passages because they know it doesn't matter.

10. Needless detail. Specificity and jargon can show expertise – unless you focus way too much on tiny details that don't matter. I see this a lot in military thrillers, and fine, your audience might want to know every spring involved as the hero slowly assembles his CMMG Resolute 300 Mk4 Semi-Automatic with a medium-tapered 4140CM steel barrel and a salt-and-nitride-finished barrel and SV muzzle brake and a full-length picatinny rail that he bought on eBay for $297.

But probably, this is going to feel like getting hit in the head by that rifle repeatedly. Don't show off that you know how to Google for "research."

11. Swearing. In certain genres, cursing is *fine*. If you want to use it, go for it. Some readers will hate it, some will love it. I'm pro-swearing, and my books with curse words outsell those without. But if you use too many, before readers care about the characters or what's happening, you might be losing half your readers with absolutely non-essential elements. Plus, too much gratuitous swearing early on will make it harder to use curse words with impact later. Occasional swearing is probably fine, but a dozen per page will be distracting even for hardened pirates.

12. Backstory. Backstory, how much is too much? You're allowed one sentence, less if possible. 3 facts maximum. Obviously these rules are flexible guidelines. What you don't want is three paragraphs of exposition on backstory in between one sentence that moves the plot forward into the action again. Rule of thumb: Stay in the room! Wherever you are, whenever you are, stay there as much as possible. Stay with what's happening. You'll be tempted to explain to readers who these people are, why this scene matters, and the underlying tensions between them because of what happened at the office party last Christmas, but don't. (Unless you can do it in under a sentence, then maybe. No wait, just don't.) Do they even *know* this information? Are they thinking about it right now; is it critical and relevant to the actual thing that's happening – do they have time to think about old stuff rather than reacting to stuff right now? If they know the info already, who are they telling? Or are they thinking out loud because they're aware of being observed by readers; in which case they are not authentically experiencing the plot events – they are simulating how they should be reacting to plot events, but stopping every few sentences to tell you about it. Is anything really happening in this section? Or are the characters just talking about stuff out loud for the benefit of the reader?

Here's a good rule of thumb: make them ask the question, before you give them the answer. Make them want to know what happened between *x* and *y* ten years ago. Make them wonder what used to be in that empty bookshelf space without the dust; or what's behind that locked door; or how that guy got the scar across his face. Because right now, they don't care. If it's important to your story (it has emotional relevance to your characters and may influence their actions or reactions) show it's *absence*. Have the question raised but refuse to answer. The more important the information, the less easy it should be for readers to access it. Also, if they have time to sit around and make small talk about trivial events that didn't have an emotional impact on them, it means your plot is too slow or stakes are too low, because your characters should need or want something much more pressing than getting to know each other or navel-gazing or reviewing things that happened earlier.

13. All big action. *Boom Zap Pow!!!* Who are these people, why is this violence and blood and gore necessary? Why do I care about these dead people? Action scenes without character depth have no emotional depth. Action can be meaningful later, when there's real danger. Does any of this actually matter to the main story – or is this the routine, ordinary world we can expect? Also, if there's this much violence now, we probably aren't going to get excited about actual, real violence later.

Violence is not conflict. The first chapter needs to make the protagonist sympathetic and provide real conflict. *What do you mean, I killed a half dozen guys!* They didn't matter emotionally; the protagonist wasn't nervous about his own safety (he didn't feel threatened); so these deaths are incidental. They can show that our protagonist is a heartless killer, fine – but that probably won't make him sympathetic; or that the villains are cruel and vicious (but that doesn't make them scary, if the protagonist is not at risk).

14. Real story vs. backstory. You have a polaroid and a movie camera. Backstories are snapshots of that sunny day at the beach when Eddie nearly drowned. Real stories are slow pans across the room and a fly buzzing in the window and the stench of cleaning supplies and the severed hand in the sink. Backstory is concluded action that has no teeth; there's no real danger, so there's no real suspense or intrigue. The results are known. Real story is unresolved conflict; the resolution hasn't happened yet; the danger is real.

Add more conflict and suspense earlier (show the stakes or danger inherent in the world) and much less backstory exposition (those things need to come out after raising questions, in the right place, when relevant… it's a tough balance but always shoot for more actual story (unresolved action) than backstory (resolved action).

15. All the answers: intrigue and suspense are caused by unresolved answers about unresolved conflict. You need to show the conflict and tension to show that the protagonist may face real consequences. Most of the plot will depend on your character's attempts to fill in knowledge gaps and figure out what's happening, in order to avoid conflict.

16. Painful trauma, emotion, heartbreak… we don't care that much because we don't know who the people are or what's happening. Is she choosing this? Forced to comply? Resisting? Is it a surprise or something she expected? This can work well for a prologue, that skips forward; or for a late-book scene (dark night of the soul) not really for a first chapter. You may think you're painting an emotional scene wrought with passion and pathos and gnashing teeth and agony… but you're probably throwing a little emo-tantrum. Characters will always seem like drama queens if you overdo their emotional reactions. To fully appreciate, understand and feel the character's pain, we need to know why this matters so much and is so traumatic. We can't empathize if we don't have the details; and you don't want to give all the details in chapter one. So these scenes will probably fall flat, unless they come later.

17. On that note... Don't use any exclamation points in chapter one. Seriously. They're almost never warranted. Definitely no more than 5, max. And if you ever have a double "Shoot!!" or confused shriek "What the hell?!" those probably need to go, too.

18. When something happens, stop writing. I know I said this already, but this one thing will immediately transform your writing. Something big happens, changes, something new and surprising and shocking. *Full stop, turn the page.* Give readers a moment to process with a scene or chapter break, right when the thing happens. Don't continue or show the reaction in the next sentence.

19. Not describing the scene: We should get the scene/setting early so we can picture what's happening, but not in huge detail, just the basics. Spotlight a couple of things that portray your unique world or setting, and the genre. Imagine you're walking into a lecture, but a little uncertain if you're in the right room. The professor keeps going and going without actually telling you what the topic is; he's in the middle of some anecdote and you're waiting for him to confirm or deny that you're in the right place so you can either pay attention or leave quickly. I like to see a little setting description so it's not just a generic landscape; but let the conflict and action happen and show the consequences.

20. Have the thing happen first. Don't explain the thing that's going to happen before/as the thing is happening. *Boom!* A bomb went off. It reminded me of the time I was in

Afghanistan fighting poppy farmers, and the time my 3rd wife slammed the door, after locking me out of my own house. I met her at a baseball game; all her family loved baseball. It's one of the things that drew us together. After getting out of the army, I was haunted by so many ghosts and PTSD, you'd think the crack of a bat hitting a home run would trigger an anxiety attack, but somehow I found the excitement comforting, without the risk of shrapnel in your skull. So anyway, about that bomb...

How to know if it's backstory/telling: who is giving all this information? Why are they giving this information right now? Is it stuff they already know? Are they just thinking through it anyway... reminding themselves of the stakes? Fine if they are debating a difficult moral decision, which builds conflict. Not fine if they're just talking out loud so readers know the details. Time yourself reading those paragraphs out loud where nothing is happening. Imagine your characters standing still and waiting for this little soliloquy to wrap up so they can get back to what they were doing. How often do you make them sit around and wait? What is actually happening? Don't make your characters wait for readers to catch up to the story.

21. Nothing is happening. Maybe there's a lot of backstory, off screen memories or flashbacks, thinking through stuff or reacting to an almost event, but actually... nothing is happening. Characters need to be faced with things that demand a response, but probably not things that demand their entire history to properly understand the central conflict or pathos. Not in the first chapter.

22. POV jumping. POV jumping is hard to pull off well; especially if you're switching a first-person "I" voice between different heads/characters. It's hard to see who is speaking. There's also danger in having different characters responding to the same events, so the plot isn't really moving forward, it's repeating the same information twice, so nothing is new or surprising. Readers should learn things as characters learn things, at the same time.

Side tip: referring to external events with words like "normally, usually" lessen the conflict; unless it's to show contrast. Gerald burst into flame, unable to control his powers. He was usually even-tempered, even cordial on my usual visits to his underground troll bank of illicit alien contraband. But the new batch of augmented security robots were scanning the neighborhood and he was clearly on edge.

23. Descriptions for each character. I scattered my father's ashes over the canyon and turned back towards the car. My wife Linda was waiting. At 5.7 she's just a few inches shorter than I am, with wafting blonde hair that contrasts with her black blazer and pearls. I climb into the red convertible and she pats me on the shoulder. I glance into the rearview mirror as Lance tosses me a bag of Cheetos. "May he rest in cheeses," he says. "Are you high? That joke's worse than usual." Lance leans forward, pushing his dark bangs off his unshaven face, revealing the clear blue eyes and dark lashes that are too pretty for his unkempt state and the jagged tattoos that run up and down his chiseled forearms.

Character description needs to be done with new information that points to personality; more than just physical markers; and connected with an action or interaction, not just your POV character checking him out and commenting about his appearance for no reason.

24. We won't feel sympathy if we don't have details; so no vague posting. It doesn't increase intrigue if you tell us what happened but skip the details. You need to show the pain without telling us why it matters, until we want to know – then hold it out, lean into the uncertainty, hook and switch. Dangle answers out of reach.

25. Bad dialogue (what is bad dialogue?) language that nobody would ever say. Clichéd lines. Exclamations or noises. Obviously unrealistic people. Real people don't talk out loud about things that they know, or share their feelings easily, or use full names and details for each other. Keep it short and simple; conflict is in subtext and nuance. People rarely exchange information or say what they mean.

Bonus: I mentioned earlier, you can use italics to show thought; but beware of interrupting the narrative every few sentences to have the character react mentally and "think" things to themselves or mutter to themselves. A good thought is probably half a sentence, a fragment that reveals mood, character, emotion or new information. If you have a sort of mental running dialogue of commentary throughout especially the first chapter, it really slows things up and can seem melodramatic. It can also be confusing if you're jumping from 1st person thoughts to 3rd person narrative.

This is especially true if the character is musing on current event of their world to share/show/introduce world-building concepts for the first time; or if they are casually laughing at themselves for being silly. High-level, reflexive self-awareness paired with jovial easy-go-lucky attitude makes it hard for anything to seem important or serious. You can have light and fun scenes or playful banter with friends, but remember, conflict is the most important thing, and the conflict should be big enough that they don't easily blow it off, forget or accept *que sera sera* (oh well, whatever, nothing I can do about it).

17 TIPS FROM VIDEO GAMES

Scene/Setting

1. Frame entrance, show reaction

This is an easy one, when you arrive someplace new, the camera shows a back view of the character, positioning the frame to catch the best view of the sweeping scenery, then shows the reaction (surprise, wonder, awe) of the main character. If there are multiple characters, they can comment on it or say "wow." Just make sure you show the description with words, not just hint at it through the character's statements. Don't let "beauty" be the end in itself; add conflict soon so that the beautiful is always fleeting or threatened, and characters don't have time to revel in nice things. Also, only characters who have never seen this before will react this way; it can be nice to add someone more experienced who is overly familiar with it.

"Wow," she said, standing near the railing. "It's beautiful."
"Well, I wouldn't call it that, but I guess it has a kind of charm. To be honest I haven't looked up in months, always keeping my head down, trying to survive. Stand out in the open like that, admiring the view, and you won't last long out here."

2. Nice view, slow down, pretty music

This one is similar, though harder to describe. When you're *supposed* to be appreciating the beauty, there's a slow, close up detail scene with pleasant music playing. You can use an emotional cue: "She sat down her bag, feeling a warmth rising in her chest as she gazed out over the view towards the horizon."

3. Force characters on to right path

Characters need to be responsible for the consequences of their actions, but also constrained by the available choices. In video games, I get frustrated by "open worlds" that are huge and sprawling, full of adventures and sidequests. I lose track of the main story. However in at least one recent release, I actually got to the ending too quickly, and now I'm going back to play through all the great sidequest content I missed. There's a difference between meaningful sidequests that influence the ending, by making an emotional impact (impossible quest)... and the trivial tasks that help them level up but focus on interesting events that show more of the world (world worth saving). To make your story believable, you need to corral characters and readers by setting hard limits and obstacles; excuses or reasons *why* they can't just find an easy solution. In video games, this will be a wall or ocean or border of some kind; it could also be a locked door or missing tool.

4. Treasure in every cave/behind every waterfall

In open-world games, anything unique or interesting about the landscape is probably a clue hinting at discoveries. In books, anything you show will be interesting (intentional). It's frustrating to climb a mountain or find a waterful that *doesn't* have a secret cave behind it with a unique treasure. As the author, you are the *only one* who knows what's important to this story; so readers will assume anything you show might have a surprise use, function or reveal. It might be a clue. It might not. Truth be told, in many videos games I'm disappointed when I don't find something where there should have been something; that makes me appreciate when my faith is rewarded and something is waiting for me. The point is, if you show something, have it feel like a discovery. Your characters will be solving problems very early in your story, and seeking solutions. That will give them narrow vision: does this help my immediate goals or not? They won't notice anything else. Give them something to want, and the landscape will be filled with purpose.

5. Clues, easy to see, bright orange (levels) – I'm a casual gamer, so I often play on "easy" mode. In certain games, I've noticed, the path is made clearer for amateurs: bright marks on the walls to show the climbing route or way forward, so I don't get lost or stuck for an hour trying to figure things out. People who like the challenge of discovery would think this is too heavy-handed. In your first draft, I recommend making the clues or turning points as big and clear as you can. Later, you can tone them down.

Raise Stakes

6. Every victory is delayed

Every time they're about to complete their current goal or mission, thwart their intentions. Every victory reveals a bigger problem or challenge. Their plans fail. Each time they find their objective and are about to realize their quest, there should be a spontaneous danger, surprise or battle (the obstacles equal to or greater than the boon they need).

7. When hanging by fingertips... fall

Don't just show them doing scary things, with the possibility of danger, that they navigate successfully. Allow the bad things to happen.

8. Increase challenges when they level up

As they gain in confidence and ability, the challenges and obstacles will always need to scale up to be formidable. They may need boss fights or enhanced enemies with new weapons. If they defeated a challenge earlier, don't make them able to defeat the same challenge again later in the same way.

9. Information quest leads to favor quest

If their current goal is simple, like find a guy and ask him about a critical piece of information, you can turn it into an extended quest: he has what they want, but he'll trade it for help with another matter. (That simple mission will prove more dangerous than they expected; and maybe when they return the guy has been killed and they still have no answers).

10. Avoid fights if possible (at first)

At least for the first half of the book, your protagonist will probably avoid conflict; and even later they shouldn't relish confrontation or violence. Conflict is usually unplanned or unexpected; until later when the stakes are high and clear, and the protagonist understands this confrontation is necessary.

11. No cheat codes (can't skip key scenes)

In some video games, you can level up quickly or skip slow cutscenes to get back to the action; but *some* of these are important to understand the main storyline. And if the game is too easy, it won't feel meaningful. Make sure the boring bits (slow scenes) are crucial because they reveal important information. Highlight the key scenes with description or emotion.

12. Need more training, advantage or abilities

In many cases, your protagonist may have a special gift, but they still need training. They *shouldn't* be able to defeat the antagonist or resolve their impossible quest easily, from the beginning – it should cost them. This means you'll probably need some form of training or mentorship, even if it's a sped-up collage (three months of brutal, repetitive training: don't show every day and every practice routine, but show a few, the improvement, and the important changes or events that take place during that period).

Side Missions

Side missions (subplots) do two things: deepen personality and character arc so we feel deeper connection; and lighter and easier challenges that frame difficult moral decisions. These

413

"in-between" scenes can demonstrate the character's moral progression.

Is the side plot necessary?
- Does she change?
- Does she get a new weapon/ability/totem that will become necessary later?
- Will it add future drama later, or heighten tension by revealing conflict?

Structure/Impact

13. Story recap between action. Discuss what happened, make new plans, remind of the stakes and obstacles (stakes are bad things that may happen; obstacles are the things that will stop you from preventing those bad things.)

14. The sidekick/buddy for humor. Many video games include a sidekick or supplementary character who accompanies the main hero on quests; this allows them to help each other access some hard to reach places, and also gives a running commentary of quips, conversation or backstory to keep things moving, especially during transit scenes. It can even be someone annoying that becomes loveable, humanizing the protagonist.

15. Preface/flashback. These can establish the skills of the character before the story starts, hint at coming dangers, or heighten the death scenes by making readers care more about characters. It can also explain character motivation and why this *one thing* they can't just walk away from.

16. Addiction is dissatisfaction. Addiction is doing the thing even while not receiving the immediate benefits. You need to delay answers, never satisfy and keep loops open. If readers are satisfied and have all the answers, then the conflict won't matter.

17. Establish rules early with real examples of harsh discipline; someone rebelling and getting punished. These are the hard limits of the world, and set the expectations and stakes. You can also show someone villainous that's way too strong or powerful; or someone ridiculously cool and heroic – figures the character will be amazed at or terrified of; but will later become, and face.

GENRE BREAKDOWN: YA DYSTOPIAN

When I started writing, I read a lot of books in my genre (young adult fantasy) looking for commonalities. I'm sharing these rough, generic summaries so you can see how to begin crafting a *potential* story that includes popular elements in a unique way.

> A very shy girl. Her only friend is a guy but she doesn't like him like that. She stands in front of a mirror and notices her flaw, something she hates about herself. Her parents are gone and she lives with a relative or adopted family. In the *first* chapter, she goes to a party or concert and meets a guy. He's the hottest guy she's ever seen. She's instantly smitten by him. He's so cool he'd never notice her... but he does. He even comes straight up to her and accuses

her of something or mistakes her for someone else. At first he is hostile and rude. Then he's cold and dismissive, or maybe cruelly flirtatious. After that incident, things slow down and we learn more about her. Maybe there's something strange about her she can't explain. Maybe she has mysterious powers that she's learned to live with and keep a secret. She doesn't know why she has them. She thinks it just makes her strange and abnormal. But then she sees the guy again – they keep running into each other, and they have a powerful response. She can't stop thinking about him. They seem to have a special, magical connection which leaves her flustered and confused. He gazes at her like she's a puzzle he can't figure out. He doesn't understand why she doesn't know who she is and what she's capable of. Her powers grow and she's probably in danger, both from accidentally hurting others and from someone who's hunting her. The hot guy finally reveals to her what he is, why they have a connection, and why she's in danger…

In any kind of YA, parentage is important. Usually one or both parents are missing – assumed dead. Later we may discover they aren't really dead. They are in prison; or they are the enemy; or something else happened. The protagonist finds out that through her parents she is irrevocably tied to the core plot. Her father started this. Her mother is the villain. She inherited powers through one of them. Maybe we find out that her parents aren't really her parents, and her new boyfriend is actually her brother. Dealing with these revelations is part of the character coming to grips with her new self.

Here's another example, that skews slightly more dystopian, and includes a love triangle; which can work well if each character represents a different class or side in the brewing conflict.

There's a big choosing ceremony or event coming up. It might be a wedding even. Whatever it is, the main character has no freedom to choose her own destiny. She might rebel or run away. Or something else unexpected happens. Whether or not the ceremony goes through, after the ceremony life is completely different. She's left her family and is learning new skills and facing new challenges. She's special: if not a princess already, she finds out that her mother or father (who she's been lied to about) was actually important and powerful. Now she feels like she has to make them proud and live up to their memory. She discovers that she has powers – powers she shouldn't even have. Nobody understands her. People are afraid of her. In the meantime there are two boys in her orbit. One is dark haired jerk, one is blond and kind. They usually have breathtaking blue or green eyes. One is poor, one is rich. One turns out to be a prince, the other turns out to be an assassin (a bad guy – in opposition to her own goals and wants). Or they could be brothers. Or best friends. Her feelings for each change as she deals with new revelations. Ultimately, she learns to control her powers, and begins fighting back. But all her plans fail, she's captured and discovered, and held captive at the mercy of the villain. She escapes certain death, defeats her enemies (for now – but not for good) and finds a safe place to regroup.

When I started writing dystopian, I was frustrated to discover that the books I'd been writing weren't in line with the most popular books in the genre. While my novels flirted with apocalyptic intrigue (the stakes are high enough that failure could mean the end of civilization), they all start in the contemporary, modern world. That means my books are going to be a little bit slower. I'll have to work harder to add in some early intrigue and establish the narrator's voice and personality.

In postapocalyptic dystopian novels, the lead characters can start off already broken and hopeless, just trying to survive. But they find hope and meaning in their love for each other. That's a simple plot. And it's exciting. You can start with the action, in an established far-future culture or society with strict rules and systems. The first scenes can be gore and violence.

I can't rewrite the novels I've already completed, but I've since realized my in-between books aren't quite what readers expect, desire or respond to. I'm missing the elements that define the genre. It has nothing to do with the *quality* of the writing, but without the expected components, I have to work much harder to keep readers enthralled in my story. In future books, I'll be more careful to write a story that features the best elements readers love:

Tyrant: A dystopian needs a tyrant, an oppressive government/society without freedom. A place with no hope. Cruel and unjust. A secret conspiracy.

Complacency: Nobody is happy… but they don't rebel. They walk the line. They don't have a leader.

Violence: Probably involving teens and kids with guns, and death and gore.

Inciting Event: The protagonist gets forced onto a path of action that's impossible for her to refuse. She does the best she can. It may involve sacrificing herself to save someone she loves.

Love interest (x2): There's usually at least two main love interests. There's a lost guy, she gives him meaning and purpose. He wants to save and protect her. She wants to be strong and pushes him away. They fight because she refuses to accept help. He can be controlling and overprotective. He's dark and secretive. The other guy is happy, confident, funny and friendly. She should like him. He likes her, but she doesn't feel that way about him. This other guy may turn out to be the bad guy. She has mixed feelings; because she does like him a little. Maybe they kiss. Maybe she's attracted to him.

A revolution: she becomes a revolutionary hero, and leads an uprising. Her role is more important than sorting out her relationships, so she stalls on that front and ignores her feelings. She won't let herself be happy until her people are free. She feels bad about killing, at first, but gets better at it.

An extensive list for YA dystopian novels might look something like this:

- A structured society with class conflict
- Second class citizens/slaves

- Feelings or authenticity is outlawed (emotional repression)
- Testing or trials used to define and position roles
- A choosing or placement ceremony
- Being an outlaw, getting jailed or executed for existing
- Can't choose how to love or marry
- No control over own life
- Social statuses can be changed suddenly or hacked
- Fancy party with fancy dress
- Rich, powerful guy takes interest in her
- Strong, handsome guy likes her (main love interest). He's tough and mean to everyone but her. He saves her and protects her… but they clash at the beginning "I don't need you to protect me!"
- Devious, fanatical villain with personal vendetta
- A class of enforcers who hunt down nonconformers (her parents might be one). She might be one too, until she's fallen and becomes hunted herself.
- A cruel mother who abandons her, or a weak father who doesn't protect
- Ungrateful siblings she needs to support
- She must break the law or risk bending the rules to protect her family
- Revolution/rebellion is already brewing, but they need a symbol
- She's already practically trained, efficient, competent (she's had to be)
- Might be an assassin, thief or hunter

- War, soldiers, or big monsters (something wild and dangerous that is hunting them).
- A secret that could destroy everything
- A special child, chosen one that was lost (might be her)

If you took out the "dystopian" part, but kept the YA – you'd still get the love interests. Instead of a tyrant, you'd have an evil force or power – she has something he wants. She's the only one who can stop him. She discovers she has powers that are mysteriously and abnormally strong.

PRODUCTIVITY (SOFTWARE, HARDWARE)

Some people need more help with the details of actually getting words on the page, so here are some pointers. Keep in mind I'm an expert, neuro-atypical procrastinator with ADHD. I'll spend 5 hours avoiding for every 20 minutes of writing. But that also means I've had more experience than most in wrestling with my resistance. I may not have defeated my demons, but I'm intimately aware of them and can offer some unique strategies to keep yours at bay.

Basically, I recommend creating a writing habit centered around timed sprints for about an hour a day (three, 20-minute sprints). I recommend doing this in *iA Writer* or a similar writing app on a smartphone or iPad, for minimal distractions, with a bluetooth keyboard. I think it helps to have a different device or space or routine for writing the words, than you have for putting it all together and doing deeper revisions and edits (I export to Dropbox, then add new scenes into my Word document.)

Resist the urge to edit, polish, rephrase or even correct typos or punctuation issues. Try to stay in the flow. There's even evidence that writing blindly (typing while closing your eyes or looking at a blank screen) can boost wordcount; something similar happens when you dictate.

Bribing your muse

A while ago I started playing with the idea of acting like the author I want to be, which includes buying myself things that make me feel like a "real" writer: the fancy laptop in the old leather bag; slight emo-goth dieselpunk attire; that sort of thing. I have a blog post up about establishing an author brand. The main thing is, it's OK to buy yourself silly things that make you feel good. Feeling good about your writing is a big deal. One of my favorite things is a wooden *Penna* keyboard, because it's so pretty, even if I don't use it often to actually write (I should, but I prefer my smaller, portable one). It cost well beyond reason. I'm trying to make writing more enjoyable, since it's not just about function. I'm bribing my muse with pretty things.

My other idea was to only eat cookies and sugar while writing, to trick my brain into being addicted to writing (getting that rush of dopamine) but I have no self control… maybe you'll have better luck. Try to make writing *feel good*; even if it's something like lighting a scented candle, filling your writing space with fun toys, or treating yourself to favorite snacks.

Best hardware and software

I did a lot of research to find a better writing setup to improve my word count. As I mentioned, I use a lightweight bluetooth keyboard with my iPhone; the *iA Writer* app has a dark screen feature. It keeps the text centered and fades out when you hit return. I share to Dropbox, then copy and paste it into my longer Word document, scene by scene. Results will vary though, so find something that works and feels comfortable for you. Here are some extra details if you intend on shopping.

I think there may be benefits to turning off the screen completely, or using stressful stuff like *Write or Die* or *The Most Dangerous Writing App*. There's also tools that allow for group sprinting or gamification, like *4thewords*. But it's mostly about setting a habit.

Three, 20-minute sprints a day is all you really need. With practice you should be able to write around 500 words in each session. 1500 a day is plenty, if you do it consistently. The difference between a three-month novel or a one-month novel is not that you write it faster (you're not actually typing more words per minute). You're just writing for 3 hours a day instead of 1.

Six steps to an unbreakable writing habit

Here's a list of some of my favorite productivity and motivation strategies. There's also a video walking through these if you'd prefer in the online *Grimoire*.

1. Clear Your Plate

Someone asked me recently how to find balance between life and writing. I don't feel qualified to answer, because I don't "find balance" – I drop the ball. If you're trying to juggle too many things, you'll never master any. Yes, we have responsibilities and need to earn a living, but you just need a few small chunks of time to write. If you can't find them, you're going to need to give something else up.

This isn't about doing everything, it's about doing less. It's learning how to say no and when to say yes. It's about putting yourself and your writing first. This may require some support from friends and family, or maybe you just let a few projects slide. You can create a lot of mental bandwidth by giving up on some items (instead of having them loom over you, creating doubt and guilt – because you haven't done them yet).

2. External Accountability

Working around other people helps keep you on task and in the zone; that's why I love doing writing retreats and surrounding myself with other authors. I made this list during a productivity camp in Thailand: every day we had to check in, set goals, and convene again eight hours later to report our progress.

You can set up your own writing group, or at least find a writing buddy (there are even sites you can use, like *FocusMate. com*, which pairs you up with someone to do a short burst of coworking). You can organize your own by getting on a group Skype call, and "writing together" even if you're far apart.

Make sure someone knows what you're trying to achieve. Try and make sure someone is counting on you to finish (teams of writers competing for word count goals can work well).

3. Timed Sprints

Set a timer for 20 minutes. Sit down and write. Do three writing sprints a day and you will finish in no time. After experimenting with the best writing apps and keyboards for writers, I have a new system that works well: I make sure I know what's going to happen in each scene (and can remember it and write it down in a sentence or two) then I move to a bluetooth keyboard and my iPhone. Small screen, no distractions, always moving forward.

It can also help to close your eyes, or turn the screen around (you can better visualize, and use the meaning of the words without focusing on the letters.)

4. Track Results

Have a calendar and put it up somewhere visible – cross off the days you hit your wordcount goal; also write down the daily wordcount. You want to build a visible chain of success, that propels you forward. There are apps that track this, but you should be able to see it all the time. You can also share an excel file in dropbox or google spreadsheet – you can set it up so your writing group can each post their daily wordcount, and it will keep a running total. Most of these I've had trouble keeping up with, so even something fun and simple like X'ing your calendar or giving yourself stickers for each day you've written something new can work.

5. Confidence Games

There are some interesting psychological tricks you can use on yourself to stay confident, but the biggest thing is to watch your language; confidence is your body and voice. Look yourself in the mirror and say "I'm the type of person who's capable of completing 50,000 words in a month" (a friend of mine is putting something together based on research that shows we are extremely fluid in our self-evaluation, it can be helpful to have someone *else* say this to you, or ask "are you the type of person I can count on to finish this book?")

You can also use less intimidating statements like, "why am I capable of writing a book in a month?" or "Why am I such a great writer?" Ask the question, not the statement, and it will have the same effect without feeling as imposing.

You can even record your own voice saying "*You* are the type of person" instead of "I'm the type of person..." You may not believe in you yet, but you can choose to install that belief with deliberate neuro-programming.

6. Energy Maintenance

Last but not least, make sure to take care of yourself and recharge. You're going to need *more* sleep and rest than usual, or your brain will catch on fire. Get sunlight, put your feet to the grass, breathe deeply. Fix your posture or change your writing set up. Try alternating to a standing desk whenever possible. Take frequent breaks to stretch and move. Drink lots of water.

Remember, don't try to do more – you'll burn out if you do too much. Focus on doing *less*, and choosing to drop some responsibilities so you can focus on your writing.

In my experience, the only real secret to writing success is consistency. Not banging out 5,000 word days, but writing a little bit, every day, over a long period of time. That said: there's also no real benefit to writing slowly. The novel you started a few years ago might never get finished, because as you grow and change and improve, you'll always see new ways to change it or make it better.

THE WRITING PROCESS

Having a map of your story, and having pictured the scenes in detail, will help with the writing process, but that doesn't mean it will be easy. Here are some final tips to help you finish writing your book.

1. Write the rough draft quickly. Don't edit, don't improve the writing, don't focus on the sentences. Just block in the conversation, setting and action in big chunks. If you get stuck, make a note and move on. Focus on hitting a certain word count, or getting through a scene a day.

2. Keep going until you get to the end. If you get stuck, go back to the beginning and start revising and cleaning things up. Every time you go through, you discover new things about your story and characters.

3. Get to the end. Clean it up enough to send to beta readers (or your mom), but keep focusing on the story, not the writing, until you're sure the story is enjoyable and satisfying. At this point, I recommend reading *The Story Grid* by Shawn Coyne and *Story Fix* by Larry Brooks, or *Nobody Wants to Read Your Sh*t* by Steven Pressfield. (Or, of course, go through *Book Craft* again for new insights).

4. Then start revising in earnest. Don't get discouraged that the writing may not be that great yet. Those sentences don't start to shine until the last few rounds of editing.

5. Kill your darlings, which means, any sentence you're really proud of because it's such great writing probably needs to be cut (readers don't want to be impressed with the writing if it distracts from the story). Stick with the story, use the words that convey the right images and emotions, but don't overdo it.

6. Writing is a learnable skill! You don't really understand what it takes to write a book until you've finished one, and even then, you're just a beginner. Be proud of yourself, but recognize you may need a professional editor, and also to finish several more books (probably both) before you start producing high quality work.

7. That said, "quality" isn't necessarily an indicator of commercial success. If you can't find an agent or publisher, don't be afraid to self-publish and get your work out there. Who knows what could happen.

8. Different genres have different expected lengths, but a normal first novel should be between 60K (young adult) and 90K (epic fantasy). If you're shooting for 60K and 60 chapters, each chapter will be around 1000 words, and shouldn't be over 2000 words—but that's on average. Some will be longer or shorter.

MOTIVATION (MINDSET, ELIXIRS)

The first chapter of *Book Craft* – Chapter 0, on courage – used to be 25K of fascinating historical trivia, but it tended to veer mostly towards creative confidence and then got pretty deep into alternative, questionable suggestions. But I have frequently encountered authors who are feeling frustrated or overwhelmed, and we've had very profitable conversations, so I wanted to include a few unconventional tips here.

Basically, we have too many tabs open, and writing demands an immense cognitive ability. Tidy your workplace, close your tabs, use the writing tips in productivity section. But let's say you're still having trouble feeling creative or inspired or motivated.

The most productive writers in history were also the most stimulated (Balzac drink 50+ cups of coffee a day). But the secret to productivity, or overcoming procrastination, is not more caffeine or stimulation – that will just turn the resistance into anxiety. The trick is to remove the block.

The problem is, if you're feeling blocked, you're probably avoiding something you don't want to do; something that feels hard, that you don't enjoy. There are tricks, like starting in 5 seconds, or scheduling a consequential writing time (*when* I finish my coffee/after lunch, *then* I'll write 500 words).

If a 500 word goal feels like an obligation and keeps you from writing, set a goal of 50 words, or just one sentence. Getting started is the hardest part. But even then... you can't really *choose* to feel differently, because it's a mental state you can't control (but thinking you can will lead to guilt and unhappiness, because you know you could or should be doing better, but you don't).

A century ago, the definition of Creative Genius was a manic state; associated with depression, the melancholic humor and black bile. Aristotle writes that all those who have become eminent in philosophy or politics or poetry or the arts are clearly of the atrabilious (melancholy) temperament. This is where it gets interesting: melancholy is tied to sadness or depression, but is also linked with mania (a kind of furor or frenzy). Ficino, in *Three Books on Life*, says that "melancholy and furor" are the same phenomenon.

Creative Genius didn't used to be a way of thinking, it was a physiological reaction. It had specific symptoms. I get these same symptoms when I'm in a manic state: breathlessness, extra sweating, increased confidence and boldness, flushing, rapid talking, insomnia... my friends and family will tell me something is off. I'll be extremely excited about everything and think what I'm doing is going to change the world. I'll get a ton of creative work done, but I could also endanger myself and others through bad decision making.

Check out this excerpt from the 11th-century *Regimen Sanitatis Salernitanum*, attributed to John of Milano, which gives the basic run-down as to the effects of too much of one humor or another:

If Sanguin humour do too much abound,
These signes will be thereof appearing cheefe,
The face will swell, the cheeks grow red and round,
With staring eies, the pulse beate soft and breefe,
The veynes exceed, the belly will be bound,
The temples, and the forehead full of griefe,
Unquiet sleeps, that so strange dreames will make
To cause one blush to tell when he doth wake:
Besides the moysture of the mouth and spittle,
Will taste too sweet, and seeme the throat to tickle.

If Choller do exceed, as may sometime,
Your eares will ring, and make you to be wakefull,
Your tongue will seeme all rough, and oftentimes
Cause vomits, unaccustomed and hatefull,
Great thirst, your excrements are full of slime,
The stomacke squeamish, sustenance ungratefull,
Your appetite will seeme in nought delighting,
Your heart still greeued with continuall byting,
The pulse beate hard and swift, all hot, extreame,
Your spittle soure, of fire-worke oft you dreame.

If Flegme abundance haue due limits past,
These signes are here set downe will plainly shew,
The mouth will seeme to you quite out of taste,
And apt with moisture still to overflow,
Your sides will seeme all sore downe to the waist,
Your meat wax loathsome, your digestion slow,
Your head and stomacke both in so ill taking,
One seeming euer griping tother aking:

With empty veynes, the pulse beat slow and soft,
In sleepe, of seas and ryuers dreaming oft.
But if that dangerous humour ouer-raigne,

Of Melancholy, sometime making mad,
These tokens then will be appearing plaine,
The pulse beat hard, the colour darke and bad:
The water thin, a weake fantasticke braine,
False-grounded joy, or else perpetuall sad,
Affrighted oftentimes with dreames like visions,
Presenting to the thought ill apparitions,
Of bitter belches from the stomacke comming,
His eare (the left especiall) euer humming.

These are real physical symptoms; even if ancient doctors were wrong about the four humors causing them, the remedies for fixing an imbalance tended to work, appearing to justify the whole system. And the most dangerous was Melancholy, which could make one experience "false grounded joy" or "perceptual sadness" or even visions. I already shared my three stages to creative confidence, but I think the "false grounded joy" and sadness go together for most creatives who are amateurs or what I call "fools" (people without experience who create for the love of it, not to make money.) "Fool" isn't meant as an insult, only a contrast with the magician from the Tarot tradition: one is not better or worse than the other, but one has more experience and skill.

The inevitable fear after the work is done whether anybody else will appreciate it, and the all-too-common indifference or dismissal of the work after you've finished, will always trigger both feelings of joy and defeat. But perhaps artistic types who want to create are also just more likely to be melancholic.

Classic melancholic personalities have these ("artistic") qualities:

- Sensitive
- Intuitive
- Self-conscious
- Easily embarrassed
- Easily hurt
- Introspective
- Sentimental
- Moody
- Likes to be alone
- Empathetic
- Often artistic
- Often fussy and perfectionist
- Deep
- Prone to depression, avarice, and gluttony

Melancholy is also tied to apparitions and dreams: In Chaucer's "The Nun's Priest's Tale," the rooster, Chanticleer, has a dream in which he was being pursued by a yellowish-red hound-like creature. He wonders if the dream is prophetic, so his wife, Pertelote, reassures him by telling him:

> Certes this dream, which ye have mette tonight,
> Cometh of the great supefluity
> Of youre rede cholera, pardie,
> Which causeth folk to dreaden in their dreams

Of arrows, and of fire with redde beams,
Of redde beastes, that they will them bite,
Of conteke [contention], and of whelpes great and lite
[little];

Right as the humour of melancholy
Causeth full many a man in sleep to cry,
For fear of bulles, or of beares blake,
Or elles that black devils will them take,
Of other humours could I tell also,
That worke many a man in sleep much woe;
That I will pass as lightly as I can.

Based on the description, this actually sounds like Sleep Paralysis, a terrifying experience that seems like it has to be caused by supernatural forces (that's the only way I could explain them, when my friends and family were flummoxed by my visions and night terrors. It's different now that we have the internet to look things up).

I think there's also a link with migraines, which can have uncanny side effects. Both can both manifest in hearing voices, distorted sensory perception, the feeling of persecution, delusions of grandeur. Migraines are associated in classical texts with black bile; and the associated dietary restrictions match up with migraine triggers pretty well).

If you aren't naturally on the bipolar spectrum, this kind of creative "flow" state can be induced. And you don't have to go full manic; you can simply support your brain's own chemistry to make sure it's getting the nutrients it needs. I actually think the four humors are related to modern understanding of important neurotransmitters.

- Dopamine
- Serotonin
- Acetylcholine
- Gaba

Each one can be supported or blocked, depending on your own brain chemistry. What I've found for me personally, especially since being diagnosed with ADHD and starting ritalin, is that ritalin doesn't speed me up or make me focused. It just takes away the block (if you don't have ADHD, try ritalin anyway, it probably *will* speed you up... which can work.) As far as that goes though, I far prefer and recommend modafinil, which makes me hyper-focused, more intelligent and more eloquent.

Modafinil also triggers recklessness and overconfidence. Genius is being bold, fervently confident in one's own infallibility, great risk and daring, fearlessness. This is what I feel on modafinil... or if I've had too much *Huperzine A* for several days – a common ingredient in most "brain boost nootropics."

Huperzine A increases the amount of acetylcholine in the brain. People with acetylcholine natures as "highly innovative, intuitive, flexible and impulsive; writers, artists and advertising are natural occupations for the acetylcholine type."

My guess is, manic and depressive states represent an imbalance of acetylcholine; and that certain types of people have a harder time regulating it – something that can be improved by avoiding certain foods, and eating other foods. The fact that food can change brain chemistry and alter mood gives credence to the original humors system, whose dietary prescriptions aren't that far off from modern counterpoints.

If these seem too experimental, another common ingredient in most cognitive boosters is theanine – one of the main compounds in green tea. While coffee can make you jittery or come with side effects like tension, tea has caffeine and theanine, which has a calming effect.

I don't actually love it (most supplements have too much theanine which feels sedative.) I like to feel crazy alert and hyper-focused. But the truth is, especially if you're writing the rough draft, you want to be a bit relaxed. Creativity comes from the more chill part of our brain; or the lateral insights flourishing between hemispheres. Strong green tea (a lot of it) should have a very nice effect. Mate (something I drank from the gourd in Argentina after polo matches) is similar to green but more stimulating with some unique properties.

Kratom is an Asian root still sold over the counter in many places, that is a bit like pure, powdered Japanese matcha (in preparation, not taste). It gives a nice mood boost and usually focus and energy. Not that I'm recommending them, but opioid-based painkillers like Vicodin remove social anxieties.

To me, the feeling of anti-social avoidance as an introvert feels exactly like my avoidance to writing or tasks I dislike. Not fear or dread or anything, just a very strong, stubborn refusal to do the thing. The feeling of being in the flow, of being "turned on" and "focused" and "inspired" – is the surplus of certain brain chemicals, mostly dopamine (pleasure) serotonin (happiness) and norepinephrine (enthusiasm). When you're firing at all cylinders, you're using these up – so you'll feel drained or uncreative the next day, until your brain makes more.

But there are things that boost or replenish these faster: supplements like L-Carnitine or N-Acetyl Tyrosine (NALT); or herbs like Ashwagandha or Lion's Mane mushroom – both help with a calm, relaxed focus, better sleep and better dreams. Even something simple like "Bullet Proof Coffee" (with butter) is basically giving your brain the nutrients it needs to do more good work. (Four Sigmatic has a "mushroom mix coffee" with Lion's Mane that's pretty great).

Gabapentin regulates dopaminergic neuron firing, which may help specifically with writer's block; St. John's Wort boost optimism and feelings of general satisfaction. If you feel general brain fog, make sure you don't have any basic deficiencies like iron, b12 or magnesium. High-quality krill oil (fish oil) might help too.

Most of these things can be found easily online or over the counter. The point is, you as a writer, have chosen to run your brain on high capacity for months at a time. Writing a book is more challenging for brains than nearly anything else. Make sure you know how your brain works, what it needs, and take that into account. You can't fill the tank with wishful thinking.

If you're in a state where marijuana is legal, you may find that it works better for you than most of the things listed above. Stay away from hybrids. Use an indica (relaxing) while brainstorming or drafting, and a sativa while editing (stimulating). And indica might make you sleepy; a sativa might make you anxious. Both are great for visualization crisp and vivid scenes, and unique flashes of insight as both sides of your brain begin to talk to each other (multi-tasking, not so much – so pick one thing to focus on, set a timer and zero-in on one project). I prefer edibles with coffee for breakfast.

As a final point – though this could be (and might be) a whole book, nearly every famous writer in history was using mind-stimulating or mind-altering substances; from opium and marijuana (Shakespeare) to more common staples like tobacco, coffee and sugar (all have significant psychoactive effects). For the past several centuries, beer was the most common, safest drink when clean water wasn't reliable; so you can assume they were semi-buzzed, if not outright drunk, as many authors were. Nearly all medicinal pain killers from the pharmacy contained opium, marijuana or even heroin.

I could argue, easily, that every "great work of literature" was drug induced, and that you'd be hard-pressed to find one that isn't; that the overlap of "brilliant" literary works from the enlightenment and modern period was not accidental, but due to the introduction of stimulants and narcotics (tea, coffee, and tobacco were once seen as dangerous elements that led to revolutionary courage).

Don't assume that your sober writing is your best writing; or that great writers of the past succeeded despite their consumptive habits, rather than because of them.

"No poem was ever written by a drinker of water."
– *Homer, Greek epic poet, (Eighth Century BC)*

DOPAMINE BRAIN

Attention is caring enough or being interested enough in the thing to keep considering it. ADHD is a type of hyper-sensitivity.

We're aware of so much, and feel it so deeply, we can't do anything. Nothing holds our attention. It's also tied with reward-deficiency.

Dopamine allows us to regulate emotional responses and take action to achieve specific rewards. People without dopamine don't care enough about any potential rewards to fake or force interest or attention towards something we have negative feelings for. The overwhelm outweighs any possible benefit; or any possible punishment. Sticks and carrots won't work on us.

Writing is probably going to be a part-time hobby for most authors, because there is no specific drive or goal towards rewards (unless you create one yourself and focus on earnings, rather than something vague like a positive review); there's also probably no real penalty or consequence if you don't get it done. You should make some, as artificial or self-imposed deadlines help, a little less than hard or real deadlines like a preorder launch date.

But even so, your biggest struggle will be maintaining your dopamine levels to stay creative over the long haul, while feeling good about it, and mostly by removing that stupid mental block that makes you watch 12 hours of Netflix when the *only* thing you had on your todo list was write 500 words.

Therefore, when I talk about "mindset" I don't recommend just positive affirmations (though those can definitely help), because motivation is rarely a simple case of forcing yourself to do the thing. You don't need to fight that beast every day; it's a battle you'll often lose twice – once when you do nothing, and again when you feel guilty about it. Instead, you can charm or distract the beast. You just may need to try a few things to see what makes it sit quietly in the corner while you get to work, with no resistance.

PS. If you're into that sort of thing, try something as simple as a tiger's eye (energy), obsidian (remove blocks) or onyx (willpower) bracelet; or a big citrine (stimulating) or rose quartz (relaxing) globe for your office. If you're really into that sort of thing, check out your Vedic horoscope gemstone recommendation based on the planets in this cycle of your life.

LOVE OR PURPOSE

A beginner's job is to fall in love with the process. To find joy. To want to do this. This is why passion matters. Passion and enthusiasm must outweigh and overwhelm the frustration inherent in becoming proficient: a practitioner's job is to get better. Practice is not about doing, it's about learning, the mind intent on improving until they are qualified to turn their joy and hobby into a profession. And the professional's job is to get paid more, while working less. To maximize profit, to write better books, faster.

You may disagree, because a handful of famous writers only write a few books which took a very long time. I would point out that they probably wasted years in creative turmoil wrestling with these very things; and that most of them did *not* earn a living from their books. It's not an easy thing, but that doesn't make it untrue. Your beliefs do not impact the work. You can choose beliefs that make it easier, or better yet, set beliefs aside entirely and focus on the Creating Your Best Work.

According to HP Lovecraft,

"Amateurs write purely for the love of their art, without the stultifying influence of commercialism."

Roald Dahl adds,

"A person is a fool to become a writer. His only compensation is absolute freedom. He has no master except his own soul, and that, I am sure, is why he does it."

Most writers, *even those who are very experienced*, are still amateurs or fools: joy and creative freedom are everything to them, and they aren't willing to adapt or change their work to suit the market.

This path, however, often leads to a debilitating crisis of faith: a boiling point. After struggling righteously and failing for years (which I, like every creative person, have certainly done) you may start to turn from love to money. Not because it's about the money – it never really is – but because you want to use your words to provide value; to impact; to share and be heard. That won't happen if nobody reads your books. And if nobody is reading them, either you don't have anything interesting to say, or you're not saying it well.

Remember the process I recommended in the book:

- Choose joy
- aim for value
- practice your craft

If you stick only with the first, remember your courage will always be offset by an appropriate amount of anxiety which cannot be resolved. You're going to experience more severe and more frequent bouts of burnout, dissatisfaction and overwhelm, and that's fine... to an extent. Practice is not about doing, it's about deliberate improvement; you can only improve if you have an aim and a clear goal. If your only goal is to continue making yourself happy, by choosing those same happy feelings and hits of dopamine, you'll be an addict chasing the next high. It is not the case that mania always leads to genius. Sometimes it's just crazy. The joy is necessary because it's the only reliable fuel. You still need to furnace, the fire, the train and the tracks, locomotion, movement, travel, destination, and purpose: to transport others, to provide value. Otherwise, it's just a destructive wildfire.

But what if you could skip the years of stumbling around in the dark: years of getting it wrong, or writing bad books, or sinking your whole heart and paycheck into your book launch and be devastated to realize this is going to be so much harder than you imagined and simply choose, right now, to become a better writer on purpose? It's possible, but you're the only person who can.

> "There was a moment when I changed from an amateur to a professional. I assumed the burden of a profession, which is to write even when you don't want to, don't much like what you're writing, and aren't writing particularly well."
> –*Agatha Christie*

CHOOSE CAREFULLY

I'm not sure if I have mentioned any specific mindset tactics, so here's one. Recently I was watching a YouTuber talk about how she instantly manifested her dream life, and her steps were nearly exactly the same as this quote from St. Paul.

> "Do not be anxious about anything, but in every situation, by prayer and petition, with thanksgiving, go present your requests" -*Philippians 4:6*

So here you have advice, from the Bible and from YouTube: the ancient and the modern, and they are saying the same thing. Whether or not you believe explicitly in the Law of Attraction, you've probably been cultured into some form of casual optimism. You might believe your thoughts have power, because, like Buddha said:

> "Watch your thoughts. They become words. Watch your words. They become deeds. Watch your deeds. They become habits. Watch your habits. They become character. Character is everything."

Actually, Buddha probably never said this: more likely, it came from the sermon of a priest from Iowa in 1856, and I like his version better:

> Plant a thought and reap a word;
> plant a word and reap an action;
> plant an action and reap a habit;

plant a habit and reap a character;

plant a character and reap a destiny.

PS. Always check quotes you find on the internet.

So without considering what type of books you want to write, or what kind of book readers want to read, consider this: when you say things like, "I don't care if I sell any" or "it's not about the money" or "I'd be happy selling just one copy of my book." What if that wasn't just humble misdirection? What if that was your order to the universe. Do you think small, limited, self-effacing beliefs like that are exciting and empowering? Are you surprised when you get exactly what you wanted, which was "I don't want to sell any books"?

Ask for what you want. Expect and accept that it is coming to you. Be grateful, but make your position clear. Authors give up their greatest powers by playing small and choosing the low-risk path to obscurity, with accidental intention. It's scary to shoot big, because it forces you to play the game. If you intend to sell 10,000 copies, any behavior that doesn't aim for that goal – including the types of books you write – will need to be modified. You can drift, allowing whatever the universe decides to grant you, or you can steer, by choosing what you want.

THE WITCHES' SYMBOL

Earlier I showed you an example of a recently discovered "witches symbol" and remarked on the similarities between it and my plotting structure. Another possible interpretation, is that it represents astronomical wisdom: the eight perceived planets rotating around the sun—secret knowledge that learned priests might have known, but kept hidden because it conflicted with biblical cosmology. I could make a strong argument that all ancient hero myths are actually based on astrology, so the "story structure" we've inherited shares a universal, celestial origin, but that's beyond the immediate scope of this book.

ABOUT THE AUTHOR

I like to think of myself as Edgar Allan Poe meets David Blaine, a gothy street magician with too much jewelry, long black hair and eyeliner. In reality, I'm an antisocial, ADHD booknerd who is either watching you in silence from across the room or spewing out fascinating historical trivia and theorizing as I chase stray cats down the street. I wrote my Master's thesis on astrological symbolism in *Harry Potter* and my PhD on the ethical inversion of modernist values in *Paradise Lost*. I've been featured by CNN for renting castles and have hit the Wall Street Journal and USA Today bestseller lists. These days, I mostly write YA fantasy about mermaids, vampires and aliens.

Visit me at:
- www.creativindie.com
- www.urbanepics.com
- www.writethemagic.com

MORE ABOUT ME

You could say my writing career started with vampires. During my PhD studies, I spent years falling asleep in Greek class, and practically living in the library. But then I stalled out: I couldn't pass the requirements necessary to graduate, which included publishing in a peer-reviewed journal. They were too competitive, and my ideas were too "out-there" and broad, rather than the academic minutiae I loathed. My wife and I traveled to literary conferences in Poland, Turkey, Scotland and Ecuador, presenting my esoteric papers that were met with polite clapping or disdainful judgment. But time was running out: if I didn't publish and graduate in time, all of my credits would be wiped clean; seven years wasted.

Unsure about the future, I applied for the prestigious Fulbright scholarship to study vampire mythology in Romania, and got rejected... twice. Just under the ticking clock, after a flurry of writing and submissions, and one false-positive when I was "accepted" by what turned out to be a scam journal built to prey on desperate grad students, I finally got something into a legit publication and dropped my final thesis off at the library. It was formatted incorrectly, but we'd already bought tickets to leave Taiwan, so I gave a classmate a fistful of cash and had him promise he'd get it sorted out.

In the end, we went to Romania ourselves. The most interesting stop was the self-proclaimed "Dracula's castle." In truth, Bram Stoker wrote his book based on a mix of accounts and illustrations, a mishmash of truth and legend, to cash in on the commercial trend of *penny dreadfuls* and the pulp fiction vampire novellas that were already becoming popular in his day. On a meta-level, the most authentic thing in the castle was a prop from the 1922 silent classic "Nosferatu: A Symphony of Horror," the first, unauthorized cinematic adaptation. The castle itself was small and cramped, interesting in its own right of course, with a colorful local history. But that's not why people from all over the world came to see it. It's the story that gave it life and value.

What I forgot to mention, somewhere in all of this, were my mostly failed self-publishing experiments, including trying to republish a version of Mircea Eliade's very early vampire novella *Miss Kristina* (which should have been public domain, but apparently wasn't) and getting a cease and desist from the family's Trust. I'd already received one from Angry Birds, for an unflattering surrealist pop art painting of Steve Jobs they didn't approve of.

Or I could go way back to the Easter Bunny I saw when I was six, the demons at twelve, the aliens at twenty-two. Until I had access to the Internet and figured out my traumatic supernatural sleep terrors were caused by a relatively common sleep disorder. Sleep paralysis was also thought to be the prime cause of supernatural experiences, angel visits, alien abductions and yes, even vampires.

As a last-ditch effort for some stability, I went to a job application at a university. I think everyone was aware how little I belonged; but my rejection was sealed when a woman brought out a copy of one of my self-published books and everyone had a good chuckle at my expense. It was wildly speculative, unprofessionally designed, and obviously self-published... of course I still thought it was great, if they'd only read it, but it wasn't the kind of thing they wanted their faculty to be associated with.

I left that meeting frustrated, vowing to prove them wrong, and within a year I'd finished my first novel – which has been called "*Twilight*, with mermaids." So again, vampires. Life imitates art, art imitates life.

I could also mention that time I tried to make a *Twilight* themed dance party. I prepared everything, but then had to charge to cover the costs and rent the space. And then... nobody came.

I mean, *nobody*. Just the DJ and me and an empty room with a box of plastic fangs and stick-on furry sideburns.

I was missing the only thing that actually matters: people. Your art, event, product, book or whatever doesn't *matter* if nobody reads it. None of it matters, none of the words you used, the organization, whether it's good or isn't, a "book" exists when it's being read for the first time by someone new. That reading experience, the precise order of those hundreds of thousands of tiny characters, form a collective meaning, that must be processed in isolation, one page at a time, it's the act of discovering what happens next and how it all fits together that can only be appreciated by a new reader. The value of a book is how the reading experience unfolds. It doesn't matter how many months or years you worked on it, why you made all the changes or edits you did, what you meant it to convey or your lofty ideals about what it means to be a writer.

Those hours a reader spends in your imagination, getting to know and love your characters, experiencing their challenges and heartbreaks, a cozy weekend on the couch; a long road trip; the weeks afterwards that the reader can't stop thinking about your story... *that's* where your book truly resides.

Once you've finished your last round of revisions and cast your spell and harnessed your lightning and gathered the dead limbs of your past experiences and created your monster ("It's aliiiive!") the book will go out to make its own way in the world, where it will either warm hearts or horrify them; be loved or shunned; inspire greatness or revulsion. This is beyond your control.

A good book awakens the reader's mind, is stimulating, is thought provoking, is magical. But *you* do not get to dictate how this magic happens, or if it happens at all.

THE END

Made in United States
Troutdale, OR
06/23/2024

20762086R00293